PADI
Adventures in Diving Manual

PADI

Student Diver

Address

City, State/Province

Telephone

Instructor   Date

PADI
Adventures
in Diving

Published by International PADI, Inc.
30151 Tomas Street
Rancho Santa Margarita, CA 92688-2125

Library of Congress Card Number 95-072809
ISBN 1-878663-09-7

Printed in the United States of America
10 9 8 7 6 5 4

PRODUCT NO. 79101 (Rev. 9/03) Version 2.3

Second Edition Acknowledgements

Editor in Chief
Drew Richardson

Development, Instructional Design, Consultation and Review
Bob Coleman, Patricia A. Fousek, John Kinsella, Drew Richardson,
Julie T. Sanders, Karl Shreeves, Brad Smith, Lori Bachelor-Smith,
Bob Wohlers

International Review and Consultation
Henrik Nimb, Terry Cummins, Colin Melrose, PADI Asia Pacific;
Randy Giles, PADI Canada; Jean-Claude Monachon, PADI Europe;
Mark Caney, Suzanne Pleydell, PADI International Ltd. Yasushi Inoue,
PADI Japan; Olle Olson, PADI Nordic; Trond Skaare, PADI Norway;

Technical Writing
Karl Shreeves

Editing
Jeanne Bryant

Layout and Design
Janet Klendworth, Dail Schroeder

Illustrations
Greg Beatty, Joe De La Torre, T.K. Lewis

Photography
Aaron Anthony, Jon Coon, Jeff Mondle, Karl Shreeves, Bob Wohlers

SEACREST PEAK PERFORMANCE
ON SUNDAY 22 BUOYANCY
8:30 DEEP

DO WRECK AND P.P.B WORKSHEETS.

Table of Contents

2 TANKS
BC
THERMOS W/ HOT WATER

Underwater Videography

Wreck Diving

Appendix

ADVENTURES IN DIVING

Introduction

Welcome to the Adventures in Diving program – the first step beyond Open Water Diver certification. Adventures in Diving offers different experience and training options that range from simple introductions to underwater activities to more challenging experiences, and ultimately to two different certifications.

By now, you've probably discovered that diving is more than an end in itself. It's a vehicle to a wide range of activities and inter-related skills that create adventure, fun and recreation no matter how varied your interests. Adventures in Diving takes you from riding diver propulsion vehicles, to taking pictures or video underwater, to looking for lost objects, to visiting your favorite reef – all of these, or none of these. You choose, with your instructor's guidance (obviously, some activities aren't possible in some environments). You can make one Adventure Dive or many – again, depending on what you want to do. As you make these dives, you develop skills that make diving more fun, more versatile and that expand the types of dives you can make.

PADI ADVENTURES IN DIVING PROGRAM OVERVIEW

The PADI Adventures in Diving program consists of 16 Adventure Dives at this writing (there are always new ones being added – check with your PADI Instructor, Dive Center, Resort or visit PADI's website, padi.com). These include an altitude dive, a boat dive, a deep dive, a diver propulsion vehicle dive, a drift dive, a dry suit dive, a multilevel dive, a navigation dive, a night dive, a Peak Performance Buoyancy dive, an AWARE fish identification dive, a search and recovery dive, an underwater naturalist dive, an underwater photography dive, an underwater videography dive and a wreck dive. To begin your adventure, you only have to make *one* – perhaps you've got a strong interest in wreck diving and you want to try it. Or, you can qualify for certifications by completing several Adventure Dives. You may try wreck diving and then try fish identification. It's up to you.

Of the certifications you can earn in the Adventures in Diving program, the first option is the PADI Adventure Diver certification. You earn the Adventure Diver certification by making three Adventure Dives that you and your instructor choose together. You can do this in as little as a day, but the schedule's flexible. Any Adventure Dives you make count toward your Adventure Diver certification (with your instructor's approval) so trying a single Adventure Dive moves you toward Adventure Diver.

Adventure Dives

- Altitude Adventure Dive
- AWARE-Fish Identification Adventure Dive
- Boat Adventure Dive
- Deep Adventure Dive
- Diver Propulsion Vehicle Adventure Dive
- Drift Adventure Dive
- Dry Suit Adventure Dive
- Multilevel and Computer Adventure Dive
- Night Adventure Dive
- Peak Performance Buoyancy Adventure Dive
- Search and Recovery Adventure Dive
- Underwater Naturalist Adventure Dive
- Underwater Navigation Adventure Dive
- Underwater Photography Adventure Dive
- Underwater Videography Adventure Dive
- Wreck Adventure Dive

After the PADI Adventure Diver course is the PADI Advanced Open Water Diver certification. For the Advanced Open Water Diver certification, you'll complete the Underwater Navigation and Deep Adventure Dives and three other Adventure Dives that you and your instructor decide on. You can go directly from Open Water Diver to Advanced Open Water Diver, but if you already have the Adventure Diver certification, those dives may count toward your Advanced Open Water Diver certification.

No matter what your interest, remember that you progress at your pace. You don't have to do everything at once – you can make an Adventure Dive here and there as your interests dictate, eventually earning the certification that interests you. Or, you can make a weekend of it and go right through.

CONTINUING THE ADVENTURES

The Adventure Dives in this program have a unique relationship with various PADI Specialty Diver courses. What you learn and practice in an Adventure Dive can be credited (at your instructor's discretion) to the corresponding PADI Specialty Diver course because it is the first dive from the course. Likewise, if you've already completed a PADI Specialty Diver certification, the first dive was the Adventure Dive that counts (again, at your instructor's discretion) toward any of the certifications in the Adventures in Diving program.

The PADI Enriched Air Diver Course

and Adventures in Diving

The relationship between the Adventures in Diving program and the PADI Enriched Air Diver (nitrox) course differs a bit from the relationship with other PADI specialty courses. After completing the knowledge development portion of the Enriched Air Diver course, your enriched air dives may integrate with Adventure Dives, with your instructor's approval. To do this, you may combine the skills for an Adventure Dive with the two required Enriched Air Dives. For example, your first enriched air dive could also be the Underwater Videography Adventure Dive and the second enriched air dive could be the Underwater Navigation Adventure Dive. This allows you to progress toward your Adventure Diver and/or Advanced Open Water Diver certification while earning your Enriched Air Diver certification.

As a scuba diver, you'll learn you have some responsibilities associated with this exciting activity. As a savvy consumer, one of your first responsibilities is to verify that the individual conducting your program is an authorized PADI Instructor. You can do this by asking to see his or her instructor card. Check the photo and make a note of the individual's instructor number, next call PADI or visit www.padi.com to verify that the individual is authorized to conduct the program you are enrolled in or plan to take. If at any time during your program you have questions about the instructor conducting your program please contact PADI. Contact information for the PADI Office nearest you is located on padi.com.

PADI Rescue Diver Course

After completing the Advanced Open Water Diver course, you're qualified to begin the PADI Rescue Diver course, which teaches you emergency prevention, intervention and management. In fact, you can get a taste of this course with the optional Rescue Diver Experience. The experience takes place at the surface, making it easy for your instructor to schedule with an Adventure Dive or as part of any course in the Adventures in Diving program.

Talk to those who've been there – almost without exception, you'll hear that the PADI Rescue Diver course is one of the most challenging and rewarding courses you can complete as a diver. Rescue Divers will tell you that it's a real confidence builder – an experience you don't want to miss. It's serious fun.

For more information about...

Rescue Diver
See the *Rescue Diver Manual* and the *Rescue Diver* video.

After Rescue Diver You Have a Choice

Once you complete the PADI Advanced Open Water Diver and Rescue Diver courses, you have two pathways to continue your diving education – Master Scuba Diver or instructor development. Master

Scuba diver is the highest non-professional rating in the PADI System of diver education. As a pathway to greater adventure, Master Scuba Diver provides recognition for expert divers that do not wish to lead or teach divers professionally.

The instructor development pathway begins with the PADI Divemaster course and is the first professional level in the PADI System. During the Divemaster course you will develop leadership skills and professional-level dive knowledge and abilities. Earning the PADI Divemaster certification distinguishes you as both an accomplished diver and a leader, at the doorstep of becoming an instructor if that interests you.

For more information about...

PADI Divemaster Course
See the *Divemaster Manual* and the *Divemaster* video.

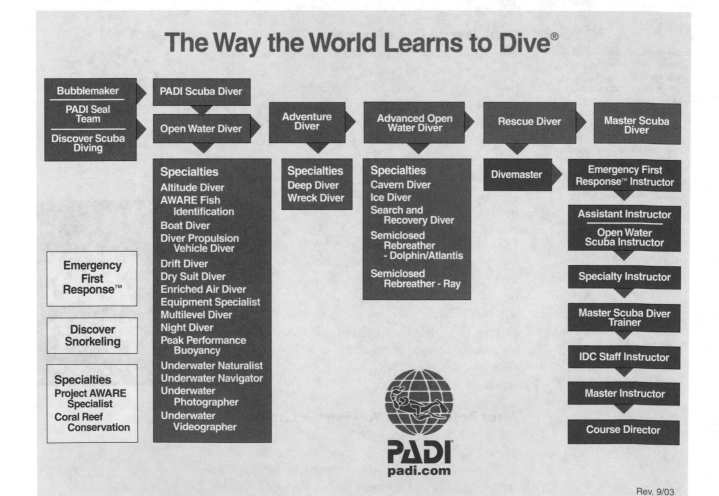

The Way the World Learns to Dive®

| Bubblemaker | PADI Scuba Diver | | | | |

- Bubblemaker
- PADI Seal Team
- Discover Scuba Diving
- PADI Scuba Diver
- Open Water Diver
- Adventure Diver
- Advanced Open Water Diver
- Rescue Diver
- Master Scuba Diver
- Divemaster

Specialties
Altitude Diver
AWARE Fish Identification
Boat Diver
Diver Propulsion Vehicle Diver
Drift Diver
Dry Suit Diver
Enriched Air Diver
Equipment Specialist
Multilevel Diver
Night Diver
Peak Performance Buoyancy
Underwater Naturalist
Underwater Navigator
Underwater Photographer
Underwater Videographer

Specialties
Deep Diver
Wreck Diver

Specialties
Cavern Diver
Ice Diver
Search and Recovery Diver
Semiclosed Rebreather - Dolphin/Atlantis
Semiclosed Rebreather - Ray

Emergency First Response™

Discover Snorkeling

Specialties
Project AWARE Specialist
Coral Reef Conservation

Emergency First Response™ Instructor
Assistant Instructor
Open Water Scuba Instructor
Specialty Instructor
Master Scuba Diver Trainer
IDC Staff Instructor
Master Instructor
Course Director

PADI®
padi.com

Rev. 9/03

HOW TO STUDY

Adventures in Diving emphasizes learning by diving. For most Adventure Dives, all you have to do is read and complete the related section, including the Quick Reviews and Knowledge Review. Before the dive, your instructor will provide a thorough overview of the dive objectives or review your Knowledge Review to assess your understanding. Remember that to obtain credit for certification, you must complete the Knowledge Review and turn it in to your instructor.

You'll notice that the Main Objectives direct you to "underline or highlight" answers as you read. It's important that you actually do this, because doing so reinforces what you're learning by helping to "write" it to your long term memory. Likewise, actually answering the Quick Quizzes (not just doing so mentally) enhances learning.

Watch for These Symbols

 As you read **Adventures in Diving**, you'll notice this symbol. It alerts you to important safety information. Pay close attention when you see this symbol and consult your instructor if you do not understand the material.

This Project A.W.A.R.E. symbol highlights information or a specific diving technique that allows you to harmoniously interact with the aquatic environment.

By the time you reach the Knowledge Review, you should be familiar with the section. However, if you find there's something you forgot, look it up so you can complete the review. If there's something you don't get despite rereading that portion of *Adventures in Diving*, have your instructor explain it to you. Remember, your instructor's first concern is that you have a safe and fun adventure on each dive. Understanding the information in each section is part of the process.

Adventures in Diving Video

 The companion video for this book (also called *Adventures in Diving*) provides the foundation you need for the Adventures in Diving program. It gives you background on most of the Adventure Dives, with emphasis on the Night, Deep and Navigation Adventures Dives, which are the three most popular ones.

You may want to watch *Adventures in Diving* before reading any sections in this manual, or you may want to read and then watch. People learn in different ways, so whichever approach you prefer is probably best for you.

STANDARD SAFE DIVING PRACTICES

When diving, you will be expected to abide by standard diving practices. These practices have been compiled to reinforce what you have learned and are intended to increase your comfort and safety in diving.

I understand that as a diver, I should:

1. Maintain good mental and physical fitness for diving. Avoid being under the influence of alcohol or dangerous drugs when diving. Keep proficient in diving skills, striving to increase them through continuing education and reviewing them in controlled conditions after a period of diving inactivity.

2. Be familiar with my dive sites. If not, obtain a formal diving orientation from a knowledgeable, local source. If diving conditions are worse than those in which I am experienced, postpone diving or select an alternate site with better conditions. Engage only in diving activities consistent with my training and experience. Do not engage in cave or technical diving unless specifically trained to do so.

3. Use complete, well-maintained, reliable equipment with which I am familiar; and inspect it for correct fit and function prior to each dive. Deny use of my equipment to uncertified divers. Always have a buoyancy control device and submersible pressure gauge when scuba diving. Recognize the desirability of an alternate air source and a low-pressure buoyancy control inflation system.

4. Listen carefully to dive briefings and directions and respect the advice of those supervising my diving activities. Recognize that additional training is recommended for participation in specialty diving activities, in other geographic areas and after periods of inactivity that exceed six months.

5. Adhere to the buddy system throughout every dive. Plan dives – including communications, procedures for reuniting in case of separation and emergency procedures – with my buddy.

6. Be proficient in dive table usage. Make all dives no decompression dives and allow a margin of safety. Have a means to monitor depth and time underwater. Limit maximum depth to my level of training and experience. Ascend at a rate of not more than 18 metres/60 feet per minute. Be a SAFE diver – **S**lowly **A**scend **F**rom **E**very dive. Make a safety stop as an added precaution, usually at 5 metres/15 feet for three minutes or longer.

7. Maintain proper buoyancy. Adjust weighting at the surface for neutral buoyancy with no air in my buoyancy control device. Maintain neutral buoyancy while underwater. Be buoyant for surface swimming and resting. Have weights clear for easy removal, and establish buoyancy when in distress while diving.

8. Breathe properly for diving. Never breath-hold or skip-breathe when breathing compressed air, and avoid excessive hyperventilation when breath-hold diving. Avoid overexertion while in and underwater and dive within my limitations.

9. Use a boat, float or other surface support station, whenever feasible.

10. Know and obey local dive laws and regulations, including fish and game and dive flag laws.

A Quick Review

Before making the Adventure Dives, let's review to be sure your basic dive knowledge is fresh. The Quick Review goes over concepts you learned in your Open Water Diver course. If you recently completed the Open Water Diver course, this will be a quick refresher. If it's been some time, the Quick Review will not only help you refresh your memory, but will help bring you up to date with changes, and alert you to anything you might want to review with your instructor.

1. You should equalize your ears and other air spaces while descending
   ☐ a. only when you feel discomfort.
   ☐ b. approximately every metre/few feet, before you feel discomfort.

2. If you feel discomfort in your ears while descending, ascend until the discomfort is gone, attempt to equalize again and continue a slow descent if successful. Never continue a descent if you can't equalize.
   ☐ True　　　☐ False

3. The most important rule of scuba diving is: Breathe continuously and never hold your breath.
   ☐ True　　　☐ False

4. If you feel discomfort during ascent due to air expansion in a body air space
   ☐ a. slow or stop your ascent and give the trapped air time to work its way out.
   ☐ b. continue ascending; the air will force an escape path.

5. If you begin shivering underwater, increase your activity to warm up.
   ☐ True　　　☐ False

6. If you become overexerted underwater
   ☐ a. stop, breathe and rest.
   ☐ b. swim quickly to the surface and signal for assistance.

7. Planning a dive should include (check all that apply):
   ☐ a. what to do in an emergency.
   ☐ b. maximum time and depth limits.
   ☐ c. a review of communication procedures.

8. If you and your buddy lose contact, the general recommendation is
   ☐ a. search for no more than a minute, then reunite at the surface.
   ☐ b. search for no more than 15 minutes, then reunite at the surface.

9. If caught in a current and exhausted at the surface when boat diving, you should signal for assistance and establish buoyancy, then rest and catch your breath while waiting to get picked up.
   ☐ True　　　☐ False

10. Which of the following reduce the chance of accidental injury by an aquatic animal? (Check all that apply.)
    ☐ a. Never tease or intentionally disturb an animal.
    ☐ b. Never look under a rock outcropping.
    ☐ c. Move slowly and carefully, watching where you put your hands, knees and feet.
    ☐ d. If you don't know what something is, don't touch it!

11. If you accidentally become entangled, you should:
    ☐ a. inflate your BCD so you pull free.
    ☐ b. avoid turning and struggling, and work slowly and carefully to free yourself.

12. You help avoid underwater problems by diving within the limits of your experience and training.
    ☐ True　　　☐ False

13. If you were to run out of air at 10 metres/35 feet and your buddy were not immediately available, your best option would be:
    ☐ a. to make a buoyant emergency ascent.
    ☐ b. to make a controlled emergency swimming ascent.

14. Unless local laws or regulations state differently, you should stay within _____ of a dive flag, and boaters and water-skiers should stay _____ away from it.
    ☐ a. 15 m/50 ft., 30-60 m/100-200 ft.
    ☐ b. 8 m/25 ft., 15-30 m/50-100 ft.

15. You prevent problems with contaminated air primarily by having your tanks filled only by reputable professional dive operations.
    ☐ True　　　☐ False

16. If you feel the effects of nitrogen narcosis, you should
    ☐ a. ascend to a shallower depth.
    ☐ b. slow your descent until they pass.

17. To prevent nitrogen narcosis,
    ☐ a. avoid deep dives.
    ☐ b. descend slowly.

18. Exceeding established depth and/or time limits can produce _____ on ascent, which causes decompression sickness.
    ☐ a. bubbles in the body tissues
    ☐ b. blood circulation to the skin

19. Signs and symptoms of decompression sickness include (check all that apply):
    □ a. numbness and tingling.
    □ b. euphoria.
    □ c. pain, often in the joints and limbs.

20. A diver suspected of having decompression sickness should
    □ a. wait six hours before diving again.
    □ b. stop diving, breathe emergency oxygen and seek emergency medical care.

21. First aid for decompression sickness and lung overexpansion injuries include preventing and treating for shock, administering oxygen and if necessary, CPR.
    □ True   □ False

22. Dive tables and dive computers
    □ a. apply a mathematical model to determine theoretical dive time limits.
    □ b. read the actual amount of nitrogen in your body.

23. Avoid the maximum limits of your dive tables or computer because
    □ a. you're more likely to run out of air.
    □ b. people vary in their susceptibility to decompression sickness.

24. No decompression, or no stop, diving means
    □ a. you never run out of air.
    □ b. that you plan dives with tables and computers so you can make a direct ascent to the surface if necessary.

25. When making a repetitive dive, it's necessary to account for excess nitrogen still in your body from the previous dive.
    □ True   □ False

26. The "formal" definition of bottom time is:
    □ a. from the beginning of descent to the beginning of a direct ascent to the safety stop/surface.
    □ b. from the time you reach the bottom to the time you reach the surface.

27. If planning three or more dives in a day with the RDP, if your ending pressure group after the second dive is Y, you should wait at least _____ hour(s) before all subsequent dives.
    □ a. 1   □ b. 3

28. After a dive to 18 metres/60 feet for 30 minutes, followed by a 30 minute surface interval and a repetitive dive to 16 metres/50 feet for 28 minutes, your ending pressure group would be:
    □ a. R   □ b. P   □ c. O   □ d. T

29. After a dive to 17 metres/56 feet for 42 minutes, followed by a 42 minute surface interval and a repetitive dive to 17 metres/56 feet for 29 minutes, your ending pressure group would be:
    □ a. X   □ b. T   □ c. V   □ d. U

30. A safety stop is a pause at _____ for _____.
    □ a. 5 m/15 ft 3 or more minutes.
    □ b. 3 m/10 ft 1 minute.

31. Always make a safety stop if (check all that apply):
    □ a. you dive to 30 metres/100 feet or deeper.
    □ b. you dive in low visibility.
    □ c. your ending pressure group comes within three pressure groups of a no decompression limit.

32. If you accidentally exceed a no decompression limit by less than five minutes:
    □ a. slowly ascend to 5 metres/15 feet and make an eight minute stop prior to surfacing, then discontinue diving for at least six hours.
    □ b. ascend directly to the surface, but don't exceed 18 metres/60 feet per minute.

33. If you accidentally exceed a no decompression limit by more than five minutes, slowly ascend to 5 metres/15 feet and make a stop prior to surfacing for no less than 15 minutes (air supply permitting), then discontinue diving for at least 24 hours.
    □ True   □ False

34. In cold water or under strenuous conditions, plan your dive as though it were
    □ a. 4 m/10 ft shallower than actual.
    □ b. 4 m/10 ft deeper than actual.

How'd you do?
1. b; **2.** True; **3.** True; **4.** a; **5.** False. Shivering is a warning sign to end the dive immediately and seek warmth. **6.** a; **7.** a, b, c; **8.** a; **9.** True. **10.** a, c, d; **11.** b; **12.** True; **13.** b; **14.** a; **15.** True; **16.** a; **17.** a; **18.** a; **19.** a, c; **20.** b; **21.** True; **22.** a; **23.** b; **24.** b; **25.** True; **26.** a; **27.** b; **28.** a; **29.** c; **30.** a; **31.** a, c; **32.** a; **33.** True; **34.** b.

If you don't understand any of these questions, consult the PADI *Open Water Diver Manual* or *Multimedia*, or see your instructor.

Rescue Divers Wanted!

Conquer the fireman's lift, perfect the rope throw and execute a flawless tired diver tow.

Challenge yourself with the most serious -- yet fun -- PADI program.

Control is what you want, and training to be the best is how you achieve it!

PADI
padi.com

WHAT

will your next entry read?

Become a **PADI Master Scuba Diver** and add:

- ✔ **Achievement**
- ✔ **Excitement**
- ✔ **Challenge**
- ✔ **Adventure**

to your adventure log!

PADI®
padi.com

Go to your local PADI Dive Center or Resort or padi.com for
details about PADI's Master Scuba Diver program.

The Way the World Learns to Dive

©International PADI, Inc. 2002

ALTITUDE DIVING

Introduction

Snowboarding, skiing, mountain biking, hiking, fishing, climbing, hang gliding, camping, bird watching, hunting and photography make the world's mountain ranges synonymous with sport, adventure and recreation. Thoughts of fresh mountain air, sheer rock faces, icy brooks and deep-blue skies conjure

images of the Rockies, the Andes, the Alps and other ranges – places to escape civilization, taste excitement or just commune with nature. It's no surprise, then, that those headed up into unspoiled heights include scuba divers.

Fresh water mountain lakes are often cool, clean and clear, with interesting aquatic life. Artificial lakes and reservoirs formed amid mountains also offer unique diving opportunities. Both these natural and man-made wonders require special procedures for altitude diving. Altitude diving is your door to dive opportunities inland, away from the ocean, and amid some of the most beautiful sur-

roundings on earth. And if you enjoy other pursuits that take you toward the top of the world, now you can bring your gear and scuba, too.

CONCEPTS

Underline/highlight the answers to these questions as you read:

1. How do you determine that a dive is an "altitude dive"?

2. Why do you need to follow special dive table and computer procedures at altitude?

3. What are the theoretical and practical differences between altitude diving, flying after diving and driving to altitude after diving?

4. What are the current recommendations for flying after diving?

ALTITUDE DIVING AND DECOMPRESSION THEORY

What's an Altitude Dive?

The decompression models used by the vast majority of dive tables and dive computers, including the Recreational Dive Planner, were developed for use at sea level. These models control the release of nitrogen absorbed during your dive by assuming that you will begin and end your dive at sea level, under a full atmosphere of pressure.

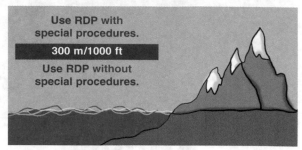

When using the Recreational Dive Planner (and most other tables and most dive computers), an altitude dive is any dive made at 300 metres/1000 feet or greater above sea level.

When you ascend into the mountains, however, you rise higher into the atmosphere where there's less air pressure. At about 300 metres/1000 feet above sea level, atmospheric pressure drops enough to question the accuracy of calculations intended for sea level. So, when using the Recreational Dive Planner (and most other tables and most dive computers), an altitude dive is any dive made at 300 metres/1000 feet or greater above sea level. An altitude dive requires special dive table or computer procedures (discussed later) to account for the atmospheric pressure difference. Diving above 300 metres/1000 feet without following proper altitude procedures increases the risk of decompression sickness.

Furthermore, there is relatively little test data for altitude diving, so altitude diving procedures apply highly conservative practices. After more than a decade of field use, these procedures have a good track record, provided you adhere to their conservatism.

Flying After Diving and Altitude Diving

Because flying after diving and diving at altitude all involve diving and ascending above sea level, you might think you can use the same or similar procedures for both. Nope, sorry. From a theoretical and practical stance, flying after diving differs significantly from altitude diving.

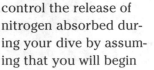

Recommendations

 The medical community offers the following general recommendations for flying after diving whether you're using the RDP, another table or a dive computer:

For Dives Within the No-Decompression Limits

- **Single Dives** – A minimum preflight surface interval of 12 hours is suggested.

- **Repetitive Dives and/or Multiday Dives** – A minimum preflight surface interval of 18 hours is suggested.

For Dives Requiring Decompression Stops

- A minimum preflight surface interval greater than 18 hours is suggested.

As with dive tables and computers, no flying after diving recommendation can guarantee that decompression sickness will never occur. These guidelines represent the best estimate presently known for a conservative, safe surface interval for the vast majority of divers. There always may be an occasional diver whose physiological makeup or special dive circumstances result in decompression sickness despite following the recommendations.

Flying after diving recommendations change over time. These are current at the time of this printing. Always check with your instructor to stay apprised of the most current ones.

In flying after diving, you dive, then ascend to altitude. Your exposure to lower atmospheric pressure *follows* your dive, usually after an interval. In altitude diving, your exposure to lower atmospheric pressure *precedes* your dive, and you return to the same lower pressure at the end of the dive. In decompression theory, these situations differ.

Don't try to apply the procedures for altitude diving for flying after diving or vice versa. Note that the recommendations for flying after diving remain the same whether you dive at sea level or dive at altitude. Also, don't mix altitudes by diving at one altitude and making a repetitive dive at a higher altitude.

The Divers Alert Network (DAN) is presently conducting a controlled study of flying after diving. At this writing, the study is ongoing. For more information on the details and progress of this study, please go to DAN's Website at www.diversalertnetwork.org/home.htm.

REVIEW

Altitude 1

1. An altitude dive is a dive made at or above an altitude higher than
   ☐ a. 300 metres/1000 feet.
   ☐ b. 3000 metres/10,000 feet.

2. The reduced atmospheric pressure at altitude and the lack of test data for diving at altitude allow for liberal dive practices at altitude.
   ☐ True   ☐ False

3. With regard to decompression theory, what is the major difference between flying after diving and altitude diving?
   ☐ a. Theoretically, there is no difference.
   ☐ b. Whether your exposure to altitude precedes or follows the dive.

4. If flying after altitude diving, you should
   ☐ a. follow the same recommendations for flying after diving at sea level.
   ☐ b. calculate your dive as though making it at the flight altitude.

How'd you do?
1. a;   2. False. These are reasons for conservative practices.   3. b;   4. a.

ALTITUDE DIVING AND PHYSIOLOGY

Key CONCEPTS

Underline/highlight the answers to these questions as you read:

1. What are two potential detrimental physiological conditions possible from altitude diving, aside from decompression sickness, what causes them and how do you avoid them?

2. What is the first aid for these two conditions should they occur?

Besides the need for special procedures to avoid decompression sickness while altitude diving, two other physiological conditions face altitude divers: hypoxia and hypothermia. Both are possible while diving at sea level, but the altitude environment makes them more likely to catch an unwary diver by surprise.

Hypoxia

Since the air at altitude has less pressure than at sea level it's less dense and "thinner." Each breath you inhale has less oxygen – fewer oxygen molecules – than each breath at sea level, even though the proportion (percent) of oxygen remains the same.

This means your body has some difficulty absorbing oxygen to meet its oxygen demands, compared to when you're at sea level. If your oxygen demand exceeds your body's ability to absorb oxygen from the less dense air (like if you exert yourself significantly), *hypoxia* – insufficient oxygen – results. Hypoxia before an altitude dive usually results from heavy exercise such as hauling equipment, donning equipment and walking to the dive site. The signs and symptoms of hypoxia include fatigue, shortness of breath, light-headedness, faintness and exhaustion. You feel like you've been exercising much harder than you actually have been.

Fortunately, hypoxia is easy to avoid. When you're at altitude, limit your activity and rest often. Allow extra time for getting ready, and take more trips carrying less than you otherwise would. Don't let yourself get out of breath. If

Altitude Diving
See the Physiology of Diving section in the *Encyclopedia of Recreational Diving*, book and multimedia.

Hypoxia can also come on suddenly at the end of an altitude dive. When you surface, you return rather quickly to the thin air. If you've been exerting yourself, or do so exiting the water, you may find it difficult to catch your breath.

you live at altitude or spend a lot of time there, your body adapts to the thinner air, making hypoxia less likely.

Hypoxia can also come on suddenly at the end of a dive. During the dive, you're under increased pressure so your body easily meets its oxygen demand. When you surface, however, you return rather quickly to the thin air. If you've been exerting yourself, or do so exiting the water, you may find it difficult to catch your breath.

If you find yourself experiencing symptoms of hypoxia, stop all your activity at once, rest and catch your breath. Resume activity at a slower pace only after fully regaining normal respiration. If exerting yourself a bit underwater, rest and catch your breath underwater *before* you surface.

Hypothermia

Hypothermia occurs when a diver has been exposed to cold water or air (both common at altitude) long enough that the body's critical core temperature drops below normal. This can occur even in a wet suit or dry suit, given sufficient time and sufficiently cold conditions. Mountain lakes tend to be cold, so while hypothermia can be a concern at sea level, you need to be more alert for it in many altitude dive environments.

Hypothermia is a potentially life-threatening condition, with signs and symptoms including shivering, numbness, and blueness in the skin. As the body core temperature drops, the victim can become uncoordinated and suffer weakness, confusion, unconsciousness and, if left untreated, death can follow.

A diver who shivers uncontrollably should end the dive and seek warmth.

You prevent hypothermia by wearing proper exposure suits for the environment and depth of your dive. In colder water, or if making several dives in cool water, you may want to consider a dry suit. Always allow yourself ample time to rewarm between dives. If you begin shivering, end the dive immediately and seek dry clothes, shelter and warmth. Shivering is a physiological warning that you should never ignore.

 Remove a diver who shivers uncontrollably from the cold, and have the diver put on warm clothes and rewarm. If a diver exposed to the cold exhibits severe numbness, weakness, confusion or any other symptom of serious hypothermia, summon emergency care, monitor the diver's breathing and pulse, being prepared to administer CPR and shock management as necessary until help arrives.

CONCEPTS

Underline/highlight the answers to these questions as you read:

1. What two dive accessories are especially appropriate for altitude diving, and how do you use them?

2. How does altitude affect the readings of a bourdon tube, capillary and electronic depth gauges, and how do you compensate for these effects?

3. What two ways can altitude diving affect buoyancy?

ALTITUDE DIVING EQUIPMENT CONSIDERATIONS

Unlike many dive specialties, altitude diving requires little specialized equipment. What does concern you at altitude, though, is how you *use* particular pieces of equipment. A couple of accessories take on added importance, depth gauges require some considerations for proper use, and altitude can affect your buoyancy.

Accessories Appropriate for Altitude Diving

Two dive accessories especially useful for altitude diving are descent/ascent lines and slates. As you'll see in a moment, ascents are extra slow at altitude and an ascent/descent line makes it easier to control your ascent rate if you won't be ascending along a sloping bottom. The line also helps measure depth.

A reference line comes in handy on an altitude dive if you don't have a sloping bottom to follow. The line helps you control ascents, which are extra slow at altitude, and it can also help you measure depth.

Slates are important for proper dive table procedures with the Recreational Dive Planner. Altitude dive planning requires converting actual depths to *theoretical* depths that you use on the RDP. For contingency table calculations, you'll want to carry actual-to-theoretical depth conversions on your slate. In addition, the proper depth for a safety/emergency decompression stop varies with altitude. You'll want to note the proper stop depth on your slate, too.

Depth Gauges and Computers at Altitude

When you dive at altitude, the lower atmospheric pressure can distort how your depth gauge reads. Depending upon the gauge, it may read shallower than actual depth, deeper than actual depth or accurately.

Digital depth gauges. Electronic digital gauges commonly adjust for altitude, either automatically or through a special setting. Consult the manufacturer's literature.

Bourdon tube depth gauges. Bourdon tube depth gauges are the most common analog depth gauges. At altitude, a bourdon tube depth gauge will read shallower than the actual depth, though many models have adjustment knobs that permit you to correct the gauge when altitude diving.

If you're using an unadjustable bourdon tube gauge, you can use this conservative approximation to determine your correct actual depth: Add .3 metres/1 foot to what the gauge reads, plus .3 metres/1 foot for each 300 metres/1000 feet of altitude. Round up fractions of 300 metres/1000 feet. For example, if you were diving at 716 metres/2350 feet altitude, you would add 1.2 metres/4 feet to the depth shown on your gauge to determine your actual depth.

For contingency table calculations, you'll want to carry actual-to-theoretical depth conversions on your slate.

At altitude, a bourdon tube depth gauge will read shallower than the actual depth, though many models have adjustment knobs that permit you to correct the gauge when altitude diving.

Capillary depth gauges. Capillary depth gauges read *deeper* than the actual depth because they're based on compressing the air in the capillary tube. Since the pressure at the surface is lower at altitude than at sea level, and that's the pressure in the tube when you start the dive, it's easier to compress the air in the tube. This makes it read deeper than you actually are.

Interestingly, this makes capillary depth gauges easy to use at altitude because it reads the theoretical depth you use on the RDP (or other table), eliminating the need to convert your actual depth to a theoretical depth. Unfortunately, capillary depth gauges are harder to use accurately for depths below 9 metres/30 feet, so you may still need a digital or bourdon tube gauge.

Capillary depth gauges are easy to use at altitude compared to other gauges because they read the theoretical depth you use on the RDP (or other table), eliminating the need to convert your actual depth to a theoretical depth.

Dive computers vary in how you use them at altitude. Some automatically adjust for new altitudes, some allow you to set them for the altitude, and some you cannot use at altitude (except as a depth gauge and timer). The mountain icons on these computers indicate that they're set for altitude diving.

Dive computers. Like digital depth gauges, dive computers vary in how you use them at altitude. Some automatically adjust for new altitudes, some allow you to set them for the altitude, and some you cannot use at altitude (except as a depth gauge and timer). You'll need to check the manufacturer literature for how to use your computer at altitude, and the maximum altitude at which you can use it.

If you have any doubt regarding depth gauge accuracy, compare it with a gauge known to be accurate or against a measured line before using it. If you compare it with a measured line, remember that gauges calibrated for salt water will read three percent shallower than your line in fresh water. You don't need to be concerned with this difference when using the RDP, by the way, because it is also calibrated for sea water.

Buoyancy at Altitude

There are a couple of points regarding buoyancy at altitude. First, since altitude dives are virtually always fresh water dives, if you're used to salt water, you'll find you have less buoyancy. On the other hand, if using a wet suit, you'll find it has more buoyancy than when diving in fresh water at sea level. This is because the lower atmospheric pressure allows the trapped gas in the wet suit material to expand, making the suit more buoyant. Of course, it compresses and loses buoyancy after you descend a short distance.

To adjust for both fresh water and for wet suit expansion, be sure to check your buoyancy before diving – you should float at eye level when fully suited up and holding a normal breath with an empty BCD. When you exhale, you should sink. If you check with a full cylinder, you may want to add about two kgs/five lbs to offset the buoyancy you gain by consuming most of the air in your tank.

Altitude 3

1. Two dive accessories especially appropriate for altitude diving are (check all that apply):
    - ☐ a. slate
    - ☐ b. altimeter
    - ☐ c. dive light
    - ☐ d. descent/ascent line

2. As a general rule, bourdon tube depth gauges read _____ than actual depth at altitude, and capillary gauges read _____.
    - ☐ a. deeper, accurately
    - ☐ b. shallower, deeper

3. Diving at altitude may affect your buoyancy compared to sea level diving.
    - ☐ True   ☐ False

How'd you do?
1. a, d;   2. b;   3. True.

USING THE RECREATIONAL DIVE PLANNER AT ALTITUDE

Underline/highlight the answers to these questions as you read:

1. What's the altitude range for using the RDP with altitude diving procedures?

2. What two steps should you follow to make a proper ascent at altitude?

3. What's the recommended maximum number of dives for one day at altitude?

4. How do you determine the proper repetitive group on the RDP when arriving at altitude from sea level?

5. What is The Wheel's advantage over the Table for planning altitude dives?

6. How do you calculate no decompression limits for single and repetitive dives at altitude, when diving in less than six hours and more than six hours after arriving at the dive site?

7. What is the maximum depth for recreational divers at altitude?

As mentioned earlier, you follow special procedures when using the Recreational Dive Planner for altitude diving. With the RDP, you must follow altitude procedures for any dive at 300 metres/1000 feet to a maximum altitude of 3000 metres/10,000 feet. At no time should you use the RDP to plan dives at altitudes above 3000 metres/10,000 feet. Dive computers vary in their altitude ranges, so consult the manufacturer literature.

When using the RDP for altitude diving, follow these procedures:

Ascents at Altitude

An altitude dive ascent has two components that differ from ascents using the RDP at sea level. First, the ascent rate is 9 metres/30 feet per minute or slower, that is, half the sea level maximum rate. This slower rate is important because your theoretical ascent rate slows at altitude. It also adds some conservatism, which is appropriate with little formal test data available. Second, you make a three-minute safety stop at the depth prescribed on the Theoretical Depth at Altitude chart on *all* dives, regardless of depth or bottom time.

Repetitive Diving

The general recommendation is that you make no more than one repetitive dive per day while altitude diving. This means a maximum of two dives in a day. (Note that for training divers with preceding shallow dives followed by a long surface interval, it may be appropriate for your instructor to conduct three dives in one day.) Don't mix altitudes by making the repetitive dive at a higher altitude than the first dive.

The maximum ascent rate at altituide is 9 metres/30 feet per minute. You make a three-minute safety stop at the depth prescribed on the Theoretical Depth at Altitude chart on all dives, regardless of depth or bottom time.

Arriving at Altitude

When you arrive at an altitude dive site, you have effectively "surfaced" from the greater pressure at sea level, and your body has a higher nitrogen level than the surrounding atmosphere. You need to account for this higher nitrogen level when planning your dive.

The simplest method is to remain at the dive site altitude for six hours or longer, permitting your body nitrogen to equilibrate with the surrounding pressure. You may then make your dive without having to account for excess nitrogen from sea level.

When you arrive at an altitude dive site, you have effectively "surfaced" from the greater pressure at sea level, and your body has a higher nitrogen level than the surrounding atmosphere. You need to account for this higher nitrogen level when planning your dive.

To dive sooner than six hours, however, you account for the nitrogen by determining a pressure group letter for use on the RDP Table or Wheel. Upon arrival at the dive site altitude, count two pressure groups for each 300 metres/1000 feet of altitude to determine your pressure group. Round up fractions of 300 metres/1000 feet. After determining your pressure group on arrival at altitude, you may allow a "surface interval" to reduce your pressure group, if you wish. If you are diving above 2400 metres/8000 feet, wait six hours before diving.

For example:

- A diver plans an altitude dive at 1500 metres/5000 feet. What is the pressure group upon arrival at the dive site altitude?

  Answer: J – Count 10 pressure groups (two for each 300 metres/1000 feet) to arrive at J.

- If the diver in the previous question waits 90 minutes after arriving at the dive site altitude, what is the new pressure group?

  Answer: B – Side Two of The Wheel or Table 2 on the Table shows that after 90 minutes, pressure group J moves to pressure group B.

If you spend six hours or more at an altitude above 300 metres/1000 feet, but ascend to a yet higher altitude to dive, you still use the same procedures as though you were arriving from sea level. If you find yourself in this situation regularly, take the PADI Altitude Diver Specialty course to learn special acclimated diver procedures. These procedures give credit for having less nitrogen than if arriving at the dive site from sea level.

- A diver plans to dive at an altitude of 2680 metres/8792 feet. What is the pressure group upon arrival at the dive site altitude?

  Answer: You can't determine a pressure group for altitudes greater than 2400 metres/8000 feet. The diver must wait six hours before diving.

Determining Theoretical Depth

As mentioned earlier, you need to convert actual depths at altitude to *theoretical* depths that you use on the RDP to account for the differences in atmospheric pressure. You can think of theoretical depths as "sea level equivalent" depths that are usable on the RDP.

Use the Theoretical Depth at Altitude Chart at the end of this section for converting the actual depth to theoretical depth:

1. Use the exact or next greater number shown on the table. Round altitudes up to the next 300 metres/1000 feet, and round depths to the next greater depth. This can mean that you round up an actual depth on the Theoretical Depth at Altitude Chart, and then round up the theoretical depth when applying it to the RDP.

2. The Wheel, with its two metre/five foot depth increments (as opposed to the Table's greater increments) helps minimize unnecessary rounding. This gives The Wheel an advantage over the Table RDP when using theoretical depths to calculate dive profiles.

3. Remember that a capillary depth gauge reads theoretical depth automatically, so you don't need to convert it.

4. The recreational diver depth limit for any altitude dive is a *theoretical* depth of 40 metres/130 feet. This means that the higher the altitude, the shallower the maximum allowable actual depth. In any case, a maximum theoretical depth of 30 metres/100 feet is generally recommended, with a maximum theoretical depth of 18 metres/60 feet for novice divers. See the Deep Diving section for more about depth limits.

You need to convert actual depths at altitude to theoretical depths that you use on the RDP to account for the differences in atmospheric pressure. You can think of theoretical depths as "sea level equivalent" depths that are usable on the RDP.

Sample Problems

Sample Problem 1 *(Use the Theoretical Depth at altitude Charts on the following pages.)*

A diver plans to dive at an altitude of 1000 metres/3300 feet to an actual depth of 15 metres/47 feet. What is the depth used on the RDP for planning this dive?

Answer: 18 metres/60 feet. Round up 1000 metres/3300 feet to 1200 metres/4000 feet on the Theoretical Depth at Altitude Chart. Round 15 metres/47 feet to 16 metres/50 feet in the "Actual Depth" column, then move right into the 1200 metres/4000 feet column. The theoretical depth shown is 18 metres/58 feet. An 18 metre/58 foot dive rounds to 18 metres/60 feet on the RDP.

Sample Problem 2

At what depth would the diver in the above problem make the required safety stop?

Answer: 4.5 metres/13 feet. Find 4.5 metres/13 feet listed under 1200 metres/4000 feet in the Safety/Emergency Decompression Stop Depth portion of the chart.

Sample Problem 3

If the diver in Sample Problem 1 arrives from sea level and dives 15 minutes after arriving at the dive site, what is the no decompression limit for the planned actual depth of 15 metres/47 feet?

Answer: 36 minutes. Upon arrival at the dive site, count eight pressure groups (two for each 300 metres/1000 feet) for Group H. On Table 2 of the Table or Side 2 of The Wheel, after 15 minutes Group H moves into Group F. On Table 3 of the Table, or Side 1 of The Wheel, a diver in pressure group F diving to the theoretical depth of 18 metres/60 feet (see Sample Problem 1) has a no decompression limit of 36 minutes.

Altitude 4

1. Altitude diving procedures for the RDP may be used at a maximum altitude of
   - ☐ a. 6000 metres/20,000 feet.
   - ☐ b. 3000 metres/10,000 feet.

2. The rate of ascent when diving with the RDP at altitude is 9 metres/30 feet per minute.
   - ☐ True   ☐ False

3. The generally recommended maximum number of dives that may be made in one day when using the RDP at altitude is:
   - ☐ a. one   ☐ b. two   ☐ c. three

4. Upon arrival at an altitude of 1653 metres/5422 feet from sea level, your pressure group is:
   - ☐ a. J   ☐ b. L   ☐ c. M

5. The Wheel's advantage at altitude is that it has altitude corrections built in.
   - ☐ True   ☐ False

6. You wish to dive to an actual depth of 24 metres/80 feet one hour after arriving from sea level to an altitude of 1382 metres/4532 feet. What is your no decompression limit? What is your no decompression limit if you wait six hours before making the dive?
   - ☐ a. 11 minutes, 29 minutes
   - ☐ b. 5 minutes, 20 minutes
   - ☐ c. 12 minutes, 20 minutes

7. The absolute maximum depth for a recreational dive at altitude is
   - ☐ a. an actual depth of 40 metres/130 ft.
   - ☐ b. a theoretical depth of 40 metres/130 ft.

How'd you do?
1. b;   2. True;   3. b;   4. b;   5. False. The Wheel's advantage is that the two metre/five foot increments minimize unnecessary rounding when using theoretical depths to calculate dive profiles.   6. c;   7. b.

Theoretical Depth at Altitude
METRIC

Actual Depth	Theoretical Depth at Various Altitudes (in metres)									
	300	600	900	1200	1500	1800	2100	2400	2700	3000
10	10	11	11	12	12	12	13	13	14	14
12	12	13	13	14	14	15	15	16	17	17
14	15	15	16	16	17	17	18	19	19	20
16	17	17	18	18	19	20	21	21	22	23
18	19	19	20	21	22	22	23	24	25	26
20	21	21	22	23	24	25	26	27	28	29
22	23	24	25	25	26	27	28	29	31	32
24	25	26	27	28	29	30	31	32	33	35
26	27	28	29	30	31	32	34	35	36	38
28	29	30	31	32	34	35	36	38	39	40
30	31	32	33	35	36	37	39	40	42	
32	33	34	36	37	38	40	41			
34	35	37	38	39	41	42				
36	37	39	40	42						
38	39	41	42							
40	41									

SAFETY/EMERGENCY DECOMPRESSION STOP DEPTH

Stop Depth	300	600	900	1200	1500	1800	2100	2400	2700	3000
	4.6	4.5	4.5	4.5	4.5	4.5	4.5	4.5	4.4	4.4

Theoretical Depth at Altitude

IMPERIAL

Actual Depth — **Theoretical Depth at Various Altitudes (in feet)**

Actual Depth	1000	2000	3000	4000	5000	6000	7000	8000	9000	10,000
0	0	0	0	0	0	0	0	0	0	0
10	10	11	11	12	12	12	13	13	14	15
20	21	21	22	23	24	25	26	27	28	29
30	31	32	33	35	36	37	39	40	42	44
40	41	43	45	46	48	50	52	54	56	58
50	52	54	56	58	60	62	65	67	70	73
60	62	64	67	69	72	75	78	81	84	87
70	72	75	78	81	84	87	91	94	98	102
80	83	86	89	92	96	100	103	108	112	116
90	93	97	100	104	108	112	116	121	126	131
100	103	107	111	116	120	124	129	134	140	
110	114	118	122	127	132	137				
120	124	129	134	139						
130	135	140								

SAFETY/EMERGENCY DECOMPRESSION STOP DEPTH

Stop Depth	1000	2000	3000	4000	5000	6000	7000	8000	9000	10,000
	14	14	13	13	12	12	12	11	11	10

PADI Altitude Diver Specialty Course

As mentioned in the Introduction, your Altitude Adventure Dive may be credited (at the instructor's discretion) toward the PADI Altitude Diver Specialty certification. In addition to what you've learned in this section and will practice on the Altitude Dive, the Altitude Diver Specialty course includes:

• rules for divers acclimated to altitudes

• altitude diving theory

• additional altitude open water experience

If you live at altitude or will dive at altitude regularly, the PADI Altitude Diver Specialty is for you.

KNOWLEDGE REVIEW Altitude Diving

1. Define "altitude dive" and briefly explain why there are special considerations when using tables and dive computers at altitude.

2. What's the main difference between altitude diving and flying after diving?

3. List the current recommendations for flying after diving.

4. List two possible detrimental physiological conditions, aside from decompression sickness, that may be concerns for altitude divers, and how to avoid them.

5. Describe how altitude affects each of the following instruments, and how to adjust for those effects:

Digital electronic depth gauge:

Bourdon tube depth gauge:

Capillary depth gauge:

Dive computer:

6. Identify the following when using the RDP at altitude:

Ascent rate:

Safety stop time/depth:

Maximum depth:

Maximum altitude:

7. What's the generally recommended maximum number of dives in a day when using the RDP at altitude?

8. You plan to dive to an actual depth of 18 metres/60 feet one hour after you arrive at an altitude of 1090 metres/3578 feet. If you were to dive to the no decompression limit, what would your no decompression limit be for a repetitive dive to the same depth after a 45 minute surface interval?

9. You plan to dive to an actual depth of 24 metres/80 feet after spending seven hours at the dive site altitude of 1226 metres/4023 feet. What is your no decompression limit? If your bottom time is 15 minutes, what would your no decompression limit be for a repetitive dive to an actual depth of 18 metres/60 feet after a one hour, five minute surface interval?

Student Diver Statement: I've completed this Knowledge Review to the best of my ability and any questions I answered incorrectly or incompletely I've had explained to me, and I understand what I missed.

Signature _____ Date_____

Altitude Adventure Dive Overview

- Knowledge assessment/ Knowledge Review
- Briefing
- Gearing up
- Predive safety check (BWRAF)
- Entry
- Descent

- Depth gauge comparison at depth
- Tour
- Ascent – safety stop
- Exit
- Debrief
- Log dive – PADI Instructor signs

Knowledge Reviews may not be reproduced in any form without the written permission of the publisher.

Altitude Diving 19

The Way The World Logs Their Dives

Keep track of your love of diving with PADI's Cordura® Adventure Log binder.

- ◆ Durable, lightweight and water resistant
- ◆ Zippered, 3-ring Cordura® binder
- ◆ Interior storage pockets, pen loops and a velcro pouch

Plan your dive, or day — then log it. PADI's Cordura® Adventure Log binder supports your love for diving and keeps you organized at the same time.

Purchase yours at a PADI Dive Center or Resort today.

PADI®
padi.com

PADI
padi.com

The Way the World Learns to Dive®

Bigger. Brighter. Better.

- Easier navigation. It gets you where you want to go fast.

- Filled with great information on everything from courses to travel.

- Multiple languages for PADI Divers worldwide.

The world of diving at your fingertips.

padi.com. Visit it today.

AWARE-FISH IDENTIFICATION

Introduction

Visit the same dive site again and again, year after year and the first thing you notice is that it changes. In remote areas, environmental preserves and other areas where we protect nature from the onslaught of human encroachment and pollution, these changes may appear neither good nor bad, but simply natural growth and adaptation of the ecosystem. In other areas, you may see the damaging effects of over fishing, pollution and coastal development, and yet in others, you may see a damaged ecosystem return to health and flourish under new protection and care.

As someone who scuba dives or snorkels, you undoubtedly see the changes in our underwater world. People care about what they love, so today snorkelers and scuba divers are among the strongest supporters of initiatives to benefit the aquatic environment. Scuba divers and snorkelers participate in underwater and beach clean-ups, support establishing underwater parks and preserves, and back legislation and regulation to protect threatened species and habitats. Snorkelers and scuba divers have become the underwater world's "natural" ambassadors because they see and care about it.

KEY CONCEPTS

Underline/highlight the answers to these questions as you read:

1. Why are scuba divers and snorkelers "natural" ambassadors for the aquatic environment?

2. What are Project AWARE's purpose and mission?

3. What steps are PADI and Project AWARE taking to protect the aquatic environment?

4. What is the Project AWARE Foundation?

PROJECT AWARE

In 1989, PADI introduced Project AWARE (Aquatic World Awareness, Responsibility and Education), responding to a growing demand to unify the voice of the dive community in preserving our aquatic environments. Originally launched as a ten-year effort, PADI professionals, divers and the international dive community embraced Project AWARE so enthusiastically that it became an ongoing project.

Since its inception in 1989, Project AWARE has increased environmental awareness in the dive community and in PADI Diver programs. It established the Project AWARE Foundation to expand aquatic environment projects, research and funding. And, it has helped propagate environmentally sound dive practices, operations and skills, matched by PADI programs and mirrored by the vast majority of PADI Instructors, Assistant Instructors, Divemasters, Dive Centers and Resorts. Project AWARE funded and/or sponsored programs have included shark conservation efforts, sea turtle protection, beach cleanups, public education videos and more.

Through interaction with PADI professionals, each year Project AWARE exposes more than a million people worldwide to environmental awareness. It is one of the dive community's largest environmental efforts, and one in which you can participate.

Project AWARE's Purpose and Mission

1. To cultivate interest in programs and initiatives within the dive community to preserve the aquatic environment and its resources.

2. To teach the public about the importance of, and our responsibility to protect the aquatic world.

3. To develop and disseminate educational materials, create public awareness, promote and organize industry efforts, provide direct financial support for worthwhile environmental endeavors, create innovative projects, and create alliances and partnerships with other organizations to strengthen common goals and commitment to the conservation of the aquatic environment.

4. To be commited to the conservation and preservation of aquatic environments and their resources.

5. To accomplish these goals by reaching people internationally who share this interest in the aquatic world, those who currently work to preserve it, and those who remain unaware that the aquatic world needs help.

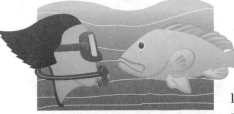

PROJECT AWARE FOUNDATION

The Project AWARE Foundation is a nonprofit, public benefit corporation (501 (c)(3) for those interested in the US legal nomenclature) that encourages and supports aquatic ecology and education. There are also Project AWARE Foundations associated with PADI Asia Pacific in Australia, PADI International Limited in the United Kingdom and PADI Europe in Switzerland. These Foundations fund projects involving aquatic environmental research, outreach, public awareness and projects that educate about the aquatic environment.

The Foundation provides this support by issuing grants, with funding coming from PADI professionals, fund raising events and programs, other sources, and PADI Divers like you. For more information about the Project AWARE Foundation, see www.projectaware.org, or the AWARE section of PADI's homepage www.padi.com.

The AWARE Diver –
Resource Manager and Environmental Advocate

As the underwater world's ambassadors to the rest of humanity, divers have a responsibility in how they dive. Divers not only observe the aquatic environment, but interact with it, either passively or actively. Therefore, divers act as more than observers. Divers are also resource managers who help determine the future health of an environment every time they visit it.

The AWARE Diver sets a good example by diving streamlined, neutrally buoyant (and not over-weighted), staying well off the bottom. The AWARE Diver doesn't allow gauges, accessories, alternate air sources or fin tips to drag on or otherwise damage sensitive organisms.

As a resource manager, the AWARE Diver assists in data collection (like you're learning to do in this Adventure Dive), and reports unusual damage, pollution or other ecological concerns to local environmental organizations or government agencies. And, the AWARE Diver participates by paying attention to proposed regulations and laws, lending supporting or opposition with an eye toward the long-term effects on the environment.

FISH IDENTIFICATION STRATEGY

Underline/highlight the answers to these questions as you read:

1. Approximately how many different fish species exist worldwide?

2. What simple strategy can you use to identify fish during a dive?

One of Project AWARE's most visible and successful efforts has been tying with REEF (Reef Environmental Education Foundation) to develop a system by which divers gather data about the diversity and abundance of fish. These data supply scientists with important information they need to determine the health of global and regional underwater ecosystems. We'll look at these fish surveys in more detail shortly, so let's begin with what you need to know to identify fish on a dive.

Current estimates say that there are more than 21,000 fish species worldwide, with more than 4000 of these found on coral reefs. Obviously, even for an ichthyologist (biologist who studies fish) it's a hopeless task to expect to learn every one of these, or even a substantial percentage.

Fortunately, you don't have to. Whether you're diving in the tropics or temperate waters, most of the fish you see belong to the same few families. This makes things more manageable. Fish watching emphasizes identifying common characteristics that let you place a fish in about 30 to 50 families instead of 21,000 species. This becomes easy with practice because in a given area, you learn to focus on the most common and representative species for these families. Through a basic understanding of key fish characteristics, plus some basic information about the local ecology, you'll have the foundation you need to classify (to the family level) most fish you see in tropical or temperate water.

Categorizing Fish

During a dive, you want a simple way to categorize fish as you spot them. One technique is to divide a slate into boxes, one for each family group you would expect to see. You might also carry a fish identification slate that reminds you about family characteristics (more detail on these shortly). When you see a fish that fits the characteristics, you note them in the appropriate family box. Later, you can confirm the family by looking up the fish in a reference book.

Through a basic understanding of key fish characteristics, plus some basic information about the local ecology, you'll have the foundation you need to classify (to the family level) most fish you see in tropical or temperate water.

Leave room on your slate to sketch or describe a fish that doesn't fit into any category. That way, you can determine its family later. As you gain experience, you'll recognize more and more local fish on sight and spend more time gathering population data.

Another important point is to leave room on your slate to sketch or describe a fish that doesn't fit into any category. That way, you can determine its family later. As you gain experience, you'll recognize more and more local fish on sight and spend more time gathering population data (described in a bit) than identifying.

Keep in mind that by its nature you must make fish watching a passive interaction. You'll see more fish and learn more about a fish by being still and by floating relaxed and neutrally buoyant than by chasing them, sculling your hands or kicking up the bottom. The more you seem like you're a natural part of the environment, the less fish regard you as a threat. For more about passive and interactive interactions, see the Underwater Naturalist section.

REVIEW

Underline/highlight the answers to these questions as you read:

1. What are the 12 groupings commonly used to identify fish in tropical or temperate waters?

2. What are the key characteristics of families (at least 30) within those groupings?

FISH GROUPS AND CHARACTERISTICS

When surveying fish in temperate or tropical waters, you can easily group most fish into one of 12 groups, each of which represents several families. These groups are:

1. Butterflyfish, angelfish and surgeonfish

2. Jacks, barracuda, porgy and chubs

3. Snappers and grunts

4. Damselfish, chromis and hamlets

5. Groupers, seabass and basslets

6. Parrotfish and wrasse

7. Squirrelfish, bigeyes and cardinalfish.

8. Blennies, gobies and jawfish

9. Flounders, scorpionfish, lizardfish and frogfish

10. Filefish, triggerfish, puffers, trunkfish, cowfish, goatfish, trumpetfish and drums

11. Eels

12. Sharks and rays

Let's look at each group and the characteristics of the families that make them up. You'll see examples of each, and your instructor may have some pictures of local representative species, too.

Butterflyfish, Angelfish and Surgeonfish

Most of these fish have thin, oval or disk shaped bodies. They typically have bright colors and patterns.

> **Butterflyfish** are usually round, small and have concave foreheads. They often have long snouts for feeding from crevices. Common types are the Banded, Foureye, Spotfin, Racoon and Lemon butterflyfish.

> **Angelfish** tend to be darker in color, have long dorsal fins and rounded foreheads. They're one of the few fish that eat sponges. Common types are the Queen, Blue, French, Gray, Rock Beauty, Flame, Emperor and Royal angelfish.

> **Surgeonfish** (also called tangs) usually have solid color, and you can identify them by the spines sticking out from each side of their tail base. They eat algae, and common types include Blue tang, Ocean surgeonfish, Doctorfish, Achilles tang, Convict tang and Longnose unicornfish.

Jacks, Barracuda, Porgy and Chub

These fish are usually silver and have forked tails. They are often some of the largest fish you see on or near a reef.

> **Jacks** (also called trevally) are large silver or bluish fish seen in open water at the reef's edge. Some species are solitary, while others school. They're strong swimming predators. Common types include Bar, Crevalle, Big-eye, Amberjack and Bluefin.

Jacks, Barracuda, Porgy and Chub continued

Barracuda are long, cylindrical and silver with faint markings. They have large mouths with visible sharp teeth. Large barracuda tend to travel alone, but smaller species may gather in schools. Common types include Great, Chevron and Pacific barracuda.

Porgies (sometimes called sea bream) are oval shaped and have steep sloping foreheads. They may have blue or yellow markings over a silvery base, and you may see them in sandy areas adjacent to the reef. Common types include Sheepshead, Saucereye and Doublebar sea bream.

Chub (or rudderfish) have elongated oval bodies, usually solid silver. You tend to see them in the water over the reef rather than close to the reef. Common types include Yellow, Bermuda and Brassy rudderfish.

Snappers and Grunts

Long tapered bodies and heads that slope toward the mouth distinguish this group. These fish are important commercial fish in many areas.

Snappers have upturned snouts and mouths, with visible canine teeth that they snap open and shut when caught (hence their name). They may be small, and travel well over the reef in loose schools. Common types include Gray, Cubera, Dog, Schoolmaster, Yellowtail, Twinspot and Bluestriped snappers.

Snappers and Grunts continued

Grunts got their name because they make a grunting noise when caught. You see them in small groups and large schools on the reef, or at night singly in sand flats and grass beds. They may be colorful with stripes; in some areas grunts are called sweetlips. Common types include French, Bluestriped, Blackspotted and Oriental grunts.

Damselfish, Chromis and Hamlets

These small, oval shaped fish dart in and out of crevices on the reef. They can be quite colorful with many different patterns and shades.

Damselfish tenaciously defend their territories, including chasing larger fish and divers. They often feed on algae, and have distinct nests or living areas. The Indo-Pacific anemonefish is a damselfish. Others include Sergeant Major, Dusky, Yellowtail, Sulfur, Humbug and Garibaldi damselfish.

Chromis are similar to damselfish but slightly different in appearance. They feed on plankton and are less territorial. They're usually elongated with deeply forked tails. Common types include Blue, Brown, Purple, Bluegreen and Bicolor chromis.

Hamlets are actually members of the seabass family, but look more like damselfish, though they have flatter, sloping head profiles. These predators are often colorful and may have stripes or markings. Common types include Barred, Indigo, Black and Blue hamlets.

Groupers, Seabass and Basslets

This group consists of big bodied (proportionately) fish with large mouths and lips. They tend to be solitary and hang out in the shadows. They're predators and highly sought after as food fish in some areas, making them prone to overfishing.

Groupers are often dark brown, black or reddish with splotchy markings. They can change color, marking and shade, sometimes making it hard to determine exact species. They have short spiny dorsal fins that taper down to the tail. Common types include Jewfish, Nassau, Yellowfin, Black, Peacock, Coral and Potato groupers.

Seabass tend to be smaller and more elongated than groupers. They're often dark, with lighter spots and varied markings. They tend to stay near the bottom, and common types include Graysby, Rock Hind, Coney, Harlequin, Soapfish and Kelp bass.

Basslets are tiny, usually colorful fish related to the seabass family. You find them on deeper reefs and walls.

Parrotfish and Wrasse

These fish add color and variety to the environment, especially in tropical reefs.

Parrotfish get their names from their beak-like teethplates and rainbow colors, much like parrots. They swim using their pectoral fins, and you see them scraping algae off hard surfaces. Common types include Rainbow, Blue, Queen, Stoplight, Redband, Longnose and Bicolor parrotfish.

Parrotfish and Wrasse continued

Wrasse are generally smaller than parrotfish, and more elongated. You see them foraging through sand and the reef for small invertebrates. Wrasse change color and pattern as they go from juvenile to adult. Some wrasse, such as the hogfish and razorfish, depart markedly from "typical" wrasse shape. Common types include Creole, Yellowhead, Bluehead, Clown, Rainbow, Senorita, Bird, and Cleaner wrasse.

Squirrelfish, Bigeyes and Cardinalfish

This group is largely nocturnal, out on the reef by night and hiding in cracks and crevices by day. Their reddish color and big eyes make them easy to spot and identify as night adapted fish.

Squirrelfish have a pronounced rear dorsal fin that sticks up like a squirrel's tail, thus the name. You see them under ledges and in crevices during the day. Common types include Longspine, Reef, Giant, Blackbar and Soldierfish.

Bigeyes differ from squirrelfish in that they have bigger eyes, a continuous dorsal fin and appear less scaly. Common types include Glasseye, Bigeye and Goggleye.

Cardinalfish are small and reddish, with short snouts and two separate dorsal fins. Common types include Barred, Flamefish and Fiveline cardinalfish.

Blennies, Gobies and Jawfish

This group has long bodies and spends time perched in small holes or on the bottom. Often, all you see is the fish's head sticking out from its hiding place.

Blennies generally perch themselves on their pectoral fins. They have fleshy appendages called cirri that look like bushy eyebrows. Common types include Saddled, Redlip, Seaweed, Chestnut and Leopard blennies.

Gobies rest on their pectorals, lying flat and motionless. Some types are cleaners, which pick parasites off of other fish. Common types include Neon, Bridled, Blue, Steinitz, Maiden and Citron gobies.

Jawfish are long-bodied fish that live in burrows they construct by moving sand and stone with their mouths. You'll see them in sand near the reef. The Yellowhead jawfish is a common type.

Flounders, Scorpionfish, Lizardfish and Frogfish

Although from different families, this group consists of bottom-dwelling fish with excellent camouflage and unusual shapes.

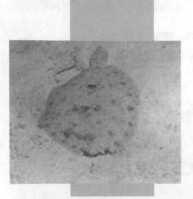

Flounders are flat fish with both eyes on one side of their body. They swim on their side. Some species can change color, and most hide by burying themselves in sand except for their eyes. Common types include Peacock, Eyed, Gulf and Panther flounders.

Flounders, Scorpionfish, Lizardfish and Frogfish continued

Scorpionfish blend in well with their surroundings, usually resembling the local flora. They have stocky bodies, and spiny dorsal fins that carry venom. Some species are quite venomous. They're hard to spot because they hold still, with injuries resulting when someone accidentally steps on or puts a hand on one. The lionfish is a scorpionfish, though it does not lie on the bottom. Common types include the Spotted and Reef scorpion fish, and the stonefish.

Lizardfish have elongated bodies and large, upturned mouths. They often rest on the bottom, camouflaged, waiting for unsuspecting prey. They may be pale, with mottled colors that match the sandy bottom. Common types include Sand Diver, Snakefish and the Common lizardfish.

Frogfish (sometimes called anglerfish) have bulky bodies and large upturned mouths. They blend in well with the bottom, and move by walking on their pectoral fins. Frogfish have an appendage that dangles in front of their mouths, which baits prey within reach. Common types include Sargassumfish, Longlure and Freckled frogfish.

Filefish, Triggerfish, Puffers, Trunkfish, Cowfish, Goatfish, Trumpetfish and Drums

All the fish in this group are free swimming, but have unusual shapes or characteristics.

Filefish and triggerfish make up a family called leatherjackets, so named for rough textured skin. These fish have ovalish or diamond shaped bodies. Filefish have an elongated dorsal fin similar to the triggerfish, only it's more spike-like. Common filefish include Scrawled, Orangespot, Whitespotted, Broom and Longnose filefish.

Filefish, Triggerfish, Puffers, Trunkfish, Cowfish, Goatfish, Trumpetfish and Drums continued

Triggerfish get their name from their elongated dorsal fin, which has a shape similar to a gun's trigger. Part of the leatherjacket family, these fish have ovalish or diamond shaped bodies. Common triggerfish include Queen, Black Durgon, Ocean, Triton, Clown and Picasso triggerfish.

Puffers get their name from the fact that they can swell their bodies up like balloons. Some have spines that stand out when they do this. All species have powerful jaws; most have dark spots or blotches.

Trunkfish and Cowfish make up the boxfish family, so-named for their triangular, boxy shape. These fish move slowly with sculling fin motions. Cowfish have two "horns" that distinguish them from trunkfish. Common trunkfish include Smooth, Spotted, and Cube trunkfish. Common cowfish include Scrawled and Honeycomb cowfish.

Goatfish have long, cylindrical bodies and barbels that hang from their chins, much like a goat's. They feed on the bottom and may gather in schools. Goatfish have many color variations, and common types include Spotted, Yellow, Red Patch, Longbarbel, and Yellowsaddle goatfish.

Trumpetfish get their name from their long, tube-like bodies and long mouths. They stalk by hanging head down, often near other vertical corals or growth that camouflages them from their prey. They may be blue-grey, bright yellow, brown or an intermediate shade.

Drums have long fore dorsal fins and striking, black and white coloring. You see them under ledges, and common types include Spotted, Jack-knife fish and Highhat drums. Some different drum species look very similar.

Eels

Eels are fish, though to the uninformed they may appear to be snakes. Most species live in holes and crevices, but may come out to feed at night. Some have singular color, while others have distinct patterns. Perhaps the most common eel is the moray; moray types include Green, Spotted, Reticulated, Viper and Giant morays. Other types include Conger, Blue Ribbon, Dragon and Wolf eels.

Sharks and Rays

Although not similar in look, sharks and rays share a group because their bodies consist of flexible cartilage and lack much true bone. You may see many types of sharks and rays, ranging from larger species to small ones. Sharks swim using their tail like other fish, whereas rays have modified pectoral fins that they use like wings, "flying" through the water. Common sharks include the Nurse, White Tip, Black Tip and Leopard sharks; common rays include the Skate, Southern stingray, Eagle Ray and Manta Ray.

AWARE-Fish ID 3

1. You spot a fish lying on the bottom. It has excellent camouflage and an unusual shape. It is probably in which grouping?
   ☐ a. Damselfish, chromis and hamlets
   ☐ b. Grouper, seabass and basslets
   ☐ c. Blennies, gobies and jawfish
   ☐ d. Flounders, scorpionfish, lizardfish and frogfish

2. You spot a reddish fish with large eyes hiding in a crack. It has a continuous dorsal fin and doesn't appear very scaly. It is probably a
   ☐ a. squirrelfish
   ☐ b. bigeye
   ☐ c. cardinalfish
   ☐ d. frogfish

How'd you do?
1. d; **2.** b.

CONCEPTS

Underline/highlight the answers to these questions as you read:

1. How can you turn your observations of reef fish into valid data for scientists to use?

2. What is the "roving diver" survey technique?

3. How do you identify a "mystery" fish?

4. How do you record, transfer and submit your observations?

FISH SURVEYS

As mentioned earlier, Project AWARE teamed up with REEF to get divers involved in gathering marine life data. The REEF Survey Project is an ongoing cooperative effort between REEF and The Nature Conservancy, which was established in 1951 to preserve plants, animals and natural communities. Through the survey project, volunteers gather species and abundance data, which REEF puts into its project database. In cooperation with biologists from the Conservancy, the University of Miami and the US National Oceanic and Atmospheric Administration (NOAA), REEF developed the procedures for gathering, transferring and organizing data. The database provides fish population data to scientists, resource managers and the conservation communities.

To participate in the REEF Fish Survey Project, you need the basic fish identification skills you're learning here and will practice in the Fish Identification Adventure Dive, and you need to be a member of REEF (www.reef.org). Alternatively, you may enjoy identifying and collecting fish information for personal satisfaction or for another scientific endeavour, in which case you record your data as needed for that purpose. Let's look at the REEF methods as an example of effective data gathering and recording.

Data Collection

The REEF Fish Survey Project uses the "roving diver" technique to gather data. This means you don't alter the way you dive, but simply swim along as usual, spotting and identifying fish as you go. You record the fish you identify on a slate.

You don't need exact fish counts, though you do need to estimate relative abundance. You can note S for a single fish (1), F for few (2-10), M for many (11-100) or A for abundant (>100). You record sightings as soon as you enter the water, and continue throughout the dive, including exploring places like sand flats, grass beds, rubble fields and looking into cracks and crevices.

The REEF Fish Survey Project uses the "roving diver" technique to gather data. This means you don't alter the way you dive, but simply swim along as usual, spotting and identifying fish as you go. You record the fish you identify on a slate

If you discover a "mystery" fish you can't identify, note its distinguishing marks and sketch it on your slate. After the dive, you can consult with some more experienced fish watchers, or check a fish guide. Include the fish in your survey data only if you positively identify the species.

Reporting Data

If you're part of the REEF Fish Survey Project, after the dive transfer your recorded sightings to the project's computer scansheet. You can record species and abundance data for a single dive, or species-only data from a series of dives. As you might expect, the species and abundance data are much more useful.

Record only those fish you identify positively, with special attention to those species marked with a black triangle on the scansheet. Next, record your position (latitude and longitude) as precisely as possible, using GPS (global positioning system) if available. Check that you've filled in all the requested information, and mail the completed sheets to REEF Fish Survey Project, PO Box 246, Key Largo FL 33037, USA.

Depending on circumstances, your Fish Identification Adventure Dive may or may not be a REEF Fish Survey. Your instructor may have you practice basic identification skills, which you will build upon later for use with the REEF survey if you wish.

AWARE – Fish Identification Specialty Course

Your Fish Identification Adventure Dive may be credited (at the instructor's discretion) toward the AWARE – Fish Identification Specialty Course certification. In addition to what you've learned in this section and will practice in the Fish Identification Adventure Dive, the AWARE – Fish Identification Specialty Course includes:

*   preparing REEF scansheets (if part of the survey project)
*   further practice identifying fish
*   practice noting fish abundance

KNOWLEDGE REVIEW

AWARE Fish Identification

1. Why are scuba divers and snorkelers the "natural" ambassadors for the aquatic environment?

2. What does AWARE stand for?

3. True or False. Project AWARE's mission includes teaching the world about the importance of preserving the aquatic environment.

4. The Project AWARE Foundation supports environmental efforts by

   ☐ a. encouraging aquatic ecology and education.

   ☐ b. funding and assisting worthwhile projects that enrich humanity's awareness and understanding of the aquatic world's fragile nature.

   ☐ c. supporting environmental research.

   ☐ d. All of the above.

5. Approximately how many different fish species exist worldwide?

6. True or False. The simple strategy for identifying fish is to focus on families rather than trying to learn every fish species.

7. Fish identification is a(n) _____ activity. Avoid _____ fish to get a better look.

   ☐ a. interactive/photographing

   ☐ b. passive/staring at

   ☐ c. passive/chasing

   ☐ d. interactive/drawing

8. List at least four common fish groupings used to identify fish in your area.

1._____

2._____

3._____

4._____

9. List some of the characteristics that assist in distinguishing between fish families.

1._____

2._____

3._____

4._____

10. Describe the "roving diver" survey technique.

Student Diver Statement: I've completed this Knowledge Review to the best of my ability and any questions I answered incorrectly or incompletely I've had explained to me, and I understand what I missed.

Signature _____ Date_____

Fish Identification Adventure Dive Overview

- Knowledge assessment/ Knowledge Review
- Slate preparation
- Briefing
- Gearing up
- Predive safety check (BWRAF)
- Entry
- Descent
- Identify fish families
- Record sightings
- Sketch/describe unfamiliar fish
- Ascent – safety stop
- Exit
- Use reference materials to identify unfamiliar fish
- Debrief
- Log dive – PADI Instructor signs

BOAT DIVING

Introduction

The anchor chain clatters and engines drone down and sputter silent; you've arrived. You and your buddy help each other gear up with anticipation; this dive promises to be great. For this dive, there's no long surface swim or entries through surf because you're only 15 metres/50 feet from the dive site – 15 metres/50 feet above it. You enter the water, and in moments, you and your buddy descend to the site.

Experiences like these attract divers to boat diving; in fact, virtually all divers end up diving from a boat sooner or later, whether it's a skiff or a giant live-aboard sailboat. Yet surprisingly, some divers learn to dive and make dozens of dives before they ever set foot on a dive boat; others learn to dive from one type of boat, but have little experience diving from others. If you fit in either group, the Boat Adventure Dive will speed your transition to diving from boats or boats you're not familiar with.

Underline/highlight the answers to this question as you read:

1. What are the advantages of diving from a boat?

ADVANTAGES OF BOAT DIVING

Diving and boats make an obvious match, though there's lots of excellent diving from shore. Even where you can shore dive, divers often prefer to go by boat to enjoy several practical advantages and because it adds to the fun and adventure, which is reason enough. To begin, boat diving gives you access to dive sites beyond a reasonable swim from shore. When boat diving, if you find poor conditions at the dive site, it's easy to move the boat to some place better. Boat diving is sometimes a bit easier in that it avoids surf, mud, or long hikes to and from the car with your equipment on. This also helps reduce wear on equipment. In some areas, there's no shore diving available – when you dive, you go by boat.

Boat diving is fun because it puts you with others who share your love of adventure and the diving lifestyle, giving you the opportunity to become friends, dive with them and learn from their experiences. Finally, one of the best reasons for diving from a boat is that boating – like diving – is a fun recreation and a great way to spend time near the water.

KEY CONCEPTS

Underline/highlight the answers to these questions as you read:

1. What are a boat's bow, stern, starboard side and port side?

2. Which is the windward side and which is the leeward side of a boat?

3. What do the following terms refer to on a boat: forward, aft, below, head, galley, bridge, wheel house, rail, transom?

BOAT TERMINOLOGY

"Avast me hearties! You there! Swab the deck or we'll haul you o'er the yardarm!"

Even the most ardent landlubber is probably aware, perhaps from television or movies, that by convention, boats have their own terminology and names for things. While some terms hang on purely through tradition, others come from practical needs, such as not confusing the boat's left with your left. Regardless of where boat terms come from, knowing the most common ones allows you to communicate effectively with the crew and others on the boat. A quick tour around a boat is all you need to become familiar with boat terminology.

Imagine you're walking on a dive charter boat. You're at the *stern*, or extreme rear of the boat. You're faced *forward*, that is, toward the front, where you can find the *bow* (the pointy end). As you face forward, the boat's *port* side is on your left (just remember "left-port" – both have four letters) and its *starboard* side is on your right. Port and starboard don't change – they're always the boat's left and right. If you turn around so you face the stern, you're facing *aft* and now starboard is on your left.

Walking around the boat, you notice a breeze blowing across the deck. The side it comes from is *windward*, with the opposite *leeward* (pronounce it "loo-ward" if you want to impress everyone with your saltiness).

You also notice a *companionway*, or passage, that leads *below* to the areas under the top deck. You go below, where you walk by the boat's *head* (toilet) and where the crew's cooking lunch in the *galley* (kitchen – but the cook is *not* the "galley slave").

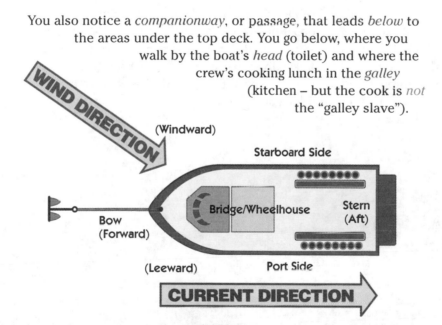

After a bite to eat, you decide to watch the captain steer the boat, and (with permission) you climb a ladder to the *bridge*, where the boat's *wheel* (steering wheel), compass and other controls are found. (On other boats, the bridge may be called the *wheel house*.) Returning to the deck, you walk aft along the *rail* – the outer edge of the boat deck – and relax, sitting near the *transom*, that is, the planking that forms the hull's stern section.

Boat Terminology

aft	toward the rear of the boat		**keel**	boat's "spine" along length of hull's center
below	below decks		**port**	when facing forward, the boat's left
bow	the front of the boat		**rail**	outer edge of boat deck
bridge	area from which the boat is controlled		**starboard**	when facing forward, the boat's right
companionway	a passage		**stern**	the back of the boat
fly bridge	bridge highly elevated for visibility		**transom**	wood or material that makes up the stern
forward	toward the front of the boat		**wheel**	steering wheel, also called "helm"
galley	kitchen		**wheel house**	houses the boat's wheel and other controls
head	restroom or toilet			
helm	controls the boat's steering		**windward**	toward the wind
leeward	away from the wind			

The boat you dive from for your Boat Adventure Dive may have all or only some of the described areas, depending upon it's size and nature. You may also hear self descriptive terms important to divers: tank racks, bunks, diver exit/entry area or brightwork. If you don't understand something, be sure to ask the crew or your instructor to define it for you. (Thought we'd slip one past you? "Brightwork" is all the shiny metal fittings the crew spends hours and hours polishing.)

Quick REVIEW

Boat 2

1. If you're on a boat facing forward, _____ is to your left, _____ is to your right and the _____ is directly in front of you.
    - ☐ a. port, starboard, stern
    - ☐ b. starboard, port, bow
    - ☐ c. port, starboard, bow
    - ☐ d. starboard, port, stern

2. To keep wind from blowing in your face, you would face the _____ side of the boat.
    - ☐ a. windward   ☐ b. leeward   ☐ c. port

3. On a boat, the restroom is called the:
    - ☐ a. bridge   ☐ b. below   ☐ c. head

How'd you do?
1. c; **2.** b; **3.** c.

TYPES OF DIVE BOATS

Dive boats range from small inflatables, to pontoon boats, to giant cruisers, live-aboards and motorsailers, and sail on everything from medium sized lakes to the high seas. Regardless of type or where it sails, there are three features that a typical dive boat needs: The first is ample deck space. "Ample" is a relative term depending on the boat's size, but dive gear takes up a lot of room, and you need adequate space for gear, you and getting kitted up. Stability is the second requirement. The less a boat pitches, the easier it is to don equipment, enter the water and exit the water. Finally, the boat needs ample engine power to drive the boat, its passengers and lots of heavy equipment to the dive site. Again, "ample" is relative, depending on the water conditions and how far you're going.

Because there are so many types of boats, it's hard to place some boats into a particular category. But to discuss the subject we need to generalize, so let's divide boats into four categories based on broad characteristics. That makes it reasonable to discuss the techniques that apply to diving from various types.

Inflatables

Where divers want fast, stable, portable and relatively inexpensive dive boats, you'll find inflatables. They range from about 3 metres/10 feet to more than 6 metres/20 feet in length and can carry two to five or six divers (or more). The "typical" inflatable is constructed from two air-filled tubes (subdivided into compartments so it won't sink with a hole in it) that converge at the bow and a solid or inflated keel. The boat's solid transom usually sports an outboard motor, and the boat may have either a rigid or flexible hull. In general, inflatables are considered "small" boats.

Hard-hull Day Boats

Hard-hull day boats range from about 3 metres/10 feet to more than 6 metres/20 feet, and typically are used for single-day, short distance excursions.

These boats include runabouts, pontoon "flat-tops," small sailboats, skiffs, ski-boats and other small-to-medium open boats. Hard-hull day boats range from about 3 metres/10 feet to more than 6 metres/20 feet, and typically are used for single-day, short distance excursions. The best dive boats in this category are designed specifically for diving or fishing, with lots of deck space; most hard-hull day boats can be trailered.

Cabin-cruisers

Ranging from about 6 metres/20 feet to well over 10 metres/30 feet, cabin-cruisers are boats with at least minimum accommodations for extended trips, including overnight trips. This group includes medium-sized sailboats, yachts and most medium-sized hard-hull boats. Some types of dive charter boats (those that carry six to ten divers) fall into this category. The best cabin-cruisers for diving are those with ample deck space.

Live-aboards

This boat category includes all the large dive boats: converted fishing vessels, large charter boats (sail or engine power), yachts and even cruise ships. The lengths start at around 10 metres/30 feet and go up from there. "Live-aboard" denotes the ability to comfortably accommodate large groups on long-distance trips, even if the boat isn't specifically used for multiday trips. Ironically, diving from the largest live-aboards may mean diving from smaller boats. Some are so large that

after cruising to a dive destination, you may use an inflatable or skiff to go from the live-aboard to various dive sites.

SAFETY/EMERGENCY EQUIPMENT FOR BOAT DIVING

When boat diving, you're often farther from assistance than when diving at many shore dive sites, so dive boats carry equipment for handling emergencies and summoning aid. As a boat diver, it's a good idea to be familiar with the purpose and location of emergency equipment available on "typical" dive boats. It's also a good idea to find out what safety/ emergency equipment is available and where it's stored when checking aboard an unfamiliar dive boat.

Personal Flotation Devices

Personal Flotation Devices, also known as PFDs, or "life preservers" include life rings, buoyant cushions, ring buoys and life jackets. In most areas, laws/regulations dictate that a boat must carry a recognized PFD for each person on board (note that your BCD is generally not a recognized life preserver, nor is it intended to be one). On smaller boats, you'll usually find PFDs tucked to the side where they're handy and visible, but out of the way. On medium-sized and larger boats, they're fre-

In most areas, laws/regulations dictate that a boat must carry a recognized PFD for each person on board (note that your BCD is generally not a recognized life preserver, nor is it intended to be one).

quently stored in marked compartments, with a few life rings hanging out to throw if someone falls overboard.

Fire Extinguishers

The problem with fire on a boat is that there's no where to run. This is why the crew takes fire prevention and smoking rules very seriously. Just in case, you'll note fire extinguishers generally placed visibly in one or more places around a boat, particularly in the galley and engine areas. Small boats like inflatables or skiffs have little to burn and may not carry one, though having one aboard is always recommended.

Sound Signaling Devices

Bells, horns and whistles warn off other vessels in low visibility, summon divers, or signal emergency and distress. On medium-to-large boats, these devices are usually controlled from the bridge. Smaller boats may rely on mouth-blown whistles or hand-held air horns. The emergency whistle on your BCD may do the job in a pinch.

Visual Distress Signals

Devices for visual signaling include flare guns and strobe lights. You use these to summon aid at long distances, especially when a marine radio isn't available. You also use these to help guide emergency vessels you have summoned by other means. These tend to be kept in the general vicinity of the bridge.

First Aid Kit

You're likely to find the boat's kit in a water-tight container in an area where it's not likely to get wet. On larger boats, it can generally be found below; on smaller boats, look under seats or in other "dry" areas.

Oxygen Equipment

As you recall from your PADI Open Water Diver course, oxygen is important for emergency care for most serious dive accidents. For this reason, it's highly recommended that oxygen be carried on dive boats. Generally, oxygen is kept near the first aid kit. (See the Deep Diving section for more about using oxygen for decompression illness first aid.)

Marine Radio

Marine radio is used for general or emergency communication (in many areas, VHF 16 is reserved for emergencies). You'll usually find the radio on the bridge, though if the bridge is fairly exposed (as on sailboats), you may find it below. Small boats may have no radio, though hand-held marine radios have become quite common. Besides marine radio, in a growing number of areas you can use mobile telephones well away from shore, and contact help that way if necessary.

Bilge Pump or Bailer

On medium and large boats, an electric bilge pump rids the boat of water washing in over the side in rough water. Electric bilge pumps are normally automatic, with manual switches near the boat's wheel. Many boats also have a manual (hand) backup bilge pump which will be below, close to the boat keel. Small boats usually don't have bilge pumps, so to handle excess water they may have plugs/valves that drain water while underway, or a "hand bailer," i.e., a bucket.

Quick REVIEW

Boat 4

1. Which are common pieces of emergency equipment on "typical" dive boats (check all that apply)?
   ☐ a. fire extinguisher ☐ b. marine radio ☐ c. first aid kit

2. Which of the following may be frequently found (or activated) on the bridge/steering area of a "typical" dive boat (check all that apply)?
   ☐ a. PFDs ☐ b. marine radio ☐ c. bilge pump

How'd you do?
1. a, b, c; 2. b, c.

KEY
CONCEPTS

Underline/highlight the answers
to these questions as you read:

1. How do you prevent seasickness?

2. What should you do if you
   get seasick?

SEASICKNESS

If there's anything that discourages would-be boat divers, it's fear of seasickness. Seasickness ranges from an unpleasant feeling of mild queasiness to severe dizziness, nausea and vomiting. It's always unpleasant and it pretty much knocks the fun out of the entire experience. Once you've had it happen, you sure don't want to repeat it.

Since the only cure for seasickness is solid ground, prevention is everything. Although its exact nature isn't completely understood (though known to be related to disturbance of balance organs in the inner ear), several tips and techniques can help you avoid seasickness.

The most common preventative is to use seasickness medication, which may be any of several drugs sold under various brand names. You take this before boarding, according to the manufacturer's instructions. Some of these may cause drowsiness or have other effects that you want to avoid while diving, so check the label and try the medication when you won't be diving. Other "medications" include ginger root and "acupressure." Little medical evidence supports the effectiveness of many of these, but many people claim they work. If you have any questions or concerns about seasickness medications, consult your physician.

Some other tips may help prevent seasickness: Get plenty of sleep, avoid alcohol and eat a balanced (but not greasy) meal before the trip. On board, stay in the fresh air and out of engine fumes. Avoid intricate tasks like reading or preparing photo equipment while underway. It may help to look at the horizon.

If you get seasick, take heart. Your illness won't be permanent. If you feel nauseous, don't go in the

If you feel nauseous, don't go in the head (its cramped quarters and stuffy atmosphere will make you worse), but instead go to the leeward rail. If the sea is rough, have someone hold your belt or arm so you don't accidentally fall overboard – avoid being on deck alone, especially while underway and at night.

head (its cramped quarters and stuffy atmosphere will make you worse), but instead go to the leeward rail. If the sea is rough, have someone hold your belt or arm so you don't accidentally fall overboard – avoid being on deck alone, especially while underway and at night. After being sick, try sipping water to settle your stomach and to avoid dehydration. Stay in the middle of the boat, which is the most stable, and away from the bow, which is the least stable.

Quick REVIEW

Boat 5

1. To prevent seasickness
   - ☐ a. take seasickness medication
   - ☐ b. stay in fresh air
   - ☐ c. avoid alcohol
   - ☐ d. all of the above may help

2. If you do get seasick and feel nauseous, go to the leeward rail alone so you don't make other people sick.
   ☐ True   ☐ False

How'd you do?
1. d; **2.** False. Go to the leeward rail with someone to hold your belt or arm to prevent you from falling overboard.

BOAT DIVING PREPARATION

Once you're at sea, up the river or out on the lake in a dive boat, you're on your own to a large extent. If something's not aboard, you're going to do without it, and if you're not physically or mentally prepared for the trip, you're probably going to have to stick it out. This is why a fun, successful boat dive starts with preparing your gear and yourself properly.

Preparing Your Equipment

The rule of thumb for anything on a boat is "as little as possible." Space is at a premium, so try to pack efficiently, use collapsible soft-sided bags, forget nothing essential and make sure everything works before leaving.

Begin by inspecting your gear carefully in advance, and have it serviced as needed. Mark each piece clearly (you may be surprised how many people on a crowded

Key CONCEPTS

Underline/highlight the answers to these questions as you read:

1. How do you prepare your equipment for a boat dive?

2. How do you prepare yourself for a boat dive?

dive boat have equipment just like yours), and use a checklist, like the one in the Adventure Log, to be sure you have everything. After you inspect each

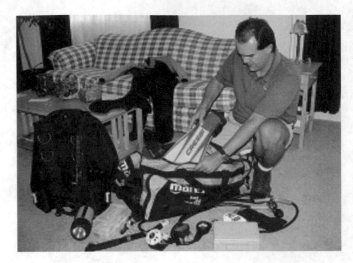

piece and have it serviced, marked and checked off, pack it in your dive bag in the reverse order that you will need it. That is, what you'll need first ends up on top, and what you need last waits at the bottom. This allows you to kit up directly from the bag without scattering everything all over the deck. Finally, have your tank(s) filled in advance and pack a separate bag with small items like dry clothes, a towel, money, etc. Don't forget your certification and dive logbook, which the crew may want to check. Also, when boat diving, place surface signaling devices in your BCD. (See Drift Diving section for more information.)

After you inspect each piece and have it serviced, marked and checked off, pack it in your dive bag in the reverse order that you will need it. That is, what you'll need first ends up on top, and what you need last waits at the bottom. This allows you to kit up directly from the bag without scattering everything all over the deck.

Although you don't want to bring anything unnecessary, do bring your save-a-dive kit. You and your buddy may want to carry some spare gear between the two of you – nothing excessive, but enough to assure you don't miss the dive due to an unexpected malfunction.

Preparing Yourself

As you learned in the previous section, preparing yourself is an important part of avoiding seasickness. The night before the dive, avoid alcohol (but do drink plenty of water, juices and other noncaffeinated liquids so you're well hydrated), eat well and get plenty of sleep. Be sure to tell someone where you're going, including the boat's name, location and destination. If you're using seasickness medication, take it sufficiently in advance according to the instructions or your physician's directions.

Boat 6

1. When preparing your gear for a boat dive, you should (check all that apply):
   - ☐ a. take as much as possible
   - ☐ b. inspect each piece
   - ☐ c. use a checklist

2. The night before a boat dive, it's best to let yourself get a little tired so you can sleep more easily underway.
   ☐ True   ☐ False

How'd you do?
1. b, c;   **2.** False. The night before a boat dive, get plenty of sleep.

Underline/highlight the answers
to this question as you read:

1. What are the general boarding procedures for a charter
   dive boat?

CHARTER BOAT BOARDING PROCEDURES

Even if most of your boat diving will be from small boats like inflatables, you're probably going to dive from charter boats from time to time. Charter boat boarding procedures vary from boat to boat, but follow the same basics:

Plan to board and check in at least half an hour prior to departure. When you arrive, ask for permission to board and wait until a crew member invites you aboard. This is important because they may have deck hatches open or completing maintenance and not be ready for passengers.

Once aboard, ask where and how to stow your equipment – the procedures for this can vary greatly from boat to boat, so check if you're not sure. Assume that anything left on the open deck will get wet – on small boats, you may want to leave anything that can't get wet either at home or in the car.

Most charter boats have a sign-in sheet and/or liability release (assumption of risk). Read and sign these

Once aboard a charter boat, ask where and how to stow your equipment – the procedures for this can vary, ranging from special lockers to simply putting your bag where it's not under foot, so check if you're not sure.

prior to the boat's departure, and attend to any other preboarding procedures the crew requires. They may have you set up your gear before the boat leaves the dock. At some point, the crew will brief you on their operating procedures. They may do this before setting sail, while underway or after anchoring. Either way, listen up, even if you've been on the boat before, because they may vary procedures depending on conditions or the dive site.

Once the boat is underway, relax and enjoy the ride. If the water's a bit rough, avoid moving around more than necessary. If you must move around, use handholds and move carefully. If you must climb a ladder, always *face* the ladder, whether going up or down.

Most charter boats have sign in procedures that may include showing the divemaster your certification and log book, signing a sign-in sheet and/or liability release (assumption of risk), or dive roster. Attend to these and any other preboarding procedures the crew requires.

Boat 7

1. Which is not part of general charter boat boarding procedures?
   - ☐ a. arrive at least one-half hour before departure
   - ☐ b. stow your equipment
   - ☐ c. leave personal belongings on the open deck
   - ☐ d. listen to briefings

   How'd you do?

   1. c.

PREDIVE PROCEDURES

Depending upon the type of boat you dive from, you can expect a predive orientation or briefing. The most extensive briefings can be expected on large charter boats, and usually include a boat facilities orientation, general characteristics of the dive site, confirming that everyone has a buddy, and a review of communication, emergency procedures and general safety rules.

During the boat facilities orientation, you can expect a description of the boat, where to find the head, galley, etc., and any areas that may be off-limits. The dive site orientation will cover the bottom depth, topography, points of interest and possible hazards, local regulations, entry and exit techniques and general suggestions for planning your dive. If you don't have a buddy, the crew will let you and other divers find and form buddy teams among yourselves, and they'll review any special buddy team procedures that may apply. (Such as if you're drift diving.) Finally, the crew will review communications, their procedures for handling emergencies and rules they expect you to follow to ensure the safety of other divers and yourself.

After the briefing and orientation, you will generally begin gearing up, but the procedure varies with the boat. Diving from a small or medium boat, you may have prepared all your equipment before leaving the dock, so that you and your buddy need only slip into your scuba units. In some cases, especially when diving from an inflatable or a hard-hull day boat, you may put your scuba units over the side on lines to put on after you enter the water, leav-

Depending upon the type of boat, you can expect a predive orientation or briefing. These may include a boat facilities orientation, general characteristics of the dive site, confirming that everyone has a buddy, and a review of communication, emergency procedures and general safety rules.

Diving from a small or medium boat, you may prepare all your equipment before leaving the dock, so that you and your buddy need only slip into your scuba units.

ing deck space for getting into your exposure suits. When diving from a private boat, part of your preparation should include having someone stay aboard to tend the boat, act as a lookout and to raise a dive flag.

On most larger boats, you'll suit up as you would when shore diving.
Have a buddy or crew member help you with your gear, if necessary, and remain seated as much as possible if the boat's rocking.

On most larger boats, you'll suit up as you would when shore diving, but work from your bag so you save space. Watch your balance if the boat's rocking, stay seated as much as possible, use hand-holds, and be sure not to leave a scuba tank unsecured – rolling loose on a boat deck, it can do a lot of damage or cause injury. Put on all equipment except your mask and fins, and conduct your predive safety check (Begin With Review And Friend) with your buddy. Being careful to steady yourself, walk to the entry/exit area. Don your mask, and then your fins just before entering the water. Some boats will have variations on suiting up procedures.

REVIEW

Boat 8

1. The topics likely to be included in a predive boat area orientation are (check all that apply):
   □ a. boat anchoring procedures
   □ b. general dive site characteristics
   □ c. boat facilities orientation

2. The procedures for suiting up on a boat
   □ a. vary with boat size and type.
   □ b. are standardized and never change.

How'd you do?
1. b, c; 2. a.

Key CONCEPTS

Underline/highlight the answers
to these questions as you read:

1. What are the general guidelines for making entries from
   various types of boats?

2. What are "trip lines," "gear
   lines," "tag lines," "descent
   lines" and "current lines"
   used for?

3. What are the procedures for
   descending while boat diving?

4. In which direction should
   you generally head when
   boat diving?

5. What are the general guidelines for exiting into a boat?

BOAT DIVING PROCEDURES

Boat Entries

By now, it's clear that boat diving techniques vary
a good bit. When making your Boat Adventure
Dive, your instructor will detail the procedures for
the specific boat you'll be on, which will probably
follow these general entry steps.

When you're ready to enter the water, make sure
your buddy is ready, too. If you're diving from a
charter boat, you'll also need to let the divemaster
log you out (in the water), which is important later
in accounting that all passengers come back
aboard. Go to the entry area with your buddy and
partially inflate your BCD. Put your regulator in
your mouth (unless you'll be donning your scuba
unit in the water, in which case breathe from your
snorkel), make sure the entry area is clear, hold
your mask firmly and enter using an appropriate
method for the boat type (more about these in a
moment). When using accessories such as cameras, have someone hand them to you after entering. After entering, signal that you're "OK" (assuming you are, of course) then clear the area so others can enter.

**Entries from inflatables
and small boats.** On small
boats close to the water,
the easiest entries are usually the sitting back-roll or
the controlled seated
entry. You may find it easiest to put your scuba unit
in the water, enter, slip
into your unit, and then
have someone hand you
your weight belt, or
weights to slip into your
weight system.

On small boats close to the water,
the easiest entries are usually the sitting back-roll or the controlled seated entry.

Entries from cabin cruisers and live-aboards.
There's more entry variety from larger boats, dictated largely by the height of the entry area. If

There's more entry variety from larger boats, dictated largely by the height of the entry area. If you're entering from a couple metres/several feet above the water, you'll probably use the giant stride.

you're entering from a couple metres/several feet above the water, you'll probably use the giant stride. One option is to make a sitting back-roll or controlled seated entry from the swim step (if the boat has one). As a general guide, remember that the best entry is usually the easiest entry. If you have a physical challenge that makes the "routine" entry unsuitable, the crew can often suggest and assist with an alternate method. Don't forget to have the crew check you "out" on the dive roster before you enter.

After entering, you may be using various lines to make swimming, equipment handling, descents or just staying in place easier. A few common lines are:

Mooring or anchor line. The mooring or anchor line is just that: the line holding the boat in place. It is commonly used for descents and ascents.

Trip lines. These lines are attached by a buoy to the anchor and rise almost vertically to the surface. Although the primary purpose of the trip line is to aid anchor retrieval, they're sometimes used to ascend and descend on. This is particularly true when the water's rough, making use of the anchor line, which jerks up-and-down as waves rock the boat, unfavorable. When ascending or descending along a trip line, take care not to pull up with great force because it may dislodge the anchor.

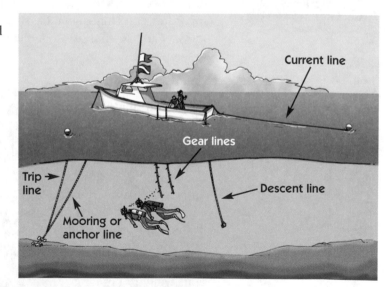

Common lines used in boat diving.

Descent lines. Also called reference lines, descent lines are heavily weighted lines dangling from the stern or other part of the boat. They're used to aid descents/ascents, particularly when using a mooring line or the anchor line is undesirable.

Gear lines. Gear lines are any lines used to suspend equipment before or after a dive. These are commonly used for accessories, or for scuba units when donning and doffing them prior to entries and exits.

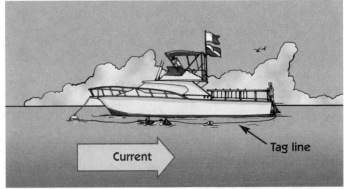

Current lines. When diving in a current, a current line is trailed behind the boat with a float. The line provides you a way to hang on without drifting away while waiting during entries and exits. It also helps after a dive if you surface and have to swim for the boat by giving you a larger target if the current carries you past the boat. Current lines are also called *stern* lines or *trail* lines.

Tag lines. Tag lines, also known as *swim* lines, run from a mooring or anchor line to the entry area or to the current line. In stronger currents, you use the tag line to pull yourself from the entry area to the mooring or anchor line, where you then descend. On your return, you take the mooring or anchor line to the tag line and then the tag line to the current line to wait your turn to exit.

Descents

Once in the water, you'll spend a brief time on the surface before descending (an exception is drift diving – see the Drift Diving section for more information about drift diving descents). Orient yourself to the boat and/or shoreline (if visible) using both natural and compass navigation techniques. Make your standard five-point descent and start downward. A current generally makes descending along a mooring, anchor,

Tag lines, also known as swim lines, run from the mooring or anchor line to the entry area or to the current line. In stronger currents, you use the tag line to pull yourself from the entry area to the mooring or anchor line, where you then descend.

descent or trip line mandatory, though you generally want to do this even without a current.

Line descents. When there's little current, it's best to use a line primarily as a visual reference. If you're diving from a small boat, for example, you might accidentally dislodge the anchor by pulling on the anchor line (if the anchor pulls loose, it can strike you with a great deal of force). When diving from a large charter boat in a current, on the other hand, you may have no choice but to hang on to the mooring or anchor line to keep the current from carrying you away. In this instance, dislodging the anchor's unlikely. Any time you ascend or descend along a line from a boat, keep in mind that the line tends to jerk up and down as the boat or mooring buoy rides swells. Avoid letting the line jerk you up suddenly, as this may cause injury.

When diving from a large charter boat in a current, you may have no choice but to hang on to the mooring or anchor line to keep the current from carrying you away.

Free descents. In calm water, you can descend without a line. If you do so, take care to avoid disorientation, watch your descent rate and maintain buddy contact.

On the Bottom

Once you reach the bottom, you usually follow a single general heading away from the boat. This normally means you dive ahead of the boat, into the current. By doing this, the current helps carry you back to the boat at the dive's end, so you're not fighting to get back. The current also establishes a navigation reference. If you're near shore, you may dive between the boat and shore to stay out of boat traffic.

Avoid long swims away from the boat. Ideally, you want to return to the boat underwater so you can ascend comfortably

Protecting the Bottom

Most boat diving occurs over sensitive bottom environments where delicate coral and bottom dwelling organisms live. To eliminate the harm done by dropping an anchor on the reef, many boats use morring buoys where they exist. Mooring buoys are permanently placed attachment systems consisting of a weighted (cement block) or anchored line with a large floating buoy at the surface. Boats pull up to the buoy and simply tie off; keeping them in place over the reef. Mooring buoys help reefs remain healthy in areas where day-to-day anchoring would do irreversible harm.

Divers can protect sensitive bottom enviornments while they boat dive as well. As you descend down a mooring or anchor line, adjust your buoyancy and be careful where your fins are once you near the bottom. Avoid making contact with the reef. Once on the bottom dive carefully and respect those creatures attached to or crawling over the reef. For more information on how to dive responsibly over sensitive bottoms, read the section Peak Performance Buoyancy in this manual.

along the anchor (or other) line. Charter boats will try to anchor in the best spots, so long swims away from the boat aren't often necessary – often, the best diving is right around the mooring anchor block or beneath the boat. Return to the ascent point with ample air to search for it if you have trouble locating it. If you find it right away, you can spend the last minutes of the dive in the immediate area.

Normally you dive ahead of the boat, into the current. By doing this, the current helps carry you back to the boat at the dive's end, so you're not fighting to get back.

Boat Diving Ascents and Exits

End the dive with a controlled ascent following the S.A.F.E. Diver guidelines in the Deep Diving section – no faster than 18 metres/60 feet per minute and make a three minute safety stop at 5 metres/15 feet. Especially if there's a current, ascend along a line – either the boat's mooring or anchor line or a weighted line – to help control your ascent rate and maintain your safety stop depth without getting carried away from the boat.

After your safety stop, come to the surface near the boat (so you're close to the dive flag), inflate your BCD and signal that you're OK. Swim back to the boat and wait your turn to exit the water. If there's a current, follow the swim line and hang on to the current line as you wait your turn to exit so you don't get carried away. When diving from a charter boat, be patient and stay out from under a diver who's climbing the boat ladder, in case the diver slips and falls, or the diver's cylinder slips loose. When it's your turn to exit, time the swells and let them carry you on to the swim step or stern platform.

If you're diving from a small boat, you'll normally slip out of your scuba unit and hang it from a gear line or pass it up to someone already aboard. Generally, only one diver climbs aboard at a time, on some boats, someone needs to counterbalance the boat's opposite side while you climb aboard.

When diving from any boat, don't remove your fins until you've made firm contact with the boat. Hand up cameras and any accessory equipment. If you have a physical challenge that makes the "standard" exit unfeasible, you and the crew will determine a suitable method to use before the dive.

Drift diving, in which you and the boat drift in the current, uses somewhat different exit procedures – see the Drift Diving section for details.

When it's your turn to exit into a large boat with a swim step, time the swells and let them carry you on to the swim step or stern platform. Stay out from under a diver who's climbing a ladder ahead of you, in case the diver or the diver's tank slips and falls.

Boat 9

1. The best entry from any boat is usually
   - □ a. the easiest.
   - □ b. a sitting back-roll.
   - □ c. a giant stride.

2. Current lines are used to keep divers from being carried away from the boat in a current.
   □ True   □ False

3. When making a descent from a small boat along the anchor line with no current, you should pull sharply on the line to ensure that the anchor's set.
   □ True   □ False

4. When diving from a boat, you should generally swim
   - □ a. behind the boat under the current line.
   - □ b. ahead of the boat, into the current.
   - □ c. generally, it makes no difference which way you go.

5. When surfacing after a boat dive, you should (check all that apply):
   - □ a. surface near the boat
   - □ b. signal that you're okay
   - □ c. wait under the boarding ladder

How'd you do?
1. a; 2. True; 3. False. Pulling sharply could dislodge the anchor. 4. b; 5. a, b.

POSTDIVE PROCEDURES

Once you're back aboard from the last dive, you want to stow your equipment as soon as possible to prevent damage to it and to keep the deck clear. A few guidelines: First, don't drop your weights, because this can damage the boat, gear and feet. Secure your weight system and your tank where they won't slide around and bash into things or people. If you're diving from a small boat, you may leave your exposure suit on and gear assembled until reaching shore. Aboard larger boats, it's usually easiest to take off and disassemble your equipment, putting each piece in your gear bag as you go. This keeps the deck clear and minimizes the probability of losing anything.

On charter boats, the divemaster or a crew member will give a roll call after each dive. This procedure makes sure everyone is aboard and accounted for before leaving the area. Don't leave the deck until your name has been called and you've been checked in. Also, never answer for another diver, even if you're "sure" the diver's asleep below or something. All divers need to be physically present for roll call.

Boat 10
1. When packing and stowing your equipment after a boat dive
   ☐ a. put each piece in your bag as you disassemble it.
   ☐ b. lay each piece on the deck so you can check it off your check list.

2. You should listen to post-dive roll calls because
   ☐ a. it ensures that all divers are aboard.
   ☐ b. it makes sure you won't lose any dive equipment.

How'd you do?
1. a; 2. a.

PADI Boat Diver Specialty Course

Your Boat Adventure Dive may be credited (at the instructor's discretion) toward the Boat Diver Specialty certification. In addition to what you've learned in this section and will practice during the dive, the Boat Diver Specialty course includes:

• spare parts and tool kits for boat diving

• optional – small boat handling and seamanship

• additional practice in planning and executing boat dives

KNOWLEDGE REVIEW
Boat Diving

1. On the illustration, label the bow, stern, port, starboard, windward and leeward.

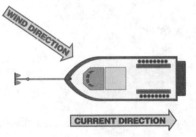

2. List eight pieces of emergency equipment commonly found on dive boats.

   1. _____   5. _____
   2. _____   6. _____
   3. _____   7. _____
   4. _____   8. _____

3. Describe how to prevent seasickness, and what to do if you become seasick.

4. Describe the "general" boarding procedures you can expect on a typical dive boat.

5. On most dive boats, you want to work from your dive bag and not take up excessive _____.

6. Explain the general guidelines for entries from various dive boats.

7. Explain the location and purpose for each of the following lines:

Trip line:

Gear line:

Tag (swim) line:

Current (trail) line:

8. Describe how to make a free descent from a boat.

9. What are the general guidelines for exiting the water into a charter dive boat?

10. Why should you listen to post dive roll calls by divemasters or crew members?

Student Diver Statement: I've completed this Knowledge Review to the best of my ability and any questions I answered incorrectly or incompletely I've had explained to me, and I understand what I missed.

Signature _____ Date_____

Boat Adventure Dive Overview

- Knowledge assessment/ Knowledge Review
- Briefing
- Gearing up
- Predive safety check (BWRAF)
- Boat Diving Entry

- Descent
- Dive for fun and adventure
- Ascent – safety stop
- Boat Diving Exit
- Debrief
- Log dive – PADI Instructor signs

LIVE
vicariously through **others** or experience it for **yourself.**

Adventure is calling.

You're already on your way!

Ask your instructor today how you can apply your advanced open water adventure dives to PADI Specialty programs. Visit your PADI Dive Center or Resort or padi.com for details.

PADI
padi.com

It's your life. Dive it well.

DEEP DIVING

Introduction

Mention a "deep dive" and watch the reactions. Novice divers want to know what it's like. More experienced divers who have been a bit deeper chat with excitement. Those qualified to venture to 40 metres/130 feet – the recommended farthest edge of recreational diving – also show enthusiasm, though somewhat tempered with respect for the challenge deep diving presents. There's something a bit attractive, exciting and mysterious about "going deep."

As a new Open Water Diver, 18 metres/60 feet marks the depth limit to which you're qualified to dive. This limit isn't arbitrary – it's based on no decompression limits, nitrogen narcosis and air supply – but even if you've only made a few dives, you may be curious about deeper dives, perhaps simply to visit specific dive sites below 18 metres/60 feet. The Deep Adventure Dive will satisfy some of this curiosity and give you access to some of those dive sites by qualifying you to dive as deep as 30 metres/100 feet, in conditions as good as or better than those in which you have training and experience.

Key CONCEPTS

Underline/highlight the answers to these questions as you read:

1. What five activities can you enjoy while deep diving?

2. What is the difference between an appropriate and an inappropriate deep dive objective?

DEEP DIVING ACTIVITIES AND OBJECTIVES

Deep diving calls for an appropriate objective, such as observing aquatic life – like bull kelp – that doesn't live in shallower water.

Have you ever wondered why a jetliner cruises at 10,000 metres/35,000 feet while a two-seater prop plane hums along at only 900 metres/3000 feet? A jetliner has to fly up where the air's thin enough to reach the high speeds necessary for crossing long distances quickly. It doesn't cruise up high "just to go up high."

Deep diving is similar. You don't make a deep dive just to go deep, but as a means to an end. Deep diving gives you access to new dive sites that lie below 18 metres/60 feet, and allows you to extend some of the activities you enjoy to new depths. Through deep diving you can observe aquatic life that doesn't live in shallower water, visit wrecks that rest in deeper water, as well as shoot photographs. In some places, deep diving makes it possible to drift effortlessly past deep water reefs (for more information, see the Drift Diving section), and in other areas, you might collect or recover objects that were lost in greater depths. Those are just five examples of the many possibilities when making deep dives.

In planning a deep dive, you must determine an appropriate objective. An appropriate deep dive objective will usually be singular because you have less no decompression time as you descend. It's a reasonable objective, too, such as participating in one of the activities listed above, and it's based on your training and experience as well as dive conditions.

An inappropriate deep diving objective is one that expects to accomplish too much in one dive, or for nothing more than the "thrill" of facing risk. It's not unreasonable to deep dive for the challenges and

For more information about...

Drift Diving
See the Drift Diving section in this textbook.

to expand your training and experience to greater depths – that's what the Deep Adventure Dive and the Deep Diver courses are for – but to simply plunge into deep water without regard for appropriate procedures is neither reasonable nor prudent.

DEEP DIVING: DEFINITION AND LIMITS

Choosing a depth to define "deep" is a bit like picking an altitude to define "high." Eighteen metres/60 feet may be "high" compared to standing on the ground, but compared to a satellite in orbit, it's "low." Clearly, both "deep" and "high" are subjective terms, though physiology and physics make defining "deep" for recreational diving a bit less subjective. In any case, you have to draw a line somewhere, if only to clearly discuss the subject.

PADI and most of the recreational diving community define a "deep" dive as 18 metres/60 feet or below, but no deeper than 40 metres/130 feet. Depths below 40 metres/130 feet lie beyond recreational diving. Given the limitations of recreational scuba equipment, the short no-stop dive times below 18 metres/60 feet and the scope and intent of recreational diver training, these depth limits serve well and have a solid track record supporting their appropriateness.

Underline/highlight the answers to these questions as you read:

1. What is a recreational "deep dive"?

2. What are the four reasons that 30 metres/100 feet is recommended as the optimal depth limit for recreational diving?

3. What five factors should you consider when determining your personal depth limit?

Although 40 metres/130 feet has been set as the maximum, for general purposes, you probably want to treat 30 metres/100 feet as the optimal maximum limit, for four practical reasons: First, the short no decompression limits and rapid air use below 30 metres/100 feet make deeper dives incredibly short. Considering the time and effort to plan and make a deep dive, the activity and objective of a 30 metre/100 foot dive has to be very satisfying to be worth only ten minutes dive time.

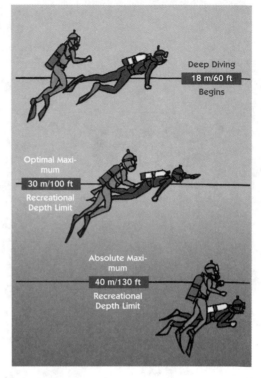

Deep Diving
18 m/60 ft
Begins

Optimal Maximum
30 m/100 ft
Recreational Depth Limit

Absolute Maximum
40 m/130 ft
Recreational Depth Limit

Second, nitrogen narcosis, the intoxicating effect of nitrogen as you go deeper, begins to have a noticable effect on most divers below about 30 metre/100 foot. While susceptibility varies from person to person, this is an important consideration.

Third, dives to depths beyond 30 metres/100 feet tend to be more associated with decompression sickness, particularly when making repetitive dives. Using a single tank of air, it's possible to overstay the no decompression limits when you're that deep, and in any case, with short no-stop times dives tend to be closer to the limits.

Using a single tank of air, it's possible to overstay the no decompression limits. It's important to watch your SPG, dive computer, depth and time closely.

Finally, in many dive environments deeper than 30 metres/100 feet it becomes very dim, or completely dark due to light absorption. This means it's not only difficult to see what's around you, but difficult to read your gauges and use your equipment.

But They're Going Deeper . . .

The dive community accepts the 40 metre/130 foot limit for recreational divers virtually without exception, yet invariably, you'll see or read about technical divers who descend well below 40 metres/130 feet. This doesn't negate the limits for recreational divers, however.

On close inspection, you'll see that technical divers each wear significantly more equipment—often four to six cylinders, multiple regulators, etc. – and it is more elaborate. Diving to depths below 40 metres/130 feet often requires special helium breathing gases, and an hour or more making stage decompression stops. As you might imagine, this type of diving requires special training, and substantial experience in recreational diving before starting that training. Even with the equipment, experience and training, technical diving by its nature entails significantly more risk than recreational diving.

When you think about it, technical divers validate the 40 metre/130 foot recreational limit with all the extra hardware, special techniques and extensive training they require to manage the risk of going beyond. Technical diving isn't for everyone, nor is it a necessary step in your progress as a diver even after thousands of dives. But, if this type of diving interests you, obtain the proper experience and training before attempting it.

A final thought: Descending below 40 metres/130 feet with a single cylinder and standard recreational scuba gear isn't technical diving. It's being stupid.

For more information on PADI's TecRec program, visit PADI's website at www.padi.com.

Developing Your Personal Depth Limit

While the dive community draws the general line for defining a "deep" dive at 18 metres/60 feet, you need to redraw that line based on the environment, your experience and your training. Nor can you overlook your buddy's experience and training when deciding the depth limit.

For example, 18 metres/60 feet may not seem deep and stressful at all when you and your buddy are properly trained, have been diving actively, and you're in warm, clear tropical water. The same dive without training after a ten-month pause in diving activity would certainly be more stressful and seem "deeper." Likewise a dive to less than 18 metres/60 feet in a cold, dark, poor-visibility lake could be considered deep even with training and experience. Obviously, depth limits need to change to meet the circumstances.

When setting your depth limit for a dive, take into account the dive site, yourself and your buddy. First, think about the environmental conditions.

Based on them, what is a realistic depth limit? Maybe you need to plan a shallower dive and gradually extend the limit in the particular environment over a series of dives. Second, ask yourself whether you're physically and psychologically fit for the dive. Are you in shape, do you have the training/experience and do you feel confident? Third, consider the depth of any previous dives, the surface interval since the last dive and your pressure group. Check your dive computer if you use one. Repetitive dives have shorter no decompression limits that restrict how deep you can go (remember, you make your deeper dive first). Fourth, evaluate your location. If you have a problem, how long would it take to get a patient to emergency medical care? Fifth, review these factors as they apply to your buddy. The more conservative personal limits – yours or your buddy's – should govern the dive.

Depth limits need to change to meet the circumstances. A dive you might consider "shallow" in warm, clear water may be a "deep" dive in a cooler, darker environment.

REVIEW

Deep 2

1. The dive community defines a recreational deep dive as
   - ☐ a. deeper than 18 metres/60 feet to 40 metres/130 feet.
   - ☐ b. deeper than 30 metres/100 feet to 40 metres/130 feet.
   - ☐ c. deeper than 40 metres/130 feet to 55 metres/180 feet.

2. The reasons 30 metres/100 feet is considered an "optimal" depth limit for recreational diving include (check all that apply):
   - ☐ a. short no decompression limits below 30 metres/100 feet
   - ☐ b. hazardous deep-water marine life
   - ☐ c. oxygen toxicity
   - ☐ d. nitrogen narcosis

3. In setting a personalized depth limit for a dive, if you've been to a certain depth before, you can dive to the same depth in all other environments.
   ☐ True   ☐ False

How'd you do?

1. a; **2.** a, d; **3.** False. You need to determine the depth limit for each dive based on that dive's circumstances.

DEEP DIVING EQUIPMENT

Like most diving specialties, deep diving has its unique equipment requirements, which you can divide into two groups: your personal equipment and specialized deep diving equipment. Additionally, deep diving calls for a support station and attention to using dive computers.

Personal Equipment

Before making a deep dive, you need to evaluate your personal equipment's suitability for deep diving. You may find that some of it needs service, and in some cases, replacement. Generally, you need to consider both equipment condition and appropriateness for use in deep water. Here are some guidelines:

Regulator. The deeper you go, the denser the air your regulator delivers. A balanced regulator breathes consistently regardless of tank pressure. Virtually all modern regulator models perform adequately within recreational limits, though you want the best performance possible. Also, regardless of model your regulator needs to be in good working order through proper maintenance and service as recommended by the manufacturer (usually, that's within the last year).

Submersible pressure gauge. Have your submersible pressure gauge serviced annually (along with your regulator) and checked for accuracy. You (obviously) want an accurate SPG for all diving, but you don't want to be at 30 metres/100 feet when you find out it reads 70 bar/1000 psi too high.

Tanks. Because you use air faster in deeper water, use a 12 liter/71.2 cubic foot or larger capacity cylinder. Remember that you want maximum air supply to provide a reserve and ample air for your safety stop, not so that you can push or exceed the no decompression limits.

BCD. Your BCD should be in good working condition. Check the BCD for leaks, either in the bladder or valves and have it serviced as necessary before deep diving with it.

Exposure suits. The suit you use in shallow water may not be appropriate for deep diving. Deeper water tends to be colder; if you drop through a thermocline (the abrupt transition to cold water you learned about in your Open Water Diver course), the temperature can plunge. On top of this, the water pressure compresses neoprene wet suits, reducing their insulation at greater depths (this isn't an issue with most dry suits). Choose your exposure suit based on the deep water temperatures.

When deep diving, be sure your gear is in good working order. Choose your exposure suit based on the temperature of the water at depth.

Alternate air source. The standard place to wear your alternate air source is clearly marked in the triangle formed by your chin and the lower corners of your rib cage. Here, either you or your buddy can easily find and control the alternate in the event of an air supply emergency. Besides an extra second stage alternate, you may want to go for a pony bottle alternate air source for deep diving. A pony bottle uses a totally independent regulator and an extra supply of air, making you more self-sufficient in the event of an emergency.

Gauges. Deep diving requires carrying a complete set of instruments: a dive computer or depth gauge and timer, plus a compass. Have your gauges' accuracy checked annually, or if they're dropped or subjected to any abuse. Many divers carry backup timers and depth gauges while deep diving.

Special Equipment for Deep Diving
Besides your personal gear, deep diving calls for some equipment that you wouldn't necessarily use for diving shallower. This equipment makes deep diving easier and in many environments, contributes significantly to safety.

Reference line. If you've already made a Night Adventure Dive, you're familiar with using a line to help maintain your orientation and control during ascents and descents. A reference line meets the same purposes in deep diving, and helps you maintain buddy contact and your safety stop depth at 5 metres/15 feet.

Choose a size line you can hang on to easily for your reference line – typically 12 mm/1/2 in. or larger – and suspend it from a separate float when shore diving to tow with you. When boat diving, you may also tow a float, but it's common to use the anchor line as the reference line. This is acceptable, provided that the water is fairly calm, but in rougher water, the anchor line may snap up and down in the first 5 to 6 metres/15 to 20 feet as the boat pitches and rolls. If you try to hold the anchor line in such conditions, you can be injured if it jerks you up suddenly. Another problem with using the anchor line is that you may not be able to locate it for your ascent if the boat had to reanchor during your dive.

Emergency breathing equipment. Short no decompression limits and safety stops make a pause at the 5 metre/15 foot level inevitable on virtually all deep dives. It's much easier to accidently exceed no decompression limits on a deep dive, thus requiring emergency decompression. You should make safety stops on all deep dives to help avoid decompression sickness.

Emergency breathing equipment at the safety stop level ensures that you have enough air to make a safety or emergency decompression stop. The most common emergency breathing system is simply a tank and regulator suspended from a line to hang at 5 metres/15 feet. Some dive boats have second stages on 6 metre/20 foot hoses that reach down from the surface, eliminating the suspended tank.

Spare weights. Although you usually account for air consumption when weighting yourself, it's common to want just a bit more weight to help you stay at safety stop depth. Typically, you put spare weights with clips on the emergency breathing equipment, either clipped to it, in a mesh bag or similar container. If needed, clip a weight to your weight belt or BCD.

Emergency breathing equipment at the safety stop level ensures that you have enough air to make a safety or emergency decompression stop. The most common emergency breathing system is simply a tank and regulator suspended from a line to hang at 5 metres/15 feet. Spare weights come in handy if you find yourself just a bit positively buoyant.

Dive light. Because some deep environments can be relatively dim due to light absorption by water, you may find a compact light useful for deep diving when you want to look in holes or cracks, or to read gauges. In some environments with low visibility, a dive below 18 metres/60 feet can be completely dark without a light. Be sure the light has been rated to 40 metres/130 feet. For more information on dive lights, refer to the Night Diving section.

First aid and emergency oxygen. It's recommended to have these available for all diving activities, but they can be extra important for rendering aid when deep diving, and in remote locations. You'll learn more about handling diver emergencies when you complete the PADI Emergency First Response program and the PADI Rescue Diver course.

Surface Support Stations

The easiest way to deploy deep dive equipment is by using a surface support station, which combines your reference line, emergency breathing equipment and spare weights into a single unit. A surface support station is simply a float with an anchored line and a weighted 5 metre/15 foot line for suspending your emergency breathing equipment and spare weights. The anchored line doubles as your descent/ascent reference line and keeps your surface support station in place. When boat diving, the boat replaces the float.

Deep Diving with Computers

Dive computers have become almost standard equipment in many environments, and it's easy to see why. Computers combine time and depth gauges (and air supply, in some models) and calculate your theoretical nitrogen uptake and release throughout a day of diving. They can extend your no decompression time on multilevel dives by giving you credit for slower nitrogen absorption as you ascend to shallow depths (like The Wheel does). Various models provide a range of information that may include ascent rates, temperature, emergency decompression and more.

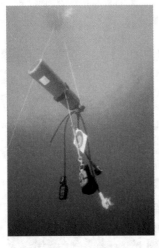

A surface support station is simply a float with an anchored line and a weighted 5 metre/15 foot line for suspending your emergency breathing equipment and spare weights.

For more information about...

Deep Diving
See the *The Recreational Divers Guide to Decompression Theory, Dive Tables and Dive Computers*, the Physiology section of *The Encyclopedia of Recreational Diving* (mulimedia and book) and Chapter Five of the PADI *Divemaster Manual*.

When diving with a computer, there are six basic guidelines to follow, along with the instructions in the computer's instruction manual. First, use the computer as a no decompression device. Stay away from required decompression stops – they greatly complicate the training and equipment requirements. Second, you and your buddy should have individual computers. Never attempt to share one between two or more divers. Third, always follow the computer with the more conservative readout, yours or your buddy's.

Fourth, if your computer fails, follow the manufacturer's instructions. If there are none, make a normal ascent at 18 metres/60 feet per minute (or the computer's rate, whichever is slower) and a safety stop, perhaps as long as your air supply permits if you think you're close to the no decompression limits. Consult the manufacturer's instructions to determine when you may dive again; you may have to wait 12 hours or more.

Fifth, whenever feasible, back up your computer by calculating your profiles with tables. This gives you a way to keep diving if your computer fails, plus it can help give you some idea of how much no stop time you'll have when planning repetitive dives. You'll find that The Wheel, with its multilevel ability, is the best choice for this. Sixth, when diving in a group in which most divers don't have computers (not unusual in a few areas), be sure the divemaster knows you and your buddy do have computers and may have more no decompression dive time available than the rest of the group.

For more information on dive computer use and multilevel diving, see the Multilevel/Computer section. Check out the PADI Multilevel Diver course for more about diving with computers.

When feasible, back up your computer by calculating your profiles with tables. This gives you a way to keep diving if your computer fails, plus it can help give you some idea of how much no stop time you'll have when planning repetitive dives. You'll find that The Wheel, with its multilevel ability, is the best choice for this.

Enriched Air Diving and Deep Diving

You may already be familiar with enriched air nitrox (a.k.a. "nitrox," "EAN," and "EANx"), which is simply air with extra oxygen blended in so that you have a greater proportion of oxygen than found in air. Air is (for practical purposes) 21 percent oxygen, 79 percent nitrogen, whereas popular enriched air blends have, for example, 32 percent oxygen, 68 percent nitrogen (EANx32) and 36 percent oxygen, 64 percent nitrogen (EANx36).

The purpose of enriched air is to extend your no decompression time by reducing the amount of nitrogen in your breathing gas. This is particularly advantageous for dives between 18 metres/60 feet and 30 metres/100 feet. For instance, using EANx36, your no stop time at 28 metres/90 feet is 40 minutes compared to 25 minutes with air.

Enriched air is an excellent and useful way to extend your no decompression time. See your PADI Dive Center, Resort or Instructor about the PADI Enriched Air Diver course.

However, enriched air brings with it concerns of oxygen toxicity, caused by breathing elevated oxygen under pressure if you exceed the maximum depth for a particular blend. For example, the maximum depth for EANx36 is 27 metres/90 feet – descending deeper presents a signficant risk of losing consciousness and drowning due to oxygen toxicity. Enriched air also has concerns regarding using equipment with elevated oxygen. For these reasons, don't use enriched air unless you're properly trained and certified in its use.

When you're properly trained and certified, you know how to avoid and minimize the risks listed above, making enriched air an excellent and useful way to extend your no decompression time. See your PADI Dive Center, Resort or Instructor about the PADI Enriched Air Diver course.

For more information about...

Enriched Air Diving
See the *Enriched Air Diver Manual* and the *Enriched Air Diving* video

Quick REVIEW

Deep 3

1. One of the considerations in determining if your equipment is appropriate for deep diving is whether it's in good working order and serviced in the last year.
   ☐ True   ☐ False

2. The special equipment for deep diving includes (check all that apply):
   ☐ a. emergency breathing equipment
   ☐ b. dive computer
   ☐ c. spare weights
   ☐ d. emergency oxygen

3. A surface support station:
   ☐ a. combines emergency oxygen and first aid equipment with a small boat.
   ☐ b. combines the reference line, emergency breathing equipment and spare weights.
   ☐ c. is only necessary for dives deeper than 30 metres/100 feet.

4. It's acceptable for two divers to share a single computer.
   ☐ True   ☐ False

How'd you do?
1. True;   **2.** a, c, d;   **3.** b;   **4.** False. Divers in a buddy team should have individual dive computers.

DEEP DIVING TECHNIQUES

Once you're properly equipped, deep diving becomes a matter of reapplying the diving techniques you already know to the deep water environment. You already know how to use the buddy system, how to check your buoyancy, how to make ascents and descents, how to handle out-of-air emergencies and other diving techniques, now you're going to the learn to apply the same skills when diving below 18 metres/60 feet.

Maintaining Buddy Contact

In your Open Water Diver course, you learned to keep contact with your buddy so you can assist each other in watching time and depth, or help each other if a problem arises. You also learned to reunite with your buddy on the surface, and then to resume your dive, if you become separated. The buddy system plays the same roles when you deep dive, but it's more important that you *maintain* buddy contact because if you're separated and forced to surface to reunite, the dive ends. You seldom have the air and no decompression time available to redescend into deep water.

To maintain contact on deep dives, watch each other during descents and ascents. Stay within touching distance and swim side-by-side just above the bottom. In poor visibility you might want to use a short "buddy-line" to maintain contact. Frequently monitor each other's depth and air supply.

It's important that you maintain buddy contact because if you're separated and forced to surface to reunite, the dive ends. You seldom have the air and no decompression time available to redescend into deep water.

Key CONCEPTS

Underline/highlight the answers to these questions as you read:

1. What are two techniques for maintaining contact with your buddy during a deep dive?

2. How should you weight yourself for a deep dive?

3. How do you make a head-up descent, and why is it important on a deep dive?

4. What are two ways you can slow or stop a descent or ascent along a reference line?

5. What are four techniques to use while descending or ascending without a visual or tactile reference while deep diving?

6. What are two ways for estimating an 18 metre/60 foot per minute or slower ascent rate?

Neutral Buoyancy at Depth

Maintaining neutral buoyancy on a deep dive differs little from a shallower dive, but keep a few points in mind. First, begin the dive properly weighted – so you float at eye level with an empty BCD and holding a normal breath. (If you check with a full cylinder, add about two kgs/five pounds to compensate for the air you use during the dive.) Second, during descents and ascents, adjust your buoyancy frequently – don't wait until you're rising or sinking rapidly. Finally, with proper weight your BCD (or dry suit if you're using one – see the Dry Suit Diving section for more about buoyancy control with dry suits) should be all you need to maintain neutral buoyancy. You shouldn't need to remove any weights at depth. See the Peak Performance Buoyancy section about protecting sensitive bottom environments by refining your buoyancy skills.

Descents and Ascents

It's usually best to descend into deep water so that you keep your feet below head level. This position makes it easier to control your buoyancy, equalize your air spaces and remain oriented.

Descents and ascents on deep dives require more attention to maintaining control because you travel through more water. A few techniques and a reference line, however, make it easy to govern your ascents/descents. This can be especially important with lower visibility since you don't have as many visual clues to keep you oriented.

Head-up descents. It's usually best to descend into deep water so that you keep your feet below head level. This position makes it easier to control your buoyancy, equalize your air spaces and remain oriented. The position also helps if you need to readjust equipment during the descent. When descending, keep your right hand on the reference line and use the left to operate your BCD and equalize your ears. When beginning your descent, don't forget to set your watch bezel or timer if necessary.

Controlling descents and ascents. It's important to control your descents and ascents to reduce the risk of squeezes or DCI. The first step in controlling your descents and ascents is to maintain buoyancy control. If you regulate your buoyancy frequently, you eliminate the vast majority of out-of-control ascents or descents.

If you need to, you can stop or slow an ascent or descent with a reference line, even with your hands occupied. The first way is to lock the line with your elbow. This is the fastest way to stop or slow on the line, but most people find the second method, wrapping your leg around the line, less tiring. This isn't as quick, but you can stay there easily if you want to hold the position for more than a few moments.

Descents and ascents without reference. It's best to descend into, and ascend from, deep water with a reference such as a line, sloping bottom or reef wall. If you can't, make these four techniques part of the descent/ascent: First, descend/ascend in a head-up position so you remain oriented. Second, face your buddy and stay close, maintaining eye contact during the descent/ascent. Third, use your computer (or depth gauge and timer) so your ascent rate doesn't exceed 18 metres/60 feet per minute. Fourth, adjust your buoyancy frequently to remain neutral and prevent a runaway ascent/descent. During an ascent, make a safety stop at 5 metres/15 feet and listen for boats and other overhead noises. Wait for any noises to pass before ascending with one hand overhead for protection.

Estimating proper ascent rate. As you know well by now, the maximum ascent rate with the Recreational Dive Planner is 18 metres/60 feet per minute. Slower is acceptable, and many dive computers expect you to go even slower.

It's easy to determine your rate when using a

If you need to, you can stop or slow an ascent or descent with a reference line, even with your hands occupied. The first way is to lock the line with your elbow.

Or, you can hold your position by wrapping your leg around a line.

computer and many electronic depth gauges because they either have ascent rate "speedometers," or they have indicators that warn you when you exceed their prescribed rate by bleeping, blinking or honking. If you're diving without a computer, use an analog depth gauge and timer to time your rate so that it takes four seconds or longer to ascend one metre, or ten seconds or longer to ascend ten feet.

When ascending from any depth, be a S.A.F.E. diver. Slowly Ascend From Every dive and make a three minute safety stop at 5 metres/15 feet.

It's easy to determine your rate when using a computer and many electronic depth gauges because they either have ascent rate "speedometers," or they have indicators that warn you when you exceed their prescribed rate by bleeping, blinking or honking.

Deep 4

1. Techniques for maintaining buddy contact on a deep dive include (check all that apply):
   - ☐ a. making feet-up descents together.
   - ☐ b. swimming side-by-side on the bottom.
   - ☐ c using a buddy line in poor visibility.

2. How do you weight yourself for a deep dive?
   - ☐ a. the same as for a shallow dive in the same equipment
   - ☐ b. slightly heavy for an effortless descent
   - ☐ c. slightly underweight so you don't have to ditch weights at the bottom

3. A head-up descent is important because it allows your feet to strike bottom first instead of your head or arms.
   - ☐ True ☐ False

4. A technique for slowing or stopping a descent/ascent on a reference line is
   - ☐ a. dropping your weights.
   - ☐ b. locking the line in your arm at the elbow.

5. When descending or ascending without a reference, stay in a head-up position, keep your back to your buddy, watch your gauges and control your buoyancy frequently.
   - ☐ True ☐ False

6. Two techniques for accurately estimating your ascent rate are to measure the rate with your depth gauge and timer, or to
   - ☐ a. use a computer or gauge with an ascent rate indicator.
   - ☐ b. ascend no faster than your largest bubbles.

How'd you do?
1. b, c; **2.** a; **3.** False. A head-up descent is important for maintaining orientation, controlling buoyancy, making equalization and equipment adjustment easy. **4.** b; **5.** False. Face your buddy and maintain eye contact. **6.** a.

MORE DEEP DIVING TECHNIQUES

Deep Diving Breathing Techniques

Even with your regulator in top condition, you can overbreathe it during stress or strenuous activity in deep water. This happens when you demand air faster than the regulator can deliver it. This causes you to feel like you can't get enough air, or that you're suffocating – a frightening experience if you don't know what's happening. The deeper you are, the more easily you can cause this because each breath requires a greater air mass than when you're shallower.

This is why you need to avoid working hard and also avoid physical demands that cause you to breathe heavily. Even on a shallow dive it's crucial to avoid overexertion while diving, but particularly while deep diving. Always breathe consistently, slowly and deeply. Don't let yourself get out of breath. If you relax and move slowly, you'll conserve air and avoid getting out of breath. If you ever feel like you can't get enough air while deep diving (or shallow), stop all activity and rest. If conditions are such that you can't continue the dive without undue exertion after catching your breath, terminate the dive and ascend properly.

Air Supply Control

From day one as a beginning diver, you learned to monitor your SPG (submersible pressure gauge) to prevent running low on or out of air. In deep diving, you and your buddy need to watch your SPGs more frequently because you use your air much more quickly. For example, you use your air about twice as fast at 30 metres/100 feet as you do at 10 metres/33 feet. Logically, you should be watching your SPG at least twice as often.

It's crucial to avoid overexertion while diving, particularly while deep diving. Breathe consistently, slowly and deeply. If you relax and move slowly, you'll conserve air and avoid getting out of breath.

Besides constantly monitoring your SPG, you can avoid air supply problems by conserving your air. Avoid overexertion, exercise or any strenuous activities, such as long swims. Deep dives should be relaxing. End the dive with an ample reserve, based on the dive specifics, so that you can return to your ascent point, ascend, make a safety stop and surface with enough air to handle the unexpected.

Finally, you can calculate your air consumption to help you plan your air supply requirements for a deep dive. See the Air Consumption Calculation sidebar.

Air Consumption Calculation

How do you know how long a tank of air will last at a given depth if you've never been that deep before? By using some simple mathematics, that's how. All you need is your air consumption rate for a shallower depth, the chart below and a sharp pencil or calculator.

DEPTH		CONVERSION FACTORS	
Metres	Feet	Converting to Surface Rate	Converting from Surface Rate
0	0	1.00	1.00
3	10	0.76	1.30
6	20	0.62	1.60
9	30	0.52	1.91
12	40	0.45	2.21
15	50	0.40	2.52
18	60	0.35	2.82
21	70	0.32	3.12
24	80	0.29	3.42
27	90	0.27	3.73
30	100	0.25	4.03
33	110	0.23	4.33
36	120	0.21	4.64
39	130	0.20	4.94

1. Start by obtaining a record of your air consumption from your dive log. The more dives you work with, the more accurate your calculations will be. For each dive, record how many bar or psi you use, the actual dive time and the depth. Dives that are more or less "flat" (you stay at or about the same depth) will be more accurate than those with several depth changes. You may want to plan a few dives to 6 metres/20 feet just for air consumption calculation.

2. Determine your bar or psi per minute surface rate with this formula:

psi or bar used divided by
actual bottom time X conversion factor
(Converting to Surface Rate for dive depth)
= surface air consumption rate

For example, on a 12 metre/40 foot dive for 20 minutes in which the diver uses 100 bar/1500 psi: 100 bar/1500 psi used divided by a 20 minute bottom time times .45 = 2.25 bar/33.7 psi per minute surface rate.

By recording your bar or psi per minute surface rate over several dives and averaging them, you can determine your normal air consumption rate. Note: Make all your calculations with the same type tank. If you use tanks that differ in capacity and/or pressure, you'll need to determine your air consumption for each independently.

3. To convert your surface rate to your planned depth rate, multiply your surface rate by the Converting From Surface Rate conversion factor for the planned depth.

Based on the previous example, if you plan to dive to 30 metres/100 feet, you can expect your air consumption to be 9 bar/136 psi per minute. (2.25 X 4.03 = 9 ; 33.7 X 4.03 = 135.8). If your tank is filled to 200 bar/3000 psi, you could expect it to last about 22 minutes (200 divided by 9 = 22.2 ; 3000 divided by 136 = 22.05). That doesn't include a reserve, so you need to plan an appropriate shorter time. Or, you can subtract the reserve pressure from your starting pressure before determining your dive time.

When calculating air supply, keep in mind that excitement, activity and cold all increase air consumption, so allow room for error and include ample reserve in your dive planning.

Anti-Silting Techniques

When you reach the bottom on a deep dive (or any other, for that matter), you want to avoid kicking up silt because doing so ruins the visibility and can make it difficult or impossible to see. On a deep dive you don't typically go as far, so causing a silt out when you hit bottom can mess up visibility over the entire area you're going to explore. And, careless bottom contact can destroy corals or other fragile aquatic life, as can a silt cloud settling on top of it.

To prevent silting out the dive, slow your descent as you near, but before you reach the bottom, and stop kicking. Establish neutral buoyancy, and when swimming, stay well off the bottom. If you must stop and maintain contact with the bottom, find a spot away from the reference line (so other divers won't descend on top of you) and free of aquatic life and sharp objects. Exhale momentarily to become slightly negatively buoyant, and then allow yourself to gradually settle, inhaling as you land gently on your knees. See? Almost no silt.

If you must stop and maintain contact with the bottom, find a spot away from the reference line and free of aquatic life and sharp objects. Exhale momentarily to become slightly negatively buoyant, and then allow yourself to gradually settle, inhaling as you land gently on your knees.

Making Safety or Emergency Decompression Stops

In your Open Water Diver course, you learned that when using the Recreational Dive Planner, or any table or computer for that matter, it's wise to make a safety stop at the end of any dive. Also, you learned that some dives with the RDP *require* a safety stop, and that if you accidentally exceed any limit on the Recreational Dive Planner, you need to make an emergency decompression stop.

It's no sweat to make either a safety or emergency decompression stop with a reference line, and you may have done it already: Ascend no faster than 18 metres/60 feet per minute (or whatever your computer likes, if you're using one) until your depth gauge/computer shows 5 metres/15 feet. It's not critical, but try to grasp the line so stop depth lies about mid-chest level if you're vertical. Maintain neutral or slightly negative buoyancy and watch your depth and time. Or, you can watch depth while your buddy watches time. Fine-tune your buoyancy as necessary.

It's not critical, but try to make the safety stop depth about mid-chest level if you're vertical. Maintain neutral or slightly negative buoyancy and watch your depth and time. Or, you can watch depth while your buddy watches time. Fine-tune your buoyancy as necessary.

When making a safety stop, it's a good practice to review the RDP time and depth limits you planned to be certain you didn't exceed them and require an emergency decompression stop – if you find you do, calculate your emergency decompression time and extend your stop to cover it.

Although it's easiest to make a stop on a reference line or on shallow bottom, you can make a safety/emergency decompression stop midwater if you need to. Make a proper ascent, slowing as you reach 5 metres/15 feet, and establish neutral buoyancy. Maintain a feet-down, head-up position while staying side-by-side with your buddy – this makes it easy to kick and/or release air from your BCD to maintain your depth. Monitor your depth and time. If there's a mild current, you may swim slowly against it, but avoid overexertion. Some divers carry small inflatable buoys/signal tubes and small reels that they can deploy from 5-6 metres/15-20 feet, which provides a reference for a stop, and provides a visual reference for a divemaster, boat captain or others at the surface.

If you miss an emergency decompression stop. Should you find that you accidentally omitted an emergency decompression stop, remain calm and stay out of the water – do not make any more dives. Tell your buddies and other supervisory personnel

that you missed the stop. Breathe 100 percent oxygen if available, and try to relax while monitoring yourself closely for any decompression illness symptoms. If any abnormalities develop, seek medical assistance immediately and stay on 100 percent oxygen.

Make a habit of stopping on *all* dives and you greatly reduce the probability of missing an emergency decompression stop. Also, US Navy procedures for handling an omitted decompression stop by reentering the water require extensive surface support and are not normally considered appropriate for recreational divers. If you miss an emergency decompression stop, do not reenter the water.

Deep Diving Along Walls

One of the most popular places to make deep dives is along walls – near-vertical drop-offs into deep water. Because there's no bottom next to many walls (well, of course there is a bottom, but practically speaking a bottom at 600 metres/2000 feet is "no bottom"), there are three special techniques to apply when deep diving along one.

First, remember that many walls are found in warm, tropical climates with extremely clear water where it's easy to be deeper than you realize. Except for your computer or depth gauge, it may not feel much different at 30 metres/100 feet than at 22 metres/70 feet, so watch your depth closely. Second, you'll probably use the wall as your reference, so stay close to keep your orientation. Hanging away from the wall in midwater is exhilarating, but it's easier to lose your orientation and end up deeper than you planned. Third, stay close to the wall, but not too close. Watch for delicate aquatic life, and avoid touching anything fragile or sensitive, just as you would on any dive.

Remember that many walls are found in warm, tropical climates with extremely clear water where it's easy to be deeper than you realize. Except for your computer or depth gauge, it may not feel much different at 30 metres/100 feet than at 22 metres/70 feet, so watch your depth closely.

Deep 5

1. The technique for breathing on a deep dive is best described as
   - □ a. deep and slow to avoid overbreathing the regulator.
   - □ b. shallow and rapid to minimize nitrogen retention.

2. You can avoid low-on-air and out-of-air situations by (check all that apply):
   - □ a. monitoring your SPG frequently
   - □ b. by avoiding overexertion and exercise
   - □ c. by calculating your air consumption

3. You should avoid stirring up the bottom by
   - □ a. descending head-first.
   - □ b. avoiding fin movement near the bottom.

4. The techniques for making a safety/emergency decompression stop, with or without a reference line, call for a feet-down vertical position.
   - □ True   □ False

5. If you discover you accidently omitted an emergency decompression stop you should
   - □ a. re-enter the water and make the stop.
   - □ b. remain calm, stay out of the water and monitor yourself for decompression illness symptoms.

6. Guidelines for wall diving include (check all that apply):
   - □ a. avoiding touching the wall
   - □ b. staying well away from the wall in midwater
   - □ c. monitoring your depth gauge closely

How'd you do?
1. a; **2.** a, b, c; **3.** b; **4.** True; **5.** b; **6.** a, c.

CONCEPTS

Underline/highlight the answers to these questions as you read:

1. At what depth range does nitrogen narcosis generally affect divers?

2. What are seven symptoms and four signs of nitrogen narcosis?

3. What five factors can speed the onset of, or amplify the effects of, nitrogen narcosis?

4. How do you prevent nitrogen narcosis and treat it if it occurs?

NITROGEN NARCOSIS

Your Open Water Diver course introduced you to nitrogen narcosis, which is the intoxicating effect nitrogen produces when you breathe it under pressure. Although the exact cause of nitrogen narcosis still eludes physiologists, most theories link it to nitrogen dissolving into a fatty material that covers nerve cells, interfering with the transmission of nerve impulses. The Deep Adventure Dive may take you deep enough to feel the first mild effects of nitrogen narcosis, so let's review and look at narcosis.

Although some divers feel "narked" at relatively shallow depths and others seem immune even at 40 metres/130 feet, the majority find narcosis first noticeable between 24 metres/80 feet and 30 metres/100 feet. The symptoms (what you feel) and signs (what you see in your buddy) may be varied, depending on the individual.

Symptoms include:

- rigid, inflexible thinking

- poor judgment and short-term memory loss

- a false sense of security

- no concern for safety or a particular task

- euphoria and elation

- sleepiness, drowsiness or complacency

- undue anxiety

Signs include:

- Inappropriate behavior

- short attention span and slow thinking

- impaired attention to safety

- stuporous behavior and semiconsciousness

All or only some of the symptoms/signs may be present when nitrogen narcosis occurs. Narcosis may be more likely or intensified by 1) hard underwater work that elevates breathing and carbon dioxide levels, 2) inexperience with deep diving, 3) use of alcohol or other drugs that produce drowsiness, 4) anxiety and 5) fatigue.

Nitrogen narcosis itself won't hurt you. It's hazard comes from the way a diver may behave under its effects, such as failing to control buoyancy, monitor air supply, depth or time limits, or being unable to react properly to a problem. At depths around 30 metres/100 feet, most divers can handle routine tasks, buoyancy adjustments and so on, but this isn't the whole picture because responses to emergencies may still be slower, less precise or improper compared to responses at shallower depths. In some environments, narcosis can combine with other conditions to create difficulties. For instance, in a cold, dark lake it can be difficult to tie a knot while wearing thick gloves by the light of a dive torch. Add narcosis and it may be impossible.

To avoid nitrogen narcosis, step one is to stay shallow. Generally, you can avoid strong narcosis by staying above 30 metres/100 feet. If you or your buddy experiences noticeable symptoms/signs of

Nitrogen Nircosis
See the Physiology of Diving section in the *Encyclopedia of Recreational Diving*, book and multimedia.

nitrogen narcosis, ascend together to shallower water until the symptoms/signs subside.

During your Deep Adventure Dive, you'll be able to gauge your reaction to nitrogen narcosis under your instructor's direct supervision by completing a simple task first at the surface, then at depth, while being timed. You may be surprised how much longer you take to accomplish the task underwater.

During your Deep Adventure Dive, you'll be able to gauge your reaction to nitrogen narcosis under your instructor's direct supervision by completing a simple task first at the surface, then at depth, while being timed. You may be surprised how much longer you take to accomplish the task underwater.

Deep 6

1. The depth range where nitrogen narcosis is generally felt by most divers is
   ☐ a. 12 metres/40 feet to 18 metres/60 feet.
   ☐ b. 24 metres/80 feet to 30 metres/100 feet.
   ☐ c. 30 metres/100 feet to 40 metres/130 feet.

2. Symptoms/signs of nitrogen narcosis include (check all that apply):
   ☐ a. limb and joint pain
   ☐ b. impaired attention to safety
   ☐ c. short-term memory loss
   ☐ d. inappropriate behavior

3. Deep diving inexperience is one of the factors that can make nitrogen narcosis more likely.
   ☐ True   ☐ False

4. Nitrogen narcosis is treated by
   ☐ a. stopping all activity and relaxing.
   ☐ b. ascending until the symptoms subside.

5. Nitrogen narcosis is prevented by
   ☐ a. staying at shallower depths.
   ☐ b. paying close attention to the dive tables.

How'd you do?
1. b;   **2.** b, c, d;   **3.** True   **4.** b;   **5.** a.

DECOMPRESSION ILLNESS

Previous discussions in this section discussed safety stops, emergency decompression stops, ascent rates and proper use of the Recreational Dive Planner and dive computers. These steps help preclude decompression sickness and lung overexpansion injuries. As you probably recall, excess dissolved nitrogen coming out of solution causes decompression sickness, and holding your breath while ascending causes serious, potentially life-threatening lung overexpansion injuries, including lung rupture (remember diving's number one rule – always breathe continuously when using scuba). Both conditions cause bubbles within the body, so they may have similar and overlapping signs/symptoms, and both require the same first aid and treatment. Therefore, together they're called *decompression illness*.

While there's always a slight possibility that a diver can get decompression illness even when correctly using dive tables or a dive computer, it's important to remember that the *primary* reason divers get decompression illness is through diver error. These errors include misusing or not using dive tables or a dive computer, improper ascent rates, inaccurately monitoring bottom time or depth and failure to adhere to conservative diving practices. Panicked, breath-holding ascents sometimes follow failure to monitor air supply, and then failure to handle the emergency as the diver learned.

Preventing Decompression Illness

To minimize the risk of decompression illness, use the Recreational Dive Planner and/or your dive computer accurately. Plus, you need to follow other dive safety practices as you learned in your entry-level course.

Never dive to the limits – always have a margin before you hit any table or computer limit. Keep in mind that because people vary in their physiology and susceptibility, no table or computer can guarantee that decompression illness will never occur, even when diving within the table limits. There are

Underline/highlight the answers to these questions as you read:

1. What is the primary reason recreational divers get decompression illness?

2. How do you minimize the risk of decompression illness?

3. What are ten factors that may increase the probability of getting decompression illness?

4. What are six symptoms and six signs of decompression illness?

5. What are the two most important steps to take when handling a case of suspected decompression illness?

6. Is there ever a time when a diver suspected of having decompression illness would reenter the water for recompression?

Decompression Illness
See the Physiology of Diving section in the *Encyclopedia of Recreational Diving*, book and multimedia.

ten physiological factors that are believed to predispose a diver to decompression illness; the more of these that apply to you, the more conservatively you should dive.

Age. As you age, your circulatory system becomes less efficient, affecting nitrogen elimination. Some people also tend to gain weight and have more fat tissue.

Fat. Nitrogen dissolves easily into fat tissue. Individuals with a larger ratio of fat to body weight may absorb more nitrogen than normal when diving.

Heavy exertion. Exertion during or after a dive increases the heart rate and affects circulation, and therefore nitrogen absorption and elimination.

Injuries and illness. Both can affect local circulation and the body's ability to handle excess nitrogen. Chest congestion can trap air in a lung or portion of a lung, creating the same condition as holding your breath.

Dehydration. Dehydration reduces the quantity of blood available to help carry off excess nitrogen.

Alcohol. Alcohol before or immediately after a dive accelerates and alters circulation. It also contributes to dehydration.

Cold water. Diving in cold water can cause your extremities to receive less circulation as they cool, which affects nitrogen elimination.

Hot showers/baths. Hot showers and baths after a dive cause skin capillaries to dilate, drawing blood away from other areas. These areas will eliminate nitrogen more slowly, while the skin experiences higher-than-normal circulation.

Carbon dioxide increase. Improper breathing and breath-holding while scuba diving can cause carbon dioxide buildup in the blood, lung overexpansion injuries, and interfere with nitrogen elimination.

Flying after diving and altitude diving. Any combination of diving and exposure to altitude greater than 300 metres/1000 feet requires special procedures. Because dive tables and computers base their no decompression limits on surfacing from a dive at sea level, at altitude where the pressure is less when you surface, tables and computers aren't accurate without special procedures that account for the pressure differences. (For more information, see the Altitude Diving section. The PADI Altitude Diver Specialty course is highly recommended if you dive at altitude regularly.)

Decompression Illness Signs and Symptoms

Because nitrogen bubbles can form in many body areas, the symptoms (what you feel) and signs (what you see in your buddy) of decompression sickness may vary considerably. Air in the body due to a lung overexpansion injury can also cause differing symptoms, depending on the nature of the injury and where the air goes.

The most common symptoms include:
- unusual fatigue or weakness
- skin itch
- pain in arms, legs (joints or mid-limb) or torso
- dizziness and vertigo
- local numbness, tingling or paralysis
- shortness of breath and/or pain breathing

Signs include:

- blotchy skin rash
- a tendency to favor an arm or leg, rubbing a joint
- staggering
- coughing spasms
- collapse
- unconsciousness

The symptoms/signs can occur independently or together, and can become apparent immediately on surfacing – usually within an hour of the dive. However, symptoms/signs can occur as long as 36 to 48 hours after a dive, or appear as quickly as during ascent at the end of a dive.

Handling Suspected Decompression Illness

Learning the special skills and techniques for handling diver emergencies, including suspected decompression illness, falls within the scope of the PADI Rescue Diver course. When you complete the PADI Rescue Diver course, you'll have taken an important step in your development as a diver.

Nonetheless, as a diver involved in deep diving, you should know the two most important steps in handling a case of suspected decompression illness. First, give patients emergency oxygen in the highest concentration possible – as close to 100 percent as you can. Breathing pure oxygen helps oxygen reach tissues receiving limited circulation due to bubble formation, and it can help the body eliminate nitrogen. Most emergency oxygen kits available to divers can supply an injured diver with 100 percent oxygen. Monitor airway and breathing, and provide cardiopulmonary resuscitation (CPR) for patients who aren't breathing and have no pulse. Keep both responsive and unresponsive patients lying down.

Give divers suspected of having DCI emergency oxygen. Most emergency oxygen kits available to divers can supply an injured diver with 100 percent oxygen. Monitor airway and breathing, and provide cardiopulmonary resuscitation (CPR) for patients who aren't breathing and have no pulse. Keep both responsive and unresponsive patients lying down.

Most cases of decompression illness require treatment under pressure in a recompression chamber.

Second, contact emergency medical care immediately and arrange for transporting the patient to an emergency medical facility. Most cases of decompression illness require treatment under pressure in a recompression chamber. Getting the patient into an emergency medical facility is the first step in proper diagnosis, continuing first aid and subsequent transport to a recompression chamber for treatment. Most areas have diver emergency services, such as DAN (Divers Alert Network) and DES (Divers Emergency Service) that coordinate and assist with patient care from emergency medical facilities to recompression. See your PADI Dive Center, Resort or Instructor about contact protocols for local emergency care and diver emergency services.

Although decompression illness treatment usually requires putting the patient back under pressure in a chamber, realize that you cannot accomplish the treatment by putting the diver back underwater. There are several reasons for this, including the facts that the required depth may be as deep as 50 metres/165 feet, drug and oxygen therapy cannot be applied and adequate air supply and thermal protection (6-10 or more hours) are seldom available. Realize that incomplete/incorrect treatment in the water will make the patient far worse, not any better.

Deep 7

1. The primary reason divers get decompression illness is diver error.
   ☐ True   ☐ False

2. Which of the following help you avoid decompression illness (check all that apply):
   ☐ a. avoiding the limits of any dive table or computer
   ☐ b. always breathe continuously when using scuba
   ☐ c. using the Recreational Dive Planner and/or a computer correctly and accurately
   ☐ d. safety stops and proper ascent rates

3. Ten predisposing factors to decompression illness include (check all that apply):
   ☐ a. age
   ☐ b. injuries and illness
   ☐ c. diving in salt water versus fresh water
   ☐ d. inactivity during the dive

4. The signs/symptoms of decompression illness include (check all that apply):
   ☐ a. limb pain
   ☐ b. unconsciousness
   ☐ c. lack of concern for safety
   ☐ d. numbness, tingling and paralysis

5. The two most important steps in handling a case of suspected decompression illness are to assure pulse and breathing and administer oxygen, and to arrange for the patient to immediately reach a medical facility.
   ☐ True   ☐ False

6. You would have a diver suspected of having decompression illness reenter the water for recompression only if it would take more than two hours to reach a recompression chamber.
   ☐ True   ☐ False

How'd you do?
1. True;   **2.** a, b, c, d;   **3.** a, b;   **4.** a, b, d;   **5.** True;   **6.** False. Do not put a diver suspected of having decompression illness back in the water.

PADI Deep Diver Specialty course

Your Deep Adventure Dive may be credited (at the instructor's discretion) toward the Deep Diver Specialty certification. In addition to what you've learned in this section and what you will practice on the Deep Adventure Dive, the Deep Diver Specialty course covers:

- Recompression chamber overview

- Examining pressure-affected objects at depth

- Practicing use of emergency breathing equipment

- Recording color changes at depth

- Practicing navigation on deep dives.

The PADI Deep Diver course is highly recommended for divers planning to make dives deeper than 18 metres/60 feet.

Deep Adventure Dive Overview

- Knowledge assessment/ Knowledge Review
- Timed task at surface
- Setting up emergency breathing equipment
- Briefing
- Gearing up
- Predive safety check (BWRAF)
- Entry
- Descent
- Timed task on bottom
- Depth gauge comparisons
- Tour
- Ascent – safety stop
- Exit
- Debrief
- Log dive – PADI Instructor signs

DIVER PROPULSION VEHICLES

Introduction

"This is how you do it," you say to yourself, rolling into a graceful turn and dipping into a channel through the reef. You squeeze the grip trigger, accelerating like a fighter jet afterburning through a canyon. Glance back over your left shoulder; your wingman – your buddy – cruises just behind; together you rise from the cut, over the reef and, still in formation, swoop into an exhilarating bank back toward the dive boat.

Top Gun? Not exactly, just a routine cruise on your DPV – Diver Propulsion Vehicle (a.k.a. "scooter"). DPVs rate a top-adventure ride in diving – they take you farther and faster so you see more. And, they're a blast to ride all in themselves. But be warned – once you've used one, it'll probably end up on your got-to-have-one list.

Key CONCEPTS

Underline/highlight the answers to these questions as you read:

1. What are the two main advantages of a DPV in recreational diving?

2. What are the two basic types of DPVs available on the market?

3. What are the five basic components common to all DPVs?

4. What eleven features do you look for when choosing your DPV?

DIVER PROPULSION VEHICLES – AN OVERVIEW

You don't even have to be a diver to realize that DPVs are fun. They look like fun, especially in a video. It's like riding a motorcycle, flying a plane and steering an astronaut jet pack on a space walk, all in one. That's all the reason you need to get one.

But suppose you have to convince a nondiving spouse or something like that, and "cool underwater ride" doesn't cut it. No worries. Besides the obvious adventure benefits, your DPV provides two significant, practical advantages for recreational diving.

First, with a DPV you'll cover more area. Although you don't necessarily go farther away (more about this shortly), you'll see more of the diving within range of the boat. This combines well with other activities. If you're engaged in a search, a DPV can let you cover the pattern more quickly. If you're an underwater photographer and take care not to disturb aquatic life with your DPV, you may find more top-notch subjects. If you're into wreck diving, a DPV lets you see more of a big sunken ship on one dive. In short, a DPV is a tool that helps you get more out of a dive. If you have a physical challenge that limits your swimming, a DPV's travel advantages proves an especially big benefit.

With a DPV you'll cover more area. Although you don't necessarily go farther away, you'll see more of the diving within range of the boat.

Second, a DPV will usually make your dive longer because you use less air. Because you exert yourself less, you don't breathe as hard so you stay down longer (no stop time allowing, of course). Not only can you see a wider area, but you have the air to do it.

DPV Types and Features

If you've yet to invest in your own DPV, when you visit your local PADI Dive Center or Resort, you may find several to choose from. Among other things, you may notice two types: some that appear fairly compact, and others that are really huge and substantially more expensive. The smaller units are *recreational diving* models, intended for easy maneuvering, reasonable transportability, modest range and a general compactness. The huge scooters are *technical diving* models. They're intended for very long range, and built for rough handling and depth. Tech diving DPVs tend to be very heavy and more cumbersome to take from place to place.

Smaller DPVs (left) are usually recreational diving models, intended for easy maneuvering, reasonable transportability, modest range and a general compactness. Technical diving models (right) are intended for very long range, and built for rough handling and depth, and tend to be very heavy and more cumbersome.

Components of all DPVs. Regardless of what DPV you look at, you'll find it has these five components: trigger mechanism, propeller and housing, handles/grips, battery access, and buoyancy characteristics. It's the variations in these that you consider in picking your DPV. Beyond these, you'll have accessories to consider, which may include chargers, lights, lanyard/tether options, T-bar "seats" or other riding attachments, instrument consoles and shipping cases.

When looking at these components, think in terms of these eleven features In choosing which DPV best suits you:

1. Ruggedness and construction. Will the scooter hold up to the type of traveling and diving you do?

2. Seals. How many o-rings and other seals do you need to maintain? How hard is it to get to them?

3. Warranty and servicing. If you have a problem, can your local dive operation handle it, or will you have to ship it somewhere?

4. Battery type. Different batteries offer different advantages in terms of cost, duration and maintenance.

5. Variable speed. This costs more, but it offers the option to save batteries and drive longer. It also makes it easier for you and your buddy to set the same cruising speed.

6. Maximum depth. Can the scooter go as deep as you want to take it? Although most will be rated to 40 metres/130 feet, there have been models with shallower ratings. It shouldn't be an issue with modern models, but it doesn't hurt to be sure.

7. On-off switch. Some are handles, some are triggers, some are magnetic activators. Each has a different feel and advantages and disadvantages.

8. Handle design. Do the grips feel comfortable in a riding position? Imagine maintaining that position for an hour or more.

9. Buoyancy characteristics. You're less likely to lose a DPV that floats during entries and exits. But you can "park" one that sinks slightly while you do something (like take a picture). Some models let you adjust the buoyancy to meet your needs.

10. Weight out of the water. Even the small ones are moderately heavy; how much vehicle can you easily get from your car to the boat?

11. Accessories. Can you get extra accessories you want or need (if any) for the type of diving you like to do?

REVIEW

DPV 1

1. The two main (practical) advantages of a DPV in recreational diving are
    ☐ a. that you can go much farther from the boat/shore and go faster.
    ☐ b. that you can cover a wider area and save air.

2. The two basic DPV types are
    ☐ a. mechanical and electrical.
    ☐ b. gas powered and battery powered.
    ☐ c. recreational and technical.

3. Basic components common to all DPVs include (check all that apply):
    ☐ a. battery access
    ☐ b. headlight
    ☐ c. propeller and housing
    ☐ d. emergency brake

4. Features to consider when choosing your DPV include (check all that apply):
    ☐ a. ruggedness
    ☐ b. warranty/service
    ☐ c. variable speed
    ☐ d. weight out of water
    ☐ e. handle design

How'd you do?
1. b.   2. c.   3. a, c.   4. a, b, c, d, e.

DPV MAINTENANCE AND TRANSPORTATION

Okay, you've got your DPV and you're ready to hit the water. Great, let's get going – but what do you need to do to keep a scooter scooting? You need to know this before you charge the batteries, much less put it in the water, so let's look at this stuff now.

The Basics

Start by reading the manufacturer's manual that comes with your DPV. Every DPV has somewhat different needs, so always go by what the manufacturer says. But, you'll probably find the basics pretty much the same from one vehicle to the next.

After each dive rinse your DPV thoroughly, like any other dive gear. Be especially careful to rinse the propeller, locking buckles and tight crevices where sand collects.

To start, after each dive rinse your DPV thoroughly, like any other dive gear. Be especially careful to rinse the propeller, locking buckles and tight crevices where sand collects. Run the unit in fresh water according to manufacturer guidelines, ideally by immersing the entire DPV. (Watch out! You're gonna get splashed.)

After rinsing, dry it off and open. Remove and clean any o-rings or other seals you're responsible for (again, the manufacturer's instructions), and charge the battery (more about battery charging in a moment). If you're not going to be using it for awhile, store the o-rings separately, or at least store the unit with the lock buckles open. Remove the battery (if possible with your model) and store it separately. Keep your DPV and battery in a cool, dry place out of direct sunlight.

Key
CONCEPTS

Underline/highlight the answers to these questions as you read:

1. What do you need to do to keep a DPV in working order?

2. What seven safety precautions apply to working with DPV batteries?

3. What eight ways can you maximize battery performance?

4. How do you transport a DPV?

The Batteries

Different battery types require different maintenance, so it's very important that you closely follow the manufacturer recommendations for your DPV. However, there are seven safety tips you want to follow when charging and handling virtually all DPV batteries.

1. Use only the charger provided or specified by the manufacturer. The wrong charger can ruin your batteries, plus create a fire or explosion hazard.

2. After recharging, unplug the charger from the wall before disconnecting the charger from the battery. This reduces spark hazard next to the battery. When charging, connect the battery to the charger before plugging in the charger.

3. Keep the battery upright while it's charging. This is especially important with liquid or gel cells that need to vent hydrogen gas while charging.

4. Don't put the battery in the DPV for at least 30 minutes (longer if manufacturer specified) after charging. You need to let the batteries vent hydrogen gas before sealing them inside the vehicle.

5. Keep flame away from the battery, and don't charge batteries in an unvented area. Again, the problem is hydrogen.

6. When you travel, make sure your charger is compatible with the local current. If it's not, you may ruin your charger, your battery or both, and create a fire/explosion hazard.

7. Be careful to connect the proper terminals (positive and negative) when connecting batteries to the charger or DPV. Doing it incorrectly can damage the battery; connecting the incorrect terminal with the charger can create a fire hazard. Many DPVs use a connection system that makes terminal mismatching unlikely.

Your DPV batteries won't last forever, and eventually they'll fail to give you the duration you need. However, you can take steps to maximize their life and performance.

1. Never fully discharge the batteries. When the propeller slows markedly, or the indicator shows low, stop. A deep drain hurts batteries, and can even ruin them.

2. Recharge the batteries as soon as possible. This is generally true, though some manufacturers may modify this.

3. Recharge the batteries completely. This is most important with Nickel Cadium (NiCad) batteries; liquid/gel batteries generally allow you to partially recharge (for a second dive, for instance) without affecting performance.

4. Replace the batteries according to manufacturer guidelines. This avoids having a dead scooter when you show up for that "dive of a lifetime."

5. Keep batteries and charger in a cool area. Excess heat destroys both.

6. Remember that as temperature drops, charging time increases. Follow manufacturer guidelines.

7. Avoid getting water (especially sea water) on your charger or the exposed battery. Avoid charging in an environment where this can happen.

8. Always follow manufacturer recommendations regarding battery charging. They vary considerably; for instance, you typically keep liquid cell batteries on charge full time during storage, whereas with NiCads you don't.

Transporting Your DPV

The one downside to a DPV is lugging it around out of water. Fortunately, with a bit of planning travel's not that big a hassle. If you're traveling by air, start by packing your DPV in its special case, with the battery disconnected or preferably, completely removed. Unless you're traveling extraordinarily light, plan on some excess baggage fees.

In many airports, your DPV may attract security attention because, frankly, under x-ray they look like bombs. Be ready to open the case (so have the key

if it locks) and explain what it is. Don't take it personally; they're just doing their job so you can fly safely.

On a dive boat, you'll usually arrive with the DPV sealed in case it gets wet. (Note: you don't seal some models until immediately before diving, however.) Keep the vehicle out of direct sunlight – cover it with a light-colored towel if necessary – and secure it so it won't roll around. A tumbling DPV can hurt people, damage equipment and you can count on it doing something expensive to itself.

Keep your DPV out of direct sunlight – cover it with a light-colored towel if necessary – and secure it so it won't roll around. A tumbling DPV can hurt people, damage equipment and you can count on it doing something expensive to itself.

REVIEW

DPV 2

1. If possible, store the batteries in your DPV.
   □ True   □ False

2. Safety precautions with DPV batteries include (check all that apply):
   □ a. always disconnect the battery before unplugging the charger.
   □ b. keep flame away from the battery.
   □ c. only use the manufacturer specified charger.
   □ d. seal batteries in the DPV immediately after charging.

3. Ways to maximize battery performance include fully and deeply discharging them whenever possible.
   □ True   □ False

4. When transporting your DPV (check all that apply):
   □ a. keep it out of the sun on a boat.
   □ b. disconnect or remove the battery for flying.
   □ c. expect to put your DPV in your carry-on luggage for flying.

How'd you do?
1. False. Store batteries out of the DPV if possible. **2.** b, c. **3.** False. Avoid completely draining batteries. **4.** a, b.

DPV DIVE PLANNING AND SAFETY

You're used to determining air and no decompression limits when you plan your dives, plus other limitations such as water temperature and physical endurance, when they apply. Guess what. Your DPV gives you a new one – battery limits. You don't want to get caught a long way from your exit with a dead scooter, so you need to account for battery life in your dive plan. Your DPV also adds some new contingencies you might have to handle, including sudden failure or a runaway. And there are other considerations such as the buddy system, the environment and other divers.

Power Planning

DPV dive planning treats battery endurance like any other limit – air or no stop time. Plan your dive well within battery limits so you don't end up towing a dead scooter on a long, tiring surface swim, or worse, you don't end up kissing it good-bye because you're too tired to tow it.

Naturally, you want to start the day with a fully charged battery. Ideally, you want to start each dive that way, but that's not always practical – but whether it's fully charged or not, you want to use your DPV conservatively. To maximize battery endurance, use the slowest speed you can for the dive.

Determining your turnaround point. Especially in shallow, warm water, DPV power may limit your dive rather than air or no stop time. But while you have an SPG and a dive computer to tell you air and no stop time remaining, many vehicles lack charge indicators that tell how much battery juice is left. And among those that do, you need to take what the indicators say with a grain of salt because battery characteristics make accurate power readings difficult. If your DPV doesn't have a battery indicator, be sure to carry a volt meter so you can confirm voltage before and between dives.

Normally, you base battery limits on your running time. The manufacturer literature usually gives an estimated run duration, which gives you a start

Key CONCEPTS

Underline/highlight the answers to these questions as you read:

1. How do you determine a turnaround point when using a DPV?

2. What should you do if your DPV fails during a dive?

3. How do you handle a runaway DPV?

4. How do you ascend and descend properly with a DPV?

5. Why do you need extra vigilance monitoring depth when using a DPV?

6. What buddy team considerations do you have when making a DPV dive?

7. How do you avoid propeller entanglements and obstructions when using a DPV?

8. What are the four guidelines for courteous and environmentally responsible DPV use?

point, but a battery loses capacity as it ages. The only way to really be sure how long your battery lasts is to test it periodically by running your DPV in controlled conditions (in a pool, in a circle close to the boat, etc.) until it slows markedly. During the dive, you track time running to gauge power use (and check the battery indicator if your DPV has one).

A dive watch with a stopwatch function comes in handy for this. It's your responsibility to track DPV run time when you're using one.

During the dive, you track time running to gauge power use (and check the battery indicator if your DPV has one). A dive watch with a stopwatch function comes in handy for this. It's your responsibility to track DPV run time when you're using one.

Since you want to always have a reserve, a good guideline is to use the rule of thirds with estimated battery power. Use 1/3 of your power (and air or no stop time, if appropriate) headed out, 1/3 headed back and 1/3 in reserve. So, if your scooter battery tests out to have an hour cruise time (most DPVs have far more than that), plan an outbound leg no more 20 minutes, leaving 20 minutes to come back and 20 minutes reserve.

Another limit to consider is how far you can swim towing a dead scooter. You don't want to be farther away than that (or it may cost you your scooter – ouch!), keep in mind that when towing, your air consumption goes up. A good strategy is to use your DPV in a circle or semicircle within an easy swim of your exit point. Instead of scootering to go farther away, scooter to see *more* within this area. This approach also lets you scooter even if you have only a partially charged battery or for some other reason you're not sure how long your batteries last.

Keep in mind that while battery power will limit some of your dives, as you go deeper and as technology increases battery capacity, air and no decompression limits will limit you on others. Watch all your gauges and stay well within all the limits.

Instead of scootering to go farther away, scooter to see more within this area. This approach also lets you scooter even if you have only a partially charged battery or for some other reason you're not sure how long your batteries last.

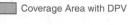
Coverage Area with DPV

Coverage Area without DPV

DPV Malfunctions

Manufacturers make very reliable DPVs, which is incredible considering that the greatest enemy of electronics is water. Through proper care, you can go years without any major problems with your DPV, but nonetheless, you need to be prepared if one happens during a dive.

Although there are several possible causes for each, ultimately only two kinds of malfunctions occur with a DPV during a dive, and they're at opposite extremes: either your DPV won't *go*, or it won't *stop*. Let's look at what you do in each situation.

DPV failure. This can happen from causes ranging from flooding, to improper power planning, to jamming something in the propeller (In most models, this breaks a safety pin or clutch so the motor runs but the propeller doesn't turn. This keeps the motor from burning out and makes repair much cheaper.). You can usually tell a flooded scooter immediately because it gets heavy, and by making a habit of checking the main o-rings for bubbles as soon as you descend with your scooter.

If your DPV quits, you tow it back to shore or the boat. It helps that most vehicles are nearly neutral, though you still need to deal with drag. If your scooter floods, it may be very heavy. If your buddy's DPV

If your DPV quits and your buddy's still functions, your buddy can tow you and your scooter to the exit — head straight there because the added load adds to the battery drain.

still functions, your buddy can tow you and your scooter to the exit – head straight there because the added load adds to the battery drain. Even if your buddy's scooter runs too low before you get there, this reduces how far you both have to swim.

Some DPV divers carry a small lift bag and a marker buoy. The lift bag comes in handy if you flood your scooter, or if you end up surface swimming due to low air. In extreme situations, such as fighting a fierce current, you might have to abandon a dead DPV for your own safety. The marker buoy increases the chances of later recovery. Some scooters have special BCDs that allow you to float the scooter at the surface, which is handy during entries and exits, as well as if your scooter floods.

If you're near the bottom with a runaway scooter, the simplest thing is to put the nose into the ground (away from sensitive aquatic life) and let the batteries run down.

Runaway DPV. This doesn't happen often, but it does happen, usually caused by something (sand or debris) jamming or damaging the trigger assembly. Often, you can ride it out to a degree, by signaling your buddy and turning toward the exit, and then riding in gentle circles at a shallow depth near the exit until the battery runs down. However, if you can't do this (perhaps due to topography), or if you reach the exit point and it's still running (likely), you'll need to take the next step.

If you're near the bottom, the simplest thing is to put the nose into the ground (away from sensitive aquatic life) and let the batteries run down. This may take awhile (you may even need to come back for it – mark it with your buoy). Don't use this method if you're well off the bottom unless you can make a slow, controlled sloping descent that allows you to equalize normally. A steep descent risks injury, such as squeezes if you can't equalize fast enough.

Your next option is to intentionally foul the prop with something – a dive mitt, goodie bag, etc. (Not to insult your intelligence, but, uh, in the heat of the moment don't use anything vital, like your dive computer, your regulator, your hand, your face, etc.) This stops the prop and usually sheers the safety pin (or similar device) in the drive connections, so the motor continues to spin until the batteries croak. If there's no safety pin in the drive, this may burn out the motor.

The easiest option, but potentially most likely to cost you the DPV, is to simply let it go. Often you'll be able to recover it, especially if you point it toward shallow water and/or the exit before you release it. But if you lose it, as painful as that may be, remember that no piece of equipment is worth more than your health and safety.

Descents and Ascents

DPVs pull you along fast, which means you need to use caution ascending and descending. If you point yours straight up or down and pull the trigger, you're going to exceed a safe descent/ascent rate, and that means unacceptable risk of ear, sinus or masks squeezes, ear drum rupture, lung overexpansion injuries and decompression sickness. You get the picture – don't do that. (Some manufacturers stipulate that you use their DPVs only for level travel.) DPVs can take you up and down faster than you might imagine, so it's important to monitor your depth closely when scootering.

Descending or ascending with a DPV requires a very gentle, shallow sloping angle (up or down). Use your computer or gauges to help you gauge your rate, breathe normally, and equalize normally. Never ascend faster than 18 metres/60 feet per minute (slower if prescribed by your computer), and never descend faster than you can equalize comfortably.

Descending or ascending with a DPV under power requires a very gentle, shallow sloping angle (up or down). Use your computer or gauges to help you gauge your rate, breathe normally, and equalize normally. **Never ascend faster than 18 metres/60 feet per minute (slower if prescribed by your computer), and never descend faster than you can equalize comfortably**. Don't neglect safety stops. If you don't have room for slow, sloping ascents/descents, make them normally while towing your scooter – not under power. Keep in mind that scooters are really ideal for horizontal use – when approaching an obstacle, it's usually easier to control your buoyancy and avoid the risks of rapid ascent by going around the obstacle rather than over it.

If you don't have room for slow, sloping ascents/descents, make them normally while towing your scooter – not under power.

DPVs and the Buddy System

When it comes to DPVs, you'll find you prefer your buddy to have one, too. When you both have DPVs, the batteries last longer, you go faster and it's more fun. Plus, if one of you has a vehicle failure, the other can tow everyone and the disabled vehicle back (or most of the way back) to the exit.

Because you crank along much faster than you can swim, it's easy to accidentally separate. One effective way to stay close is for the diver with the slower DPV to lead, with the follower maintaining the same relative position. This is important so the leader can confirm contact easily and frequently, and doesn't inadvertently leave the follower far behind with a dead scooter or some other problem. In either position, be careful maneuvering near your buddy, other divers and objects – although DPV speeds aren't that great, they're faster than you can swim and the mass of a diver and vehicle has the potential to injure.

It's important that the lead diver check on the following diver very frequently. And, because it can be difficult to signal while scootering, you may need to establish signals that only need one hand, or be prepared to stop when you need to communicate.

Sometimes, you may find you're the only diver with a DPV. Does this mean you don't get to use it? Not necessarily. You can tandem ride a DPV if you plan the dive accordingly. For one, you reduce your range and you reduce your speed. If the DPV conks out, you don't have another to tow you both back. When tandem DPVing, plan your dive so you stay within an easy swim of your exit (a good idea in any case). Ride tandem to cover more area, rather than more distance.

One effective way to stay close is for the diver with the slower DPV to lead, with the follower maintaining the same relative position. This is important so the leader can confirm contact easily and frequently, and doesn't inadvertently leave the follower far behind with a dead scooter or some other problem.

You can tandem ride a DPV if you plan the dive accordingly. For one, you reduce your range and you reduce your speed.

Propeller Entanglement and Obstruction

Perhaps the most common problem unique to DPV diving is getting something caught in the propeller. Usually, this is a piece of dive gear, though you can sometimes have problems with kelp or other debris.

You always want to dive streamlined, with nothing dangling or protruding, especially your SPG and alternate air source. Eliminate all loose ends, dangling straps and unsecured lanyards. This really pays off with DPV diving because you eliminate the primary entanglement causes; needless to say, getting your alternate second stage sucked into a DPV prop does neither the DPV nor the alternate any good.

Make a habit of checking your streamlining when scootering, since water drag can pull things loose. You may also prefer an adjustable alternate second stage that you can desensitize slightly, since streaming water can cause a slight free flow.

Use caution around thick kelp, water hyacinth or any other heavy vegetation that easily gets pulled into props. Power down and tow your DPV through such areas, especially when scootering on the surface.

When you ride your scooter, you shouldn't block normal water flow into the prop, nor should you feel the prop wash coming out. Doing either hampers your DPV's performance; ride your vehicle as intended by the manufacturer. If you feel any unusual sound or vibration while scootering, stop because this may indicate something's wrong. If you don't find an immediate cause, tow your scooter to the exit to avoid permanent damage.

Courtesy and Environmental Responsibility

A DPV can be a bit like a jet ski or a skate board. It's a lot of fun, but it can annoy a lot of people if you're not considerate. Plus, DPVs create some environmental concerns. To keep you and your DPV welcome among your fellow divers, stick to these four guidelines:

1. Be courteous of other divers. DPVs make a loud hum that can disturb aquatic life, and buzzing the reef like an F-18 on a bombing run doesn't help either. Give other divers a wide berth so you don't disturb the aquatic life they came to see, and so for them, the silent world remains relatively silent.

2. Be cautious around sensitive life. You'd do this anyway, but remember that you're going faster and that means an accidental brush with something has more potential to damage.

3. Watch your fin tips. You may not be kicking, but your fins can still do harm to the environment by dragging across the reef or bottom. Try to stay well above the reef, and ride neutrally buoyant and level.

4. Avoid disturbing the bottom. Cruising close to the bottom can suck up sand and silt, blast a cloud behind you, and risk pulling in something that jams the prop. Or, you can cruise along with the prop wash blowing downward, churning up silt as you go. Either way, your fellow divers won't appreciate it, and you can harm sensitive aquatic life that the silt settles on. Stay well off the bottom, and dive properly weighted and neutrally buoyant so you don't have to aim the prop down to maintain your depth. Make stops well above the bottom because when you're cruising, the DPV tends to offset being somewhat negatively buoyant. When you stop, you may sink a surprising amount before you reestablish neutral buoyancy. By stopping well above the bottom, you have time to do this before blundering into a sensitive bottom.

Stay well off the bottom, and dive properly weighted and neutrally buoyant so you don't have to aim the prop down to maintain your depth.

REVIEW

DPV 3

1. When determining your turnaround point with a DPV, it's important to
   ☐ a. rely on the vehicle's battery indicator.
   ☐ b. know the run time you can expect from your batteries.

2. If your DPV fails during a dive (check all that apply):
   ☐ a. you tow it back to the exit.
   ☐ b. use your buddy's DPV to tow both of you and your DPV back to the exit.
   ☐ c. you may, in extreme circumstances, have to abandon your DPV.

3. If you have a runaway DPV (check all that apply):
   ☐ a. put the nose in the bottom.
   ☐ b. let it go.
   ☐ c. point it straight up so you surface rapidly.

4. To ascend or descend properly with a DPV, point it straight up or down and "pump" the trigger.
   ☐ True   ☐ False

5. You need extra vigilance monitoring depth when using a DPV because
   ☐ a. you can ascend or descend faster than expected.
   ☐ b. most DPVs are only rated for very shallow water.

6. It's acceptable for two divers to share a DPV if you plan the dive accordingly.
   ☐ True   ☐ False

7. To avoid entanglements and obstructions (check all that apply):
   ☐ a. swim with your body directly over the water intake.
   ☐ b. streamline yourself and secure all equipment.
   ☐ c. be cautious around heavy vegetation.

8. Guidelines for DPV use include (check all that apply):
   ☐ a. cruising close to other divers so they can share in your fun.
   ☐ b. cruising close to the bottom so you can observe small organisms.
   ☐ c. staying negatively buoyant so you can stop at any time.
   ☐ d. None of the above.

How'd you do?

1. b.   2. a, b, c.   3. a, b.   4. False. Either ascend/descend normally without using DPV power, or use a very gentle slope.   5. a.   6. True.
7. b, c.   8. d.

DIVING YOUR DPV – STEP BY STEP

Okay, let's go for a cruise. Here's much of what you'll do during a normal (if there is such a thing) day of diving with your DPV.

Predive Preparation

Start with your battery adequately charged (usually, fully charged) according to manufacturer guidelines, installed and connected. Assemble and seal the unit, maintaining o-rings as needed. Check your DPV over, making sure everything's put together properly. Look closely at the propeller and drive area. Take your time completing these steps so you don't omit anything.

Next, test run your scooter for 10 seconds or less (long runs out of water can damage DPVs). Keep everything clear of the spinning prop, especially fingers and toes. An irregular noise (grating, grinding sound) can indicate a damaged propeller shaft seal. A strong wobble can indicate a bent shaft. If you find either, the scooter stays dry. Have it serviced before using it again.

If everything checks out, put the DPV somewhere out of the sun until you're ready to get in the water.

Test run your scooter for 10 seconds or less (long runs out of water can damage DPVs). Keep everything clear of the spinning prop, especially fingers and toes.

Entries

From shore. Shore entries usually mean carrying your DPV until you reach water deep enough to cruise without hitting bottom obstructions or sucking up debris. Hold your DPV so that you won't accidentally trigger it. Wade until you reach deep enough water (usually around chest deep) and then let the scooter pull you out. Keep your DPV completely submerged when surface cruising; a partly submerged propeller meets an unbalanced resistance, which in turn causes a severe vibration that can damage your drive assembly.

When boat diving, it's best to enter the water and have someone hand in your DPV, or lower it in on a line ahead of time. Show anyone who helps you how to handle it without accidentally powering it.

From boats. Like a lot of accessory gear, enter the water from a boat and have someone hand in your DPV, or lower it in on a line ahead of time. If someone hands it to you, show that person how to handle it without accidentally powering it. If you tether it on a line, it's a good idea to let the crew know so they're sure it's gone before moving the boat.

Using Your DPV at the Surface

You may use your DPV at the surface to save air until you reach the dive site. Keep the vehicle completely submerged as just mentioned, and hold it deep enough as necessary to ensure unblocked water flow. Make sure all your gear's secure and use brackets, clips, or whatever means necessary to make sure any accessory equipment stays clear of the props.

When snorkeling, adjust speed for your comfort; if you go too fast, turning your head can dislodge or flood your mask. A low profile snorkel shakes less and produces less drag when surface cruising. And here's a tip: save battery power by kicking when you take off, which reduces the initial load of getting you moving.

Riding Tandem

As you read earlier, although tandem riding greatly reduces your speed and range, it can be effective for covering more area within swimming distance of the exit. It's also useful if you're just going to and from an area, leaving the scooter "parked" while you explore.

The tandem rider usually rides by holding onto the DPV driver's tanks valve, BCD (at the bottom on either side of the cylinder), or calf/ankles. The further back the tandem rider hangs on, the more streamlined (generally speaking), but the more awkward the control for the driver.

The tandem rider usually rides by holding onto the DPV driver's tank valve . . .

... or calves or ankles. The further back the tandem rider hangs on, the more streamlined (generally speaking), but the more awkward the control for the driver.

When riding tandem, it's a good idea to agree on communication while dive planning. You can create signals based on taps, tugs or squeezes, which reduces the starts-and-stops you'd need otherwise to communicate.

Steering

Most people find steering a DPV pretty much instinctive. You sort of point it and that's where it goes. If you analyze the way divers drive DPVs, you find two basic types of turns: pivoting and banking.

Pivoting is much like steering a bicycle or motorcycle; you push-pull the DPV grips like you would handlebars, which creates a pivot point in the new direction between you and the DPV. Pivot turns allow you to make abrupt course changes.

Banking turns are less instinctive, but more fun and feel a bit like the way an airplane turns. To turn, you roll slightly (30 to 40 degrees) toward the turn, and tilt the DPV up slightly. This puts you in a gentle sweeping curve, using your fins to maintain the bank. Banking turns are graceful, and they're the best way to steer without slowing down, but you can't make abrupt turns with them.

Banking turns are less instinctive, but more fun and feel a bit like the way an airplane turns. To turn, you roll slightly (30 to 40 degrees) toward the turn, and tilt the DPV up slightly. This puts you in a gentle sweeping curve, using your fins to maintain the bank.

As you read earlier, make depth changes very, very gradual if you change depth under power. Always pay attention to your descent/ascent rate, breathe normally and equalize early and often. Stop and switch to an unpowered descent/ascent if necessary.

Final Ascent and Exit

Although you may gradually ascend while cruising, typically you'll make the last ascent stages to safety stop depth unpowered, either holding the vehicle or with it secured by a lanyard or tether. After your three minutes at 5 metres/15 feet, it's usually simplest to finish the ascent unpowered, then cruise on the surface if you're some distance from the exit.

Typically you ascend to the safety stop depth unpowered. After your three minutes at 5 metres/15 feet, it's usually simplest to finish the ascent unpowered, then cruise on the surface if you're some distance from the exit.

If you're exiting into a boat, either hand your DPV up to someone aboard, or tether it to retrieve later (reverse of getting in). If you use the tether, take off your tank and BCD once aboard and then pull up your DPV as soon as possible. This avoids the boat taking off with it still over the side, which would basically beat it to death.

If you're exiting onto shore, be careful not to cruise into water that's too shallow. Stop about chest deep, stand up, take off your fins and then wade ashore, carrying the DPV in a manner that avoids triggering it. Avoid dragging it through mud or sand, which has a way of working itself into the drive seals and other tight nooks and crannies.

Post Dive

After the dive, immediately get your DPV out of direct sun, and if aboard a boat, secure it so it won't roll about, get stepped on, tripped over or have weights dropped on it. Rinse your DPV in fresh water as soon as possible and before opening it to recharge. Recharge it according to manufacturer guidelines.

QUICK REVIEW

1. When preparing your DPV for a dive, be sure to
   ☐ a. run the propeller for at least a minute to verify operation.
   ☐ b. run the propeller for no more than 10 seconds to check for noise or wobble.

2. When entering the water with a DPV, standard practice calls for holding it in a way that avoids accidentally triggering the propeller.
   ☐ True   ☐ False

3. When surface cruising with your DPV, keep the propeller partially out of the water to reduce resistance and save power.
   ☐ True   ☐ False.

4. When riding tandem (check all that apply):
   ☐ a. the tandem rider holds on to the driver's tank valve.
   ☐ b. the tandem rider holds on to driver's SPG and alternate air source hoses.
   ☐ c. the tandem rider holds on to the driver's ankles.

5. A _____ turn allows you to make an abrupt direction change.
   ☐ a. pivot
   ☐ b. bank
   ☐ c. roll
   ☐ d. None of the above.

6. When exiting with a DPV (check all that apply):
   ☐ a. hold it so you don't accidentally trigger the prop.
   ☐ b. retrieve a tethered DPV as soon as possible.
   ☐ c. cruise into water as shallow as possible, ideally calf deep.

7. Postdive DPV care includes (check all that apply):
   ☐ a. rinsing it in fresh water.
   ☐ b. keeping it out of the sun.
   ☐ c. securing it (on a boat) so it doesn't receive or cause damage.

How'd you do?
1. b. **2.** True. **3.** False. Keep the propeller entirely submerged to avoid damage. **4.** a, c. **5.** a. **6.** a, b. **7.** a, b, c.

PADI Diver Propulsion Vehicle Specialty Course

Your Diver Propulsion Vehicle Adventure Dive may be credited (at the instructor's discretion) toward the Diver Propulsion Vehicle Specialty certification. In addition to what you've learned in this section and will practice on the Diver Propulsion Vehicle Adventure Dive, the Diver Propulsion Vehicle course covers:

- additional maneuvering practice
- touring a wide area

KNOWLEDGE REVIEW
Diver Propulsion Vehicle

1. List two advantages of using a DPV.

2. What are five features common to all DPVs?

3. Why is it important to secure your DPV when traveling by boat?

4. What is a good guideline when using battery power (or air supply) to determine your turnaround point?

5. True or False. In extreme situations, you may need to abandon your DPV.

6. True or False. When using a DPV, you should never exceed 18 metres/60 feet per minute ascent rate, or a slower rate if specified by your computer.

7. List two ways to avoid propeller entanglements or obstruction.

8. True or False. You should never ride tandem on a DPV. Each diver must always have a separate vehicle.

9. Explain the procedures for entering the water from shore with a DPV.

10. What two things can you do to avoid damaging aquatic life while using your DPV?

Student Diver Statement: I've completed this Knowledge Review to the best of my ability and any questions I answered incorrectly or incompletely I've had explained to me, and I understand what I missed.

Signature _____ Date _____

Diver Propulsion Vehicle Adventure Dive Overview

- Knowledge assessment/ Knowledge Review
- DPV preparation
- Briefing
- Gearing up
- Predive safety check (BWRAF)
- Entry appropriate with DPV
- DPV use at surface
- Descent with DPV
- Steady/level riding

- Adjusting depth
- Turning
- Tandem riding
- Parking
- Towing a failed DPV
- Underwater tour
- Ascent with DPV – safety stop
- Exit and post dive procedures
- Debrief
- Log dive – PADI Instructor signs

DRIFT DIVING

Introduction

If until now your experience has been that currents are something you fight to swim against; drift diving will give you a whole new perspective. Drift diving grew out of the philosophy, "If you can't beat 'em, join 'em," and is the prevailing practice in many areas with nearly continuous strong currents.

Drift diving can give you a real adrenaline pump. At some drift dive sites, the current rips you along far faster than you could swim, or even cruise with a DPV (diver propulsion vehicle), sailing you along effortlessly. Some divers compare drift diving in clear water to hang gliding or horizontal sky diving – but no airplane needed and you don't have to worry about your chute opening.

Underline/highlight the answers to these questions as you read:

1. What are four advantages of drift diving?

2. What are four concerns of drift diving?

GOING WITH THE FLOW

When you first became a diver, you learned that you need to consider currents when you plan your dives, that strong currents can wear you out and that they limit the distance you cover. Sometimes currents can prevent diving entirely. When you drift dive, the current works for you instead of against you.

Drift diving usually requires little effort. During the dive, you just go along for the ride, buzzing through the scenery with the current "swimming" for you.

Divers associate four advantages with drift diving. First, drift diving usually requires little effort. During the dive, you just go along for the ride, buzzing through the scenery with the current "swimming" for you. Second, drift diving opens up dive sites that are nearly impossible to visit any other way. In particular, rivers and some reefs are constantly in a strong current that precludes nondrift dive techniques. Third, since you're floating along in the current, you cover more area and see more on a drift dive. Finally, many types of drift diving relieve you of having to return to or look for a specific exit point. The boat travels with you.

But you are diving in moving water, so drift diving does have some concerns that make using appropriate drift techniques important. You and other divers need to closely coordinate exit and entry procedures, for one, and you need extra vigilance in maintaining buddy contact for another. Most forms of drift diving call for coordinating with surface support and supervision. A fourth concern is that you usually need a long, extensive bottom topography, such as along a reef, wall, river or series of dive sites strung in line with the current to drift dive. Otherwise, you spend a lot of time floating along looking at nothing (although there are some spots where you can drift onto a wreck or other specific site).

The techniques you'll learn in this section, plus additional ones you can gain in the PADI Drift Diver Specialty course, help you maximize the fun and excitement drift diving offers, while addressing its unique concerns.

REVIEW

Drift 1

1. The advantages of drift diving include (check all that apply):
   - ☐ a. requires little effort
   - ☐ b. covers more area
   - ☐ c. easier to plan

2. The concerns of drift diving include (check all that apply):
   - ☐ a. coordinating entries and exits
   - ☐ b. avoiding pelagic aquatic life
   - ☐ c. maintaining buddy contact

How'd you do?
1. a, b; 2. a, c.

Underline/highlight the answers to these questions as you read:

1. In what environments do you commonly find drift diving?

2. Where is a current slower, and why?

3. If you need to swim against a current, where is the easiest place to do it?

Drift Dive Environments

Drift diving takes place in many environments and in different kinds of currents. Some drift diving requires a boat, and some is done from shore. You can even drift dive in inland rivers.

In the ocean, the earth's rotation and the wind cause major offshore currents that flow virtually nonstop. In locations like Cozumel, Mexico, Palau or off West Palm Beach, Florida, USA, you almost always have these currents, thus making drift diving one of the most common dive techniques. Other coastal areas may experience longshore currents, which are caused by waves. Longshore currents are

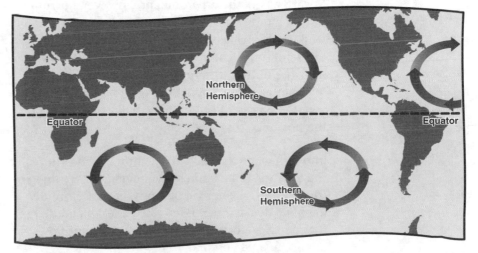

In the ocean, the earth's rotation and the wind cause major offshore currents that flow virtually nonstop.

temporary and run parallel to the shore, making drift diving possible from a boat, or simply by entering the water at one point and getting out farther down shore.

Tidal currents flowing in and out of sounds and bays as the tides change offer drift dive opportunities. A unique aspect of drift diving in tidal currents is that you can visit the same dive site drifting in different directions, depending on the tide.

Currents don't flow uniformly, but tend to be faster near the surface and slower near the bottom where they encounter resistance. If you must swim against the current for any reason, the easiest place to do so will usually be on the bottom.

Inland, freshwater divers drift dive down rivers and streams, either accompanied by a boat, or with a car left downstream for the drive back. A few locations have services for driving rafters back upstream that divers can take advantage of.

Regardless of the environment, however, currents have a characteristic that you need to keep in mind while drift diving: Currents don't flow uniformly, but tend to be faster near the surface and slower near the bottom where they encounter resistance. If you must swim against the current for any reason, the easiest place to do so will usually be on the bottom.

In rivers where the flow frequently rounds curves, the location of fast and slow moving water can vary (depending on river topography, etc.). Before diving a particular river, reference experienced divers for specific information about how current flows along the area you plan to dive.

Drift 2

1. Drift diving is common in offshore current areas, along coasts when longshore currents are present and in rivers.
   ☐ True ☐ False

2. Currents generally tend to be slower
   ☐ a. at the surface.
   ☐ b. midwater.
   ☐ c. near the bottom.

3. The easiest place to swim against a current is
   ☐ a. near the surface.
   ☐ b. near the bottom.

How'd you do?
1. True; **2.** c; **3.** b.

Underline/highlight the answers to these questions as you read:

1. What are the two general types of drift diving and when would you use each?

2. Why is some form of surface supervision recommended for most forms of drift diving?

TYPES OF DRIFT DIVING

Different types of environments call for different techniques when drift diving, so several variants have sprung up, each suited to the unique needs of the local sites and the divers. Your instructor will fill you in on the exact techniques you'll be using on your Drift Adventure Dive, but here is a basic description of the two broadest drift diving categories:

Drift Diving with a Surface Float

In this type of drift diving, a group of divers follows a surface float towed by a line-handler, who usually leads as well. The dive boat follows the float, and all divers keep the group leader/line-handler in sight at all times.

Drift diving with a surface float makes surface supervision easy and helps warn other boats away from the divers. This technique is especially useful in limited visibility, when the bottom topography is generally flat with little depth reference for descending and when surface conditions are rougher, making it harder for a boat to follow diver bubbles.

Drift diving without a Surface Float

Many drift dives call for divers to stay together in a group, but to ride the current without a surface float. When supervised by

When drift diving with a float, a group of divers follows a surface float towed by a line-handler. The dive boat follows the float, and all divers keep the line-handler in sight at all times.

a dive boat, the boat follows the group's bubbles, and the group stays together by following a group leader.

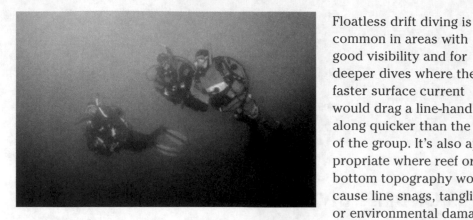

Floatless drift diving is common in areas with good visibility and for deeper dives where the faster surface current would drag a line-handler along quicker than the rest of the group.

Floatless drift diving is common in areas with good visibility and for deeper dives where the faster surface current would drag a line-handler along quicker than the rest of the group. It's also appropriate where reef or bottom topography would cause line snags, tangling or environmental damage. Floatless drift diving is also common when diving rivers where a float could entangle in overhanging trees and surface obstructions.

Surface Supervision

Whether drift diving with or without a float, you usually want surface supervision whenever possible, preferably from a boat. It's important to have someone to look out for divers to keep track of where they are.

Boat-based surface supervision can lend assistance if necessary, and picks up the group at the end of the dive, avoiding a tiring swim back to shore. Surface supervision can also be useful if an emergency arises. Boat operation for drift diving requires maneuvering and close coordination between the boat crew and the divers, so anyone involved in operating the vessel should be completely familiar with drift dive procedures.

Even when drift diving from shore, such as in river diving, surface supervision is less common, but may be possible by having a car or truck follow along the shore.

DRIFT DIVING EQUIPMENT

Underline/highlight the answers to this question as you read:

1. Beyond your regular gear for the local environment, what two pieces of equipment are important in drift diving?

Drift diving doesn't require much equipment beyond the gear you would wear in the same environment when not drift diving. In fact, you probably already use two pieces, which are a float and line, and a surface signaling device. For some drift diving, you may not even need the float and line.

Float and Line

For drift diving with a float, you generally need a float large enough to be highly visible and too buoyant to get pulled under by divers pulling, ascending, making safety stops or resting on it. The size depends partly on the number of divers; larger groups may need something pretty big, though a smaller one may be more appropriate for two or three divers and for use in rivers.

Appropriate line will be heavy-duty, at least three millimetres/one-eighth inch in diameter, and stored on a spool or reel for deployment and retrieval. Lines thicker than six millimetres/one-quarter inch may be appropriate in some conditions, but may be a hassle to reel in and out. Sometimes the leader has a hook/anchor on the reel to make it easier to stop during a drift dive.

For drift diving with a float, you generally need a float large enough to be highly visible and too buoyant to get pulled under by divers pulling, ascending, making safety stops or resting on it. The size depends partly on the number of divers; larger groups may need something pretty big, though a smaller one may be more appropriate for two or three divers and for use in rivers.

Surface Signaling Devices

In drift diving, if you become separated from the group you may need to attract the boat's attention. It's a lot easier with the right equipment. One way to handle this is to keep a whistle attached to your BCD inflator, where you can blow it without digging in your pocket for it. An inflatable signal tube makes you easier to see; this compact (about the size of a roll of coins) tube unrolls and inflates into a two metre/six foot tall, bright colored tube. Inflatable signal tubes make you much easier to spot, and take up so little space that many divers always carry one – drift diving or not. You can inflate some types of inflatable signal tubes or diver carried buoys and let them ascend on a line from 5-6 metres/15-20 feet. This provides a reference for a safety or emergency decompression stop, and alerts the boat to your presence.

Inflatable signal tubes make you much easier to spot, and take up so little space that many divers always carry one – drift diving or not.

Drift diving at night calls for carrying more than one, highly visible light since it's important that the boat be able to find you in the dark. Night drift diving has more potential hazards, and is generally an activity for divers with ample experience in both drift and night diving. See the Night Diving section for more about procedures for diving after dark.

Quick REVIEW

Drift 4

1. Pieces of equipment for drift diving include (check all that apply):
   ☐ a. surface signaling device
   ☐ b. strobe marker
   ☐ c. dive light
   ☐ d. float and line
   ☐ e. chemical light

How'd you do?

1. a, d.

Key CONCEPTS

Underline/highlight the answers to these questions as you read:

1. What five considerations go into planning a drift dive?

2. What is the most important factor when preparing to enter when drift diving?

3. What are the differences between a buoyant and a negative drift dive entry, and when would you use each?

4. What are the two procedures for beginning a drift dive with a float?

DRIFT DIVE TECHNIQUES AND PROCEDURES – BEGINNING THE DIVE

Planning Drift Dives

Like all dives, drift dives begin with planning. In planning a drift dive, don't forget to take these five considerations into account, in addition to other dive planning factors:

1. Surface conditions and current strength. In evaluating the surface conditions, assess whether it will be easy to follow bubbles (if you're not using a float) and how much difficulty divers would have climbing into a boat or returning to shore. Be sure the current isn't too swift to meet the dive objective.

2. Water visibility. Moving swiftly along a reef in poor visibility poses a risk of running into something. Make sure you can see well enough for the current's speed. Poor visibility can also make it hard for the group to stay together.

3. Dive objective. Most drift dives are tours, but some may include searches or photography. If you need to stop in the current, is it weak enough for you to do so?

4. Number and size of dive groups. Are there too many divers for one group? If you have poor visibility, it may be difficult to keep a group larger than three or four divers together. If small groups would be better, can several groups go in the water at once, or should groups take turns? This depends upon how many leaders are available and whether the dive boat can keep track of more than one group.

Like all dives, drift dives begin with planning. In planning a drift dive, take into account surface conditions, water visibility, the dive objective, the group size and diver experience in addition to other dive planning factors.

5. Experience levels. The less experienced the divers on your dive, naturally the more conservative you plan the dive. Remember that less experienced divers are more likely to surface sooner than more experienced divers. Divers less experienced with drift diving will be better off with a relatively simple dive plan.

Preparing for the Entry

The most important factor in preparing to enter the water on a drift dive is that the group needs to be ready at the same time. For some types of drift diving, this is the only way to keep the group together during descent and the dive (discussed shortly). Some techniques allow for more variation in readiness.

On many drift dives, you want to be ready, including having your mask on and regulator in place so that you and all other divers can enter quickly at the same time. This can be especially important when drift diving from a boat because it may have only one or two minutes to get everyone in the water after disengaging the propellers.

When drift diving from a boat, the crew will give you ample notice so that everyone can be ready when reaching the entry spot. Go through your predive safety check carefully because forgotten or misadjusted equipment on a drift dive can cause considerable disorganization and stress. Have your mask on and regulator in place so that you and all other divers can enter quickly at the same time. This can be especially important when drift diving from a boat because it may have only one or two minutes to get everyone in the water after disengaging the propellers. After that, the boat may drift or blow off course.

Entries. In most drift dives with less experienced drift divers, the dive starts with a buoyant drift dive entry, in which all divers enter the water with BCDs partially inflated. The advantage to this is that you can handle a problem before the group descends.

Other instances call for a negative drift dive entry, in which all divers enter the water with empty BCDs and descend as a group immediately. The negatively buoyant entry is normally used when the dive must begin on a particularly small site. More experienced divers find this an exhilarating, team-oriented entry with everyone peeling out of the boat and dropping, one after another like paratroopers as the divemaster signals, "Dive! Dive! Dive!"

Beginning Descents with Floats

When drift diving with a float, you'll probably use a variant of two common procedures that help ensure that the group stays with the float. One is based on buoyant entries and the other on negative entries.

The first procedure calls for trailing the float line behind the boat, like a current line. When the crew signals you to enter the water (Important note: NEVER enter the water before signaled by the crew to do so!), swim to the line and hold on about three-quarters of the way to the buoy. When everyone's on and ready to go, the line-handler (usually the group leader) disconnects the line and descends with the end (sometimes attached to a reel for retrieving the line at the end of the dive). The rest of the group follows down along the line, (but not hanging on to it – more about descending shortly).

One procedure for beginning a drift dive descent with a float calls for everyone to get into position on the float line behind the boat. When everyone's ready, the linehandler unhooks the line and descends with the group following along the line.

The second procedure normally calls for a negative entry. At the crew's signal, the line-handler enters with the float and with the line on a reel or in a coil. The remainder of the group follows immediately behind; after checking that there are no problems, the line-handler descends, unreeling the line. The group descends along the line, again, not hanging on to it.

Both procedures may be modified, depending upon the local environment, so your instructor will detail the procedures you'll follow on your Drift Adventure Dive. If you're diving without a float, your descent begins immediately – we'll look at floatless diving in a moment.

NEVER enter the water when drift diving from a boat before signaled by the crew to do so.

Drift 5

1. Things to consider when planning a drift dive include (check all that apply):
   ☐ a. surface conditions
   ☐ b. diver experience
   ☐ c. visibility

2. One important factor in entering for a drift dive is that everyone be ready at the same time.
   ☐ True   ☐ False

3. During a _____ entry, everyone enters the water with their BCDs inflated. It is a useful technique for _____.
   ☐ a. buoyant, small dive sites
   ☐ b. negative, small dive sites
   ☐ c. buoyant, inexperienced drift divers
   ☐ d. negative, inexperienced drift divers

4. There are two different procedures for beginning a descent with a float, but both begin with the line extended behind the boat.
   ☐ True   ☐ False

How'd you do?
1. a, b, c; 2. True; 3. c; 4. False. One calls for the line extended behind the boat and the other calls for a line-handler to deploy the line.

DRIFT DIVE PROCEDURES AND TECHNIQUES – DESCENTS, ASCENTS AND EXITS

Descents

CONCEPTS

Underline/highlight the answers to these questions as you read:

1. When drift diving with and without a float, how does the group stay together while descending to the bottom?

2. What are several techniques for keeping the group together during the tour portion of a drift dive?

3. How do techniques for ascending as a group differ from ascending as individual buddy teams, and what considerations go in to choosing which to use?

4. How do you safely exit the water into a boat after a drift dive?

It's important to keep the group together on many drift dives, especially when diving from boats, so you use special techniques that maintain both buddy contact and the group leader contact. If you're using a surface float, after the line-handler starts down (either by unhooking the line or by unreeling it), follow the line down. Use it as a visual guide only and follow it. If necessary, you can make a loose "OK" sign around the line to maintain contact, but don't pull on it. Pulling won't pull you down, but it will pull the line-handler up. Another reason is that since you're in the faster upper current, you may act like a sail and drag the line-handler across the bottom.

As you descend, maintain buddy contact and stay with the line – don't drop straight to the bottom. Doing so could separate you from the group. If you have trouble equalizing or another descent problem, ascend along the line, clear the problem, then follow it back down. Swim around any divers having descent difficulties (stay with your buddy, of course) and continue your descent by following the line.

At the bottom, the line-handler will normally watch to make sure everyone has made it down. Depending upon the local conditions, the handler may stop on the bottom, or simply wait drifting in the current (which isn't a problem because everyone's drifting together, staying with the line).

If you're diving without a float, everyone descends at the same time to stay together. Descending along a reef slope or wall for reference helps the group have a more controlled descent to the planned dive depth.

At the bottom, the line-handler will normally watch to make sure everyone has made it down. Depending upon the local conditions, the handler may stop on the bottom, or simply wait drifting in the current.

If you have equalization or similar problems during a floatless drift dive and you can't descend, the proper action depends upon the group, the environment and the conditions. You and the group plan for this in advance, and may include returning to the surface with your buddy for pickup by the boat, or (if the water's sufficiently clear) following the group from above until you can descend.

If you have equalization or similar problems during a floatless drift dive, the proper action depends upon the group, the environment and the conditions.

During the Dive

After descent, the line-handler/group leader accounts for all divers and makes sure no one has problems. If this is done while stopped on the bottom, the handler checks the current direction and indicates the travel direction. As you go, keep close contact with your buddy and the leader/line-handler. Stay neutral and avoid bottom contact so you don't damage aquatic life – or yourself. Keep gauges and alternate air sources secure so they don't dangle; snagging one while drifting can be rather awkward.

You can stay with the group more easily if you try to stay up-current from (behind) the group leader/line-handler. Watch for signals, and if the leader stops, maintain position by swimming into the current or by holding on to a nonliving part of the reef.

You can stay with the group more easily if you try to stay up-current from (behind) the group leader/line-handler. Watch for signals, and if the leader stops, maintain position by swimming into the current or by holding on to a nonliving part of the reef. If a course change is

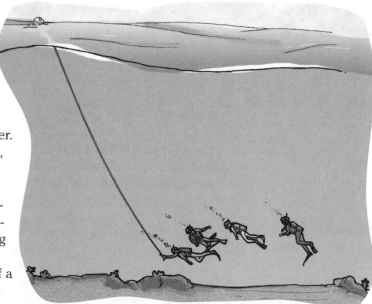

part of the plan (to visit a particular reef area, for example), the change will begin well in advance and allow for the current speed.

Ascents

Drift dive ascents either call for the entire group to ascend together, or for individual buddy teams to ascend as necessary, allowing those with sufficient air and no-decompression time to continue the dive.

For group ascents, the ascent begins when the first diver signals "low air" to the group leader/line-handler, or when the group reaches the planned maximum dive time. The group ascends normally, preceding the group leader/line-handler. If using a large float, you may use the line to assist your ascent, but with small floats, pulling on the line may sink the float. At 5 metres/15 feet, the group makes a safety stop together before surfacing. At the surface, stay in a group and listen for the group leader's/line-handler's directions.

When you use individual buddy team ascents, you and your buddy ascend on your own when you reach low air or your dive time limit. Generally, operations use this technique under good dive conditions and with experienced divers. When a buddy team reaches a limit, it signals the group leader/line-handler and ascends normally.

When ascending along a float line, again, don't hold the line and become a "sail" that drags the line-handler on the bottom. Safety stops may be more difficult to perform than when ascending with a group, particularly when you don't have a float, but you can usually manage by staying neutral, watching your gauges and using the line as a visual reference. If conditions make performing a safety stop in buddy teams difficult or impossible, it may be best to plan the dive for a group ascent.

Exiting

Once at the surface on a group dive, everyone stays together. If using a surface float, the leader will gather the line to prevent tangling, but if the line gets in the way before it's retrieved, remember to swim over, rather than under it. On the surface as a buddy team, stay with your buddy and signal the boat (if boat drift diving), which will maneuver to pick you up.

When drift diving from a boat, remember that for safety, the boat must disengage the propellers before you approach, so don't swim toward the boat until directed to do so by the crew. Keep clear of the boarding ladder until it's your turn to board, but stay with the boat and the group/your buddy. In some instances, the boat may extend a trail line for you to hang on to while waiting to exit, or the line-handler may attach the float and line for the same purpose. Generally, the group leader/line-handler exits last to be available to help someone if necessary.

When drift diving from a boat, remember that for safety, the boat must disengage the propellers before you approach, so don't swim toward the boat until directed to do so by the crew.

REVIEW

Drift 6

1. When descending along a float line during a drift dive,
   ☐ a. pull yourself down the line to speed your descent.
   ☐ b. use the line as a reference only.

2. During the tour portion of the dive, which techniques help keep the group together (check all that apply)?
   ☐ a. Stay up current from (behind) the group leader/line-handler.
   ☐ b. Watch for the group leader's/line-handler's signals.
   ☐ c. Maintain close buddy contact.

3. An important consideration in choosing to ascend as a group as opposed to ascending in individual buddy teams is whether conditions would allow individual buddy teams to make a safety stop.
   ☐ True   ☐ False

4. When exiting the water into a boat while drift diving, it's important
   ☐ a. to approach the boat immediately.
   ☐ b. to not approach the boat until directed to do so by the crew.

How'd you do?
1. b; **2.** a, b, c; **3.** True; **4.** b.

DRIFT DIVING HAZARDS AND PROBLEMS

The above techniques reduce the likelihood of problems in drift diving, but it's wise to understand possible concerns, how to avoid them and some solutions should they occur.

Currents

Drift diving makes the current do most of the work of swimming for you. When a diver tries to fight the current, however, the current will eventually win and exhaustion becomes a possible hazard. Signs and symptoms of exhaustion include fatigue, labored breathing, air starvation, headache, cramping and stress, which can elevate to near-panic.

You prevent exhaustion by keeping exertion below levels that induce heavy breathing. Underwater, stay at or near the bottom where the current is slower if you must work against it for a short distance. You may try pulling yourself along the bottom against the current by holding on to nonliving portions of the reef. If you can't swim against a current, don't try to fight it.

If you're out of position and can't fight the current, ascend no faster than 18 metres/60 feet per minute or as stipulated by your computer, inflate your BCD at the surface and rest. When drift diving from a boat, signal "okay" over head, and the boat will come to you. When drift diving from shore, swim for shore without fighting the current by swimming across it.

Besides exhaustion, currents can create psychological stress for divers who aren't used to them. In the grip of stress, a diver may try to swim against or fight the current, leading to exhaustion. The prevention is remembering to use proper drift dive techniques, and to not try to fight the current.

A final problem currents can cause is buddy separation. During a descent or ascent, a buddy who delays in descending (perhaps due to equalization

Key CONCEPTS

Underline/highlight the answers to these questions as you read:

1. How can diving in currents contribute to exhaustion, stress and buddy separation, and how do you avoid these problems?

2. What constitutes "being lost" while drift diving, and how do you rejoin the group?

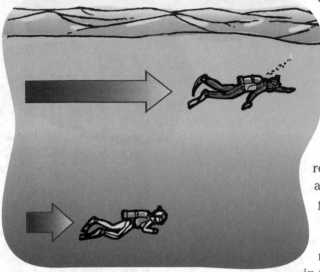

problems) will drift faster in the more rapid surface current than a deeper buddy. Or, on the bottom, if one buddy grabs something and stops, the other buddy can be carried far down current before noticing. Just be careful where you grab the bottom – protect living reef creatures. You can easily avoid these problems with good buddy contact. Stay close together during ascents and descents, and always signal each other before stopping in the current.

Currents can cause buddy separation. During a descent or ascent, a buddy who delays in descending (perhaps due to equalization problems) will drift faster in the more rapid surface current than a deeper buddy.

Getting Lost

During a drift dive from a boat, there's generally no exact exit point. The float or the dive group itself is the dive boat's reference to pick you up. If you separate from the group, the boat may not have this reference when you surface. Getting lost can also be a problem when shore drift diving if only the group leader is familiar with the appropriate exit location. This is why it's important for the group to stay together.

For the purposes of drift diving, a diver is "lost" when the diver can't see the float line or the group. The diver and buddy may be together and have a feel for where they are, but for the purposes of drift diving, the team is lost.

If you should find yourself "lost," with or without your buddy, look around for the group for no more than a minute before ascending to the surface at 18 metres/60 feet per minute or slower, or as stipulated by your dive computer. If you think you're up current from the group, you might try swimming to catch up. If you believe you're down current, you can try swimming against the current (but not at a pace that would cause exhaustion) or holding on to a nonliving portion of the bottom to see if the group catches up with you.

Keep in mind though, that if the group changed course, the current may be separating you farther.

Should you fail to find the group and begin surfacing, look for the float line (if used) and bubbles. If you spot them during the ascent, try to stop your ascent (time and air allowing) and rejoin the group. When diving from a boat, ascend carefully so you don't surface in the path of the boat. Upon reaching the surface, inflate your BCD and signal for the boat to pick you up. If you reach the surface but cannot see the boat, inflate your signal tube.

Drift 7

1. To avoid exhaustion in a current you should (check all that apply):
   ☐ a. swim steadily against the current.
   ☐ b. never fight a strong current.
   ☐ c. stay near the bottom where the current is weaker.

2. If you are drift diving from a boat and lose track of the group, but not your buddy, you're not considered lost.
   ☐ True   ☐ False

How'd you do?
1. b, c;   **2.** False. Any time you can't see the group when you're drift diving from a boat, you're considered lost and should follow the procedures for being lost.

PADI Drift Diver Specialty Course

Your Drift Adventure Dive may be credited (at your instructor's discretion) toward the PADI Drift Diver Specialty certification. In addition to what you've learned in this section and will practice on the Drift Adventure Dive, the Drift Diver Specialty course includes:

- the role of the line-handler
- a closer look at the nature of currents
- choosing the ideal drift dive boat

If you'll be drift diving on a regular basis, or just want to extend the fun you have on this dive, take the PADI Drift Diver course.

Drift Adventure Dive Overview

- Knowledge assessment/ Knowledge Review
- Briefing
- Gearing up
- Predive safety check (BWRAF)
- Entry
- Group descent
- Drift dive for fun
- Ascent – safety stop
- Exit
- Debrief
- Log dive – PADI Instructor signs

KNOWLEDGE REVIEW

Drift Diving

1. List and explain four advantages and four considerations for drift diving:

   Advantages

   1._____

   2._____

   3._____

   4._____

   Considerations

   1._____

   2._____

   3._____

   4._____

2. Explain why it's recommended that you have some form of surface supervision for most forms of drift diving.

3. List five considerations to include when planning a drift dive.

   1._____

   2._____

   3._____

   4._____

   5._____

4. Describe the differences between buoyant and negative drift dive entries, and explain when you would use each.

5. Explain the procedure for descending with a float so that a group stays together on a drift dive.

6. Describe several techniques used to stay with the group during the underwater tour portion of a drift dive.

7. Describe how to ascend as a group, and as individual buddy teams. Explain when buddy teams may ascend individually from a group drift dive.

8. Describe the procedures for safely exiting the water onto a boat after a drift dive.

9. Explain how to avoid exhaustion in a current.

10. Define "being lost" in the context of drift diving, and how you might rejoin the group if you were "lost."

Student Diver Statement: I've completed this Knowledge Review to the best of my ability and any questions I answered incorrectly or incompletely I've had explained to me, and I understand what I missed.

Signature _____ Date_____

DRY SUIT DIVING

Introduction

Water may cover seven-tenths of the earth, but without exposure suits, you wouldn't see much more than a relatively narrow band straddling the equator. That would indeed be too bad, because some of the best diving lies well north and south of tropical waters, in lakes at altitude and at deeper depths that constantly remain cool.

Without protection from the cold, you'd miss some of the best diving around.

Of the exposure suit types available, the modern dry suit opens the door to comfortable diving in the coolest water – in some instances, you may be warmer diving than topside preparing to go in! Depending on where you are, a dry suit may mean the difference between diving or missing the fun, between a long comfortable dive and a short shivering one, or between diving year round versus only a few months in the warm seasons.

While the dry suit offers the most insulation, it does re

quire you to learn special techniques you don't need with other exposure suits. But these aren't a big deal, and like most dry suit divers, you'll probably have fun learning them. And, the first time you try it, diving without getting wet is pretty cool. Well, warm. You know what we mean.

CONCEPTS

Underline/highlight the answers to these questions as you read:

1. What is hypothermia?

2. Why can mild hypothermia be a serious problem for scuba divers?

3. How do you avoid hypo-thermia?

HEAT, WATER AND THE DIVER

When you took your PADI Open Water Diver course, your instructor probably explained that water absorbs heat about 20 times faster than air, so that even "warm" 27ºC/ 80ºF water chills you pretty quickly if you're not in a wet suit. This is why you need an exposure suit while diving.

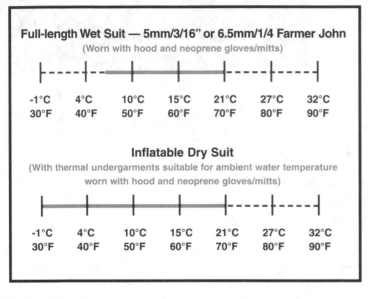

Full-length Wet Suit — 5mm/3/16" or 6.5mm/1/4 Farmer John
(Worn with hood and neoprene gloves/mitts)

-1°C	4°C	10°C	15°C	21°C	27°C	32°C
30°F	40°F	50°F	60°F	70°F	80°F	90°F

Inflatable Dry Suit
(With thermal undergarments suitable for ambient water temperature worn with hood and neoprene gloves/mitts)

-1°C	4°C	10°C	15°C	21°C	27°C	32°C
30°F	40°F	50°F	60°F	70°F	80°F	90°F

Blue lines indicate temperatures where specific exposure suits should be used.

"Cold" is a relative term, and how fast you "get cold" on a dive depends on not just the exposure suit, but on the water temperature, the dive duration, your physical fitness and body shape (which affect your ability to generate and retain heat) and your acclimation to cooler water. You're also warmer if you're active and swimming about (in the short term), than you are holding still.

The biggest concern for divers regarding temperature is hypothermia, which is the body core temperature dropping below normal. The early symptoms include uncontrollable shivering and numbness, followed by blueness in the skin, sleepiness and stupor. Unchecked, severe hypothermia leads to unconsciousness and death.

Even at its early stages, mild hypothermia can be a problem because it interferes with clear thinking, reducing a diver's normal decision-making abilities. Hypothermia also saps away strength and endurance.

You avoid hypothermia by always wearing adequate thermal protection before, during and after

For more information about...

Hypothermia
See the Physiology of Diving section of the *Encyclopedia of Recreational Diving*, book or multimedia.

the dive. If you start to shiver uncontrollably, end the dive, get dry and get warm. You can learn more about handling hypothermia emergencies in the PADI Rescue Diver course and the Emergency First Response program.

Dry Suit 1

1. Hypothermia occurs when
   ☐ a. the body core temperature drops below normal.
   ☐ b. hand and foot temperature drop below normal.
   ☐ c. you breathe too fast.

2. Even mild hypothermia can be a serious problem because
   ☐ a. you can't prevent it.
   ☐ b. it interferes with decision-making abilities.

3. To avoid hypothermia problems (check all that apply):
   ☐ a. abort a dive if you shiver uncontrollably.
   ☐ b. wear adequate thermal protection.

How'd you do?

1. a;   2. b;   3. a, b.

WET SUITS AND DRY SUITS

To understand how dry suit diving differs from diving with other exposure suits, let's back up and review how wet suits and dry suits insulate you.

A wet suit is made of foam neoprene, which is rubber with thousands of trapped nitrogen bubbles – a good insulating material. When you dive in a wet suit, a small amount of water seeps into the suit and gets trapped, where your body quickly heats it. Provided there's little water circulation (which is why a wet suit must fit snugly), the neoprene insulates you and retards heat loss. To get more thermal protection, you wear thicker neoprene.

Dry suits consist of a water-tight shell and an insulating undergarment, or foam neoprene (like a wet suit), with water-tight seals and zippers, so you stay dry inside. Dry suits provide more thermal protection because the air layer adds insulation you lack with a wet suit. But this air compresses and expands as you change depth, which is what

Underline/highlight the answers to these questions as you read:

1. How do wet suits and dry suits insulate?

2. What are at least three advantages and three disadvantages to using a dry suit versus using a wet suit?

makes dry suit diving different from diving with a wet suit or other exposure suit.

So, with a wet suit, you're insulated by neoprene, whereas with a dry suit, you're insulated by air, an undergarment and the suit shell, or in the case of a neoprene dry suit, by air and neoprene. Note, by the way, that neither suit "keeps you warm" in most cases, even though that's how we say it. Rather, both slow down how fast you lose heat – dry suits slow heat loss the most, but except in fairly warm water, given enough time (but longer than you'd be on a dive) you'll chill in a wet suit or dry suit.

Dry Suits Versus Wet Suits

When comparing dry suits to wet suits, you'll find both advantages and disadvantages.

Advantages. The primary dry suit advantage is warmth (insulation). Thanks to its superior thermal protection, you dive in cooler water with more comfort, use less air, reduce hypothermia risk and make more dives. A second advantage is that most dry suits don't lose insulation as you go deeper, whereas a wet suit does as pressure compresses the neoprene. Fit is a third advantage; wet suits must fit snugly, but a dry suit is much more forgiving because a tight fit isn't as important. Before and after a dive, a fourth advantage for dry suits is that you stay warm in the undergarment, and you're dry when you take the suit off (a big plus if it's nippy out when you surface). Finally, when you get in the water, a dry suit avoids the cold "rush" that's typical to wet suits.

Disadvantages. The most noticeable disadvantage of a dry suit is that its initial cost is typically higher than that of a comparable quality wet suit. (But, once you figure in making more dives and longer dives, your cost-per-underwater-hour may be lower than with a wet suit.) A second drawback is that dry suits require more maintenance and postdive care than wet suits. In the water, dry suits have more bulk, making long swims more tiring, and they're often more buoyant, so that you need more weight for neutral buoyancy (though usually not a lot more). Dry suits require more care in controlling buoyancy, and, if you don't equalize them when descending, can cause a "suit squeeze" (you'll learn how to control buoyancy and avoid suit squeeze as part of this section). Finally, because they insulate well, divers are more likely to overheat before the dive when using a dry suit on a hot day.

REVIEW

Dry Suit 2

1. The most obvious difference between a wet suit and a dry suit is that a dry suit insulates you with air as well as other materials.
   ☐ True   ☐ False

2. Advantages of a dry suit when compared to a wet suit include (check all that apply):
   ☐ a. ease of maintenance
   ☐ b. added warmth (insulation)
   ☐ c. less need for custom fit
   ☐ d. less weight required

3. Disadvantages of a dry suit when compared to a wet suit include (check all that apply):
   ☐ a. ease of maintenance
   ☐ b. added warmth (insulation)
   ☐ c. less need for custom fit
   ☐ d. additional weight required

How'd you do?
1. True; 2. b, c; 3. a, d.

DRY SUIT TYPES AND FEATURES

Dry Suit Types

Like all other dive gear, dry suits exist in a variety of types and styles to choose from. Suit types alone could take an entire book, but thankfully for practical purposes you can put all modern dry suits in either of two broad categories: neoprene dry suits and "shell" dry suits.

Neoprene dry suits. These dry suits are basically "wet suits that aren't wet." Neoprene dry suits are made from neoprene, similar to wet suits, and therefore insulate without undergarments (more about undergarments in a moment). Although at one time the mainstay in diving dry, neoprene dry

Underline/highlight the answers to these questions as you read:

1. What are the two basic dry suit types and how do they differ?

2. What two materials do manufacturers make dry suit seals from?

3. What are the two valves you find on a dry suit?

4. What options do you have regarding dry suit hoods and boots?

Neoprene dry suits are made from neoprene, similar to wet suits, and therefore insulate without undergarments.

suits aren't as common as they once were, though they're still made and popular in some quarters.

Shell dry suits. Most dry suits available are shell dry suits. Shell dry suits consist of two suits: a water-tight "shell" outer suit that keeps you dry, and an undergarment that insulates. You can choose from several materials for both shells and undergarments.

Common shell materials include coated fabric, crushed neoprene, vulcanized rubber and trilaminate, each with benefits and differences regarding cost, durability and buoyancy characteristics. Shell materials are incompressible (for all practical purposes) and provide almost no thermal protection.

Neoprene suits (second from left) differ from shell suits, which come in materials including (from left) coated fabric, trilaminate and vulcanized rubber. Shell suits require an insulating undergarment, but don't lose insulating ability with depth.

Undergarment materials include bunting, polypropylene, Thinsulate™, and open cell foam. Each material has benefits with regard to cost, maintenance and ability to insulate when wet (a consideration in case of a leak). The undergarment provides thermal protection by trapping air and creating an insulating layer between the diver and the cold shell/water. See your PADI Dive Center, Resort, or Instructor about the best suit material/undergarment combination for the diving you're planning.

Different undergarment materials have benefits with regard to cost, maintenance and ability to insulate when wet (a consideration in case of a leak). The undergarment provides thermal protection by trapping air and creating an insulating layer between the diver and the cold shell/water.

Dry Suit Seals

Dry suit seals keep water out of the suit at your wrist and neck (and sometimes at the face), and are generally made of thin rubber latex or neoprene. Latex seals offer greater flexibility, sealing and ease in donning/doffing, but are more fragile and require more care. Neoprene seals are tougher and may last longer, but often don't seal quite as well and are often more difficult to put on.

This raises an important point: Dry suits are dry, but not without some dampness. First, a sealed watertight/airtight suit doesn't "breathe," so your nat-

Dry suit seals keep water out of the suit at your wrist and neck, and are generally made of thin rubber latex (left) or neoprene (right).

ural perspiration creates some dampness. Second, if you have very narrow, lean wrists, water may seep in on occasion around your wrists when your tendons cause grooves and channels under the seal as your arm/hand flexes. But used properly, you should expect a suit in good repair to keep you essentially dry, with no more than some incidental dampness near your wrists.

A second important point is the *carotid sinus reflex*. A neck seal that's too tight can constrict the carotid arteries in your neck, causing changes in your heart rate and possible unconsciousness. The seal has to be pretty tight – you'd notice it and probably be quite uncomfortable. Don't dive with an overly tight neck seal. If it's uncomfortable, it's too tight.

Dry Suit Valves

A dry suit is an air space like any other, which means you add air to it as you descend and release air as you ascend. So, like your BCD, your dry suit has two valves: an inflator valve and an exhaust valve.

A dry suit is an air space like any other, which means you add air to it as you descend and release air as you ascend. So, like your BCD, your dry suit has two valves: an inflator valve and an exhaust valve.

You typically find your inflator valve on or near the chest center. A long hose, similar to your BCD inflator hose, supplies air from your regulator, permitting you to add air at the touch of a button. Normally, you connect the hose after putting on your scuba unit, and disconnect it before removing your scuba unit.

Look for your exhaust valve on your upper left arm or upper chest. Virtually all modern dry suit exhaust valves vent air automatically (you set its sensitivity), with manual venting by depressing it. A few older models required manual venting at all times. We'll look at adding and releasing air from your suit a bit later.

Boots, Hoods and Gloves

Hoods and boots may be attached to your suit, or may be separate items. With most dry suits used

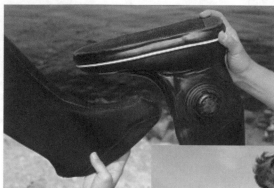

by recreational divers, you have boots built into the suit. However, a high-end alternative is a suit with crushed neoprene socks that keep your feet dry, with a matching set of special boots. This is especially suitable if you shore dive a lot and need to walk over rocks, or long distances, wearing your dry suit. Note

Your dry suit comes with either built in boots, or with separate rock boots (right) that fit over a water tight crushed neoprene sock.

that either way, dry suit boots typically tend to be large and bulky, often requiring larger fins than you usually use – be sure to check fin fit before your Dry Suit Adventure Dive.

Detached hoods are more common than attached hoods, and are normally neoprene wet suit hoods with narrow collars if your dry suit has an insulating (neoprene) neck seal, or a bibbed hood that tucks into place over a noninsulating neck seal (latex). Some dry suits have attached latex or neoprene hoods, however.

Detached hoods are more common than attached hoods, and are normally neoprene wet suit hoods with narrow collars.

Depending on the water temperature, you either wear reef-type protective gloves, or wet suit gloves or mitts. Although you can get dry gloves for your dry suit, few recreational divers bother with these (they're primarily for commercial divers).

Dry Suit 3

1. _____dry suits require no undergarments, but _____ dry suits have no thermal protection without them.
   - ☐ a. Shell, neoprene
   - ☐ b. Neoprene, latex
   - ☐ c. Neoprene, shell

2. Wrist seals are made from (check all that apply):
   - ☐ a. shell
   - ☐ b. neoprene
   - ☐ c. polypropylene
   - ☐ d. latex

3. The _____ valve lets you add air to a dry suit and the _____ valve lets you release air.
   - ☐ a. fill, exhaust
   - ☐ b. inflator, deflator
   - ☐ c. inflator, exhaust

4. On dry suits, hoods and boots are
   - ☐ a. sometimes attached and sometimes separate.
   - ☐ b. never required.
   - ☐ c. always attached.

How'd you do?
1. c; **2.** b, d; **3.** c; **4.** a.

PUTTING ON YOUR DRY SUIT

If you're familiar with wet suits, but not with dry suits, you're about to discover that you put them on differently. Wet suits usually require little or no assistance, but some dry suits require buddy assistance. You usually have to tug and pull a wet suit into place, but a dry suit slides on, except for the wrist and neck seals.

Because dry suits vary in design details such as zipper location and features, consult the manufacturer instructions, your dive center/resort or instructor for the specifics of donning your suit. But you can apply four guidelines to getting into virtually all types.

Underline/highlight the answers to this question as you read:

1. What are four general guidelines for donning a dry suit?

Timing
A dry suit can be very warm out of water. If the air's cold, or if you may get wet getting to your dive site, you may want to get into your suit as soon as possible to keep warm. More likely, though, you'll want to wait until the last possible moment. Most dry suit configurations permit you to put the suit on up to your waist, allowing you to keep cool but partially suited up.

Handle with Care
When putting your hand and head through the

seals (especially latex seals), be careful not to damage them. You can use talcum powder as needed or recommended by manufacturer so your hands slide easily though the seals. Remove rings, watches, hair pins and anything else that could catch on the seal and puncture or tear it. Stretch seals gently and no more than necessary, then smooth them out flat in place, making sure no hair or dirt gets trapped, creating a leak.

Zip All the Way

With some dry suits – such as those with zippers running across the shoulders, you'll have to get a buddy to zip you up. Others, such as those with the zipper across your chest, you can manage yourself. Waterproof zippers are more fragile than regular zippers – pull smoothly, gently and steadily, making sure no lint or other debris gets caught in the zipper. Pull it all the way tight or it will leak. If your buddy zips you up, it's a good idea to grab the zipper at the end yourself and give it a tug, just to be sure no one's playing a joke on you. You make zipping easier by lubricating the zipper according to manufacturer instructions.

When putting your hand and head through the seals (especially latex seals), be careful not to damage them. You can use talcum powder as needed or recommended by manufacturer so your hands slide easily though the seals.

Purge Excess Air

After your suit's on and zipped, purge the excess air so it doesn't balloon when you enter the water. Do this before donning any more equipment by pulling the neck seal open, (or pressing the exhaust valve), and squatting with your arms held in tightly. You'll feel air rush out past the seal; replace the seal and then stand back up. The suit will feel snugger and tighter against your body.

Dry Suit 4
1. The general guidelines for donning a dry suit include (check all that apply):
    ☐ a. valve lubrication
    ☐ b. timing
    ☐ c. purging excess air
    ☐ d. making sure the zipper is closed completely

    How'd you do?
    1. b, c, d.

DRY SUIT BUOYANCY CONTROL

Dry Suits and Weight

Earlier you learned that dry suits often require more weight than wet suits because the suit's trapped air creates extra buoyancy. Most of the special techniques necessary for dry suit use deal with that air and resulting buoyancy.

Although you'll (probably) need more weight with a dry suit, you do have some options in distributing it. First, use a shot weight belt or several bullet weights so you can distribute the lead evenly around your waist. Second, you can use ankle weights to get up to three kg/six lbs off your weight belt, but be cautious that this doesn't make you swim feet-low, stirring up the bottom and possibly damaging sensitive aquatic life. Third, you can distribute the weight between your weight belt and a BCD weight system. If you're properly weighted and distribute weight evenly between a weight system and a weight belt, ditching either should give you ample buoyancy in most emergency situations.

You establish correct weighting with a dry suit much like you do wearing any other exposure suit. Wearing the dry suit (purged of excess air with the automatic exhaust valve set all the way open) and undergarments, all your regular equipment and with an empty BCD, you should float at eye level while holding a normal breath. When you exhale, you should sink. If you do this check with a full cylinder, add about two kg/five lbs to compensate for the air you use during the dive. You should be able to maintain a 5 metre/15 foot safety stop.

You'll find it helpful to establish your weight in confined water the first time, and then fine-tune it at the dive site as needed. Avoid overweighting because you'll have to use extra suit air to offset the weight. Excess air causes the majority of dry suit diving difficulties.

Key CONCEPTS

Underline/highlight the answers to these questions as you read:

1. Why may you need more weight for a dry suit than a wet suit?

2. How can you distribute weight on your body (three ways)?

3. How do you adjust the weight worn with a dry suit to permit neutral buoyancy at the surface and a 5 metre/15 foot safety stop?

4. How do you establish positive buoyancy at the surface while wearing a dry suit?

5. How do you establish and maintain neutral buoyancy underwater while wearing a dry suit?

6. How should you add air to a dry suit underwater?

7. How should you vent air from a dry suit underwater?

After setting your weight, you may want a bit more buoyancy for surface swimming. Use your BCD for extra buoyancy at the surface – not your dry suit. Extra air in your dry suit restricts movement, puts pressure on your neck and makes you uncomfortable.

Dry Suit Buoyancy Control Underwater

When you're ready to descend, put your regulator in your mouth, vent your BCD and exhale. If you're properly weighted, you'll descend. At this point, stop using your BCD for buoyancy control and use primarily your dry suit. Use your BCD at the surface, or in case of emergency. To attain and maintain neutral buoyancy underwater, add to and release air from your dry suit.

Using your dry suit for buoyancy control has two main benefits. First, it simplifies buoyancy control because you're only controlling one system. Second, it minimizes the possibility of suit squeeze.

Using your dry suit for buoyancy control has two main benefits. First, it simplifies buoyancy control because you're only controlling one system. Second, it minimizes the possibility of suit squeeze. A dry suit is an air space added to your body (like your mask) and *must be equalized* as you descend, like any other air space. Forgetting to equalize can cause pinching and discomfort, but the process of controlling buoyancy with your dry suit keeps it equalized because you add air to it as you descend. You should also add air if the suit begins to feel excessively tight during descent, before you feel any discomfort.

Add air to your suit as necessary in short, light bursts. This assures precision control, and avoids valve freezing in very cold water. As you descend, simply tap the inflator valve button frequently. If you need to use long air bursts to maintain buoyancy control, you're probably overweighted. If air vents from your exhaust valve as fast as you add it, close it half a turn and try again. Set the exhaust valve so your suit holds the amount of air you need to attain neutral buoyancy; if you must close the valve more than a full turn, you're probably wearing too much weight.

During ascents, the suit must vent expanding air. Your exhaust valve should do this automatically, provided you're in a vertical, feet-down position with the exhaust valve raised. If automatic venting doesn't release air fast enough, you can vent manually by depressing the valve.

REVIEW

Dry Suit 5

1. A dry suit may require more weight than a wet suit because
   - ☐ a. dry suit material is lighter than wet suit material.
   - ☐ b. dry suits are full of trapped air.
   - ☐ c. a dry suit doesn't require more weight.

2. One way to distribute weight is to put small bullet weights in your undergarment pockets.
   ☐ True   ☐ False

3. When properly weighted with a dry suit purged of excess air, you should float at eye level while holding a normal breath and with the BCD
   - ☐ a. deflated.
   - ☐ b. partially inflated.
   - ☐ c. absent.

4. To attain positive buoyancy at the surface while wearing a dry suit
   - ☐ a. put air in your BCD.
   - ☐ b. put air in your dry suit.

5. You use your _____ primarily for buoyancy control under water.
   - ☐ a. BCD
   - ☐ b. dry suit

6. When adding air to the dry suit, use
   - ☐ a. steady, long bursts.
   - ☐ b. frequent, short bursts.

7. When venting air from the dry suit
   - ☐ a. maintain a horizontal position.
   - ☐ b. maintain a vertical, feet-down position.

How'd you do?
1. b;   **2.** False. Weight can be distributed with smaller weights on the belt, with ankle weights, or by splitting it between the belt and a weight system.;   **3.** a;   **4.** a;   **5.** b;   **6.** b;   **7.** b.

CONCEPTS

Underline/highlight the answers to these questions as you read:

1. What should you do if you get too much air in your dry suit?

2. What should you do if you get too much air in the legs/feet of your dry suit?

3. What should you do if you accidentally drop your weights while dry suit diving?

4. What should you do if your dry suit floods?

HANDLING DRY SUIT EMERGENCIES

With practice and training during the Dry Suit Adventure Dive and in the Dry Suit Diver Specialty course, you'll find using a dry suit pretty straightforward. However, malfunctions and "user error" can create "emergencies" that you should know how to handle.

Excess Air
Your suit can become over inflated by a stuck inflator valve, a jammed exhaust valve, a nonfunctioning automatic exhaust valve or failure to vent the suit adequately during ascent. This can lead to a rapid runaway buoyant ascent.

If your inflator mechanism starts to freeflow, disconnect the inflator hose to avoid excess buoyancy, and then end the dive.

Action – Disconnect the inflator hose if that started the problem. Immediately dump air from the exhaust valve, or, if the exhaust valve has jammed shut, by pulling open your neck seal or a wrist seal (you may get wet doing this). To slow a rapid ascent, it helps to flare your body horizontal and create drag while you dump air. Be sure not to hold your breath during the ascent!

Excess Air in the Feet/Legs

This can have the same causes as excess air, except this time you're in a head-down position with the air in your legs where you can't exhaust it. You can also have this happen if you're diving overweighted and begin to ascend with your feet higher than your shoulders. A few dry suit models have exhaust valves in the feet to help avoid this, though they shouldn't be necessary when you dive properly weighted and use proper technique.

Action. Rapidly and forcefully tuck into a ball while rolling on to your back. This should force the air into the upper part of your suit, where you can dump it through the exhaust valve or wrist/neck seals. If you can't roll over, you may end up ascending rapidly to the surface – don't hold your breath! If you find yourself floating head down with inflated legs at the surface and can't swim upright, use your BCD to bring you up (only use the BCD for this at the surface).

Dropped Weights

If you accidentally drop your weight belt or dump your weight system and can't grab it, you'll have to contend with sudden positive buoyancy.

Action. Control your ascent by dumping as much air as possible, flaring back to create drag and grasping an ascent line if one's available. Exhaust air through your exhaust valve, or a seal if necessary, to help control your buoyancy as you ascend. Be sure not to hold your breath during the ascent.

Flooded Suit

A dry suit can flood by having the zipper partially open, through a seal tear, dirty exhaust valve or a seam failure. The immediate problem will be a sudden loss of buoyancy, followed by rapid chilling.

Action. Terminate the dive immediately. First, use your BCD to regain buoyancy. Drop your weights only if necessary, taking care not to start an uncontrolled ascent if you do so. Flare back to control ascent if needed.

After any dry suit problem resulting from a malfunction, don't use the suit until it has been serviced by a qualified professional.

Dry Suit 6

1. If you have excess air in your suit you should first (check all that apply):
   - ☐ a. tuck into a ball and roll on to your back.
   - ☐ b. exhaust the air through the valve or a seal.
   - ☐ c. ditch your weights.
   - ☐ d. use your BCD.

2. If you have excess air in the legs/feet of your suit underwater, you should (check all that apply):
   - ☐ a. tuck into a ball and roll on to your back.
   - ☐ b. exhaust the air through the valve or a seal.
   - ☐ c. ditch your weights.
   - ☐ d. use your BCD.

3. If you accidentally drop your weights you should (check all that apply):
   - ☐ a. tuck into a ball and roll on to your back.
   - ☐ b. exhaust the air through the valve or a seal.
   - ☐ c. use your BCD.

4. If your dry suit floods, you should first (check all that apply):
   - ☐ a. tuck into a ball and roll on to your back.
   - ☐ b. exhaust the air through the valve or a seal.
   - ☐ c. ditch your weights.
   - ☐ d. use your BCD.

5. During any emergency that could potentially cause a rapid or runaway ascent, be sure you
   - ☐ a. don't hold your breath.
   - ☐ b. maintain adequate warmth.
   - ☐ c. use your BCD.

How'd you do?
1. b; 2. a, b; 3. b; 4. d; 5. a.

DRY SUIT CARE

As you've already learned, dry suits require more maintenance than wet suits. But it's not difficult, though it takes a bit more time than wet suit care.

Every dry suit manufacturer has specifics for maintaining its particular products, and so consult the manufacturer's recommendations for your suit. The following general guidelines apply to most dry suits:

Underline/highlight the answers to these questions as you read:

1. What are the general guidelines for dry suit care?

2. Where should you look to find out how to fix a leak on a specific dry suit?

Most dry suits include a patch kit for repairing small holes and leaks. Because different suit materials require different patches and glues, use materials recommended by the manufacturer for your suit. You can get leak repair information from the suit's instruction booklet, the manufacturer or from your PADI Dive Center, Resort or Instructor.

After each use, wash the suit in fresh water. If the suit leaked, drizzled at the wrists or you were sweating, wash the interior, too (or as recommended by the manufacturer). Flush fresh water through the exhaust valve and low pressure inlet (especially if the hose was disconnected while underwater). Hang the suit over a thick bar or rounded surface, bent at the knees or waist and allow it to dry thoroughly inside and out before storage. Don't leave the suit hanging for more than 24 hours after it's dry, and keep it out of direct sunlight.

Most dry suits require attention to the wrist and neck seals and zipper – consult the manufacturer's directions for specifics. Do not use silicone lubricants on the zipper. Roll the suit loosely and store it away from heat, chemicals, oil and direct sunlight. Launder the undergarments according to manufacturer directions.

For transport to the dive site, keep the suit loosely rolled in a separate bag, away from other equipment that can puncture it or smash one of the valves.

Most dry suits include a patch kit for repairing small holes and leaks. Because different suit materials require different patches and glues, use materials recommended by the manufacturer for your suit. You can get leak repair information from the suit's instruction booklet, the manufacturer or from your PADI Dive Center, Resort or Instructor.

REVIEW

Dry Suit 7

1. One of the most important steps in general dry suit care is to store it hanging up.   ☐ True   ☐ False

2. The best place to get repair information is from the dry suit's instruction book or from the manufacturer.
☐ True   ☐ False

How'd you do?
1. False. Store a dry suit loosely rolled.; **2.** True.

DRY SUIT DIVING GUIDELINES

The following are recognized guidelines released by dry suit manufacturers. Heed these as you use your dry suit:

1. Stay up-to-date with the latest dry suit diving procedures and techniques.

2. Use a BCD for surface floatation and for backup buoyancy control. Underwater, use your dry suit to control buoyancy.

3. Be familiar with your equipment and know how to conduct emergency procedures with it.

4. Practice dry suit diving skills and techniques under controlled conditions until they're second nature.

5. Dive with a buddy who understands your dry suit system.

6. Use the correct amount of insulation for the water temperature and your activity rate.

 7. Weight yourself for neutral buoyancy at the surface and avoid overweighting. You should be able to make a safety stop at 5 metres/15 feet with 30 bar/500 psi in your tank.

8. Check your suit valves, zipper and seals before each dive.

9. Clean your suit and valves after every dive and store your suit properly. Check for leaks and have your suit serviced annually by qualified repair technicians.

10. Know your dry suit limitations and don't exceed them. If you begin to experience uncontrollable shivering, end the dive immediately and seek dryness and warmth.

Dry Suit 8

1. Which is not included in the ten dry suit guidelines (check all that apply)?
   ☐ a. Always weight for neutral buoyancy.
   ☐ b. Always wear a BCD.
   ☐ c. Always dive with two buddies.
   ☐ d. Always practice skills under controlled conditions.
   ☐ e. Always check your valves and seals before diving.

How'd you do?
1. c.

PADI Dry Suit Diver Specialty Course

Your Dry Suit Adventure Dive may be credited (at the instructor's discretion) toward the Dry Suit Diver Specialty certification. In addition to what you've learned in this section and will practice on the Dry Suit Adventure Dive, the Dry Suit Specialty course includes:

• exposure suit overview

• dry suit material comparisons – pros and cons

• undergarment comparisons – pros and cons

• more on handling problems

• leak repair techniques

The PADI Dry Suit Diver Specialty course is highly recommended as the ideal way to begin using your dry suit. Also, a growing number of manufacturers and dive operations require dry suit certification before they sell or rent one.

KNOWLEDGE REVIEW
Dry Suit Diving

1. Explain why even mild hypothermia can be a problem for divers, and how to avoid it.

2. How do you check for proper weighting when diving in your dry suit?

3. Why is it important to not dive with an excessively tight neck seal?

4. How should you attain positive buoyancy at the surface, attain and maintain neutral buoyancy underwater, and prevent dry suit squeeze when dry suit diving?

5. Describe how to add air to your dry suit while underwater.

6. How do you vent air from your dry suit while underwater?

7. What should you do if you become too buoyant due to excess air in your suit?

8. How do you cope with too much air in your dry suit legs/feet?

9. What should you remember about breathing if caught in a runaway or rapid ascent?

10. List what you should do if your dry suit floods.

Student Diver Statement: I've completed this Knowledge Review to the best of my ability and any questions I answered incorrectly or incompletely I've had explained to me, and I understand what I missed.

Signature _____ Date_____

Dry Suit Adventure Dive Overview

- Knowledge assessment/ Knowledge Review
- Briefing
- Gearing up
- Predive safety check (BWRAF)
- Entry
- Descent
- Neutral buoyancy – hovering

- Dry suit dive for fun
- Ascent – safety stop
- Remove/replace scuba unit and weight system at surface
- Exit
- Debrief
- Log dive – PADI Instructor signs

GO DRY
and GET WET

Experience PADI's Dry Suit program and dive anytime, anywhere!

Visit your PADI Dive Center or Resort or padi.com for details about this and other PADI Specialty programs.

PADI
padi.com

It's your life. Dive it well.

MULTILEVEL AND COMPUTER DIVING

Introduction

For its first 30 years or so, recreational dive time underwater was the no decompression limit of the deepest depth reached. Period. But no more. Today, multilevel diving – gaining more no decompression time by ascending to shallower depths where nitrogen absorption is slower – is more the rule than the exception. Thanks to multilevel diving, in most environments you can stay underwater as long as you have air and warmth; this breakthrough springs from modern dive computers, The Wheel version of the Recreational Dive Planner and other advances in decompression theory.

Whether you favor coral reefs or inland lakes, most dive sites have opportunities to multilevel dive. Any place you find a sloping reef, wall or other topography that allows you to start deep and move to shallower depths, you can plan a multilevel dive with your computer or The Wheel. Even many wreck dives will allow multilevel dives in which you start on the deeper parts of the wreck, and gradually ascend to the wreck's upper structure. Multilevel diving is your ticket to more of what you got into diving for – time underwater. No wonder more and more divers consider their computers as essential as their masks and regulators.

The performance requirements for this section require you to use the Recreational Dive Planner, The Wheel. Be sure you can use The Wheel to calculate single, repetitive and multilevel dives before going any farther. To learn to use The Wheel, or for a review, consult the Instructions for Use and Study Guide packaged with The Wheel, watch the **Diving With The Wheel** video tape, consult the **Open Water Diver Multimedia**, or see your dive center, resort or instructor.

MULTILEVEL DIVING THEORY

Key CONCEPTS

Underline/highlight the answers to these questions as you read:

1. What is multilevel diving?

2. What is the only way to determine no decompression limits?

3. What are the three types of diving that make a decompression theory mandatory?

4. How far can you rely on decompression theory to produce an acceptable probability of decompression sickness?

5. What are two reasons that you shouldn't attempt multilevel diving with conventional tables?

6. What dive planner can you use for multilevel diving?

Multilevel Diving Theory
See the *Recreational Divers Guide to Decompression Theory, Dive Tables and Dive Computers*

Multilevel diving is a technique for extending your bottom time beyond the no decompression limit (a.k.a. "no stop" limit) of the deepest depth you reach. You accomplish this by ascending to shallower levels during the dive; as you ascend, your body absorbs nitrogen more slowly than if you remained at the deepest depth for the entire dive. Because you absorb nitrogen more slowly, you have more time available within the no decompression limits.

Multilevel diving – whether you use a computer, The Wheel or both – draws directly upon decompression theory, so a rudimentary understanding of this theory helps you understand some of the limitations of multilevel diving and other dive practices. You'll find that guidelines you use with dive computers and tables come from what we know – and don't know – about decompression.

No Decompression Limits

Reviewing what you know from your PADI Open Water Diver course, your body absorbs nitrogen from the air you breathe during a dive. The deeper you dive, the faster you absorb nitrogen and the longer you dive, the more you absorb. Your body tolerates some amount of excess nitrogen when you surface without developing decompression sickness; dive tables and computers track theoretical nitrogen absorption to keep your body nitrogen within tolerable limits. (Note that in these discussions, we're concerned with decompression sickness, rather than the more broadly defined decompression illness. See the Deep Diving section if you're not familiar with the distinction.)

Interestingly, the "tolerable limits" – the no decompression limits for recreational divers – are the starting point for decompression theory. No theory of human physiology or decompression alone can predict the no decompression limits. They're determined only one way: through the actual results of human dives, preferably test dives.

The Decompression Model

Since no decompression limits are determined

through the results of actual dives, if you limited your diving to one single-depth dive in a day, you wouldn't need a decompression theory. You would just memorize the limits established by successful dive results.

Virtually all recreational dive computers and dive tables grew from various modifications of a decompression model published by physiologist John Scott Haldane in 1908.

But you don't want to make only one dive, you want to multilevel dive and you want to be ready for emergency decompression, just in case. Repetitive diving, multilevel diving and emergency decompression theory have too many variables to test all the possible combinations of dives, levels and surface intervals, so physiologists use mathematical decompression models to apply test results to this multitude of diving variables. Virtually all recreational dive computers and dive tables grew from various modifications of a decompression model published by physiologist John Scott Haldane in 1908.

Briefly, a decompression model works by *mathematically* predicting how much nitrogen the human body absorbs during a specific dive. As dynamic and useful as decompression models are, however, physiologists have learned that decompression theory is imperfect, and that decompression models can predict as "safe" dive profiles that may not be so safe. For that reason, you can only rely on decompression theory to produce an acceptable risk of decompression sickness as far as it has been successfully tested. Even then, because people vary in their physiology and susceptibility to decompression sickness, no dive table or computer can guarantee decompression sickness will never occur, even when diving within the table or computer limits. This is one reason why it's important to dive conservatively, well within table or computer no stop limits.

Mounting evidence suggests that repetitive deep dives produce an unacceptably high rate of decom-

Repetitive Deep Dive Tests

A series of tests by the British Royal Navy demonstrates why it's important to test decompression model limits. In 1982, the Royal Navy tested the following profile: 46 metres/150 feet for 5 minutes, 60 minute surface interval, 46 metres/150 feet for 5 minutes, 60 minute surface interval, 46 metres/150 feet for 5 minutes.

Although it's not likely anyone would actually dive this way in normal circumstances, according to mathematics and decompression models, this series of dives should have produced no cases of decompression sickness (in fact, some dive computers will permit this profile). But, the test divers had multiple cases of decompression sickness.

pression sickness, despite the predictions of mathematical models. For this reason, plan your repetitive dives no deeper than 30 metres/100 feet, regardless of what your dive table or computer might say it permits.

Tables and Multilevel Diving

Obviously, you can use dive computers for multilevel diving – that's perhaps their prime function. Computers calculate your exact dive profile and apply a decompression model to "write" a custom dive table for your dive.

On the other hand, you can't use conventional dive tables for multilevel diving, even by "interpolating" repetitive groups, because doing so can permit dives beyond what human dives show to work. A second concern is that attempting to calculate multilevel dives with conventional tables is at best tedious and at worst complex and error-prone. Not a good place to have an "oops."

The Wheel differs, though, because it was designed and tested with multilevel diving in mind. It keeps your dive plan within accepted limits, and its design simplifies planning.

Multilevel 1

1. Multilevel diving is
    ☐ a. a technique for safely making decompression dives.
    ☐ b. a technique for safely extending no decompression dive time.

2. No decompression limits for recreational diving can only be established
    ☐ a. through actual human dive results, preferably tests.
    ☐ b. by extensive computer analysis.
    ☐ c. through experiments with rats.

3. A decompression theory is made mandatory by (check all that apply):
    ☐ a. multilevel diving.
    ☐ b. single dive no decompression diving.

    ☐ c. repetitive diving.
    ☐ d. decompression diving.

4. You can rely on decompression theory to produce acceptably minimal risk of decompression sickness
    ☐ a. as far as you wish to extend the mathematics.
    ☐ b. only as far as it has been successfully tested.

5. You don't use conventional dive tables for multilevel diving because planning with them is complex and
    ☐ a. doing so infringes on international patent laws.
    ☐ b. they may permit profiles well beyond those that have been successfully tested.

6. The dive planner that has been designed and tested for multilevel diving is
    ☐ a. The Wheel.
    ☐ b. the U.S. Navy Multidepth Tables.

How'd you do?
1. b; 2. a; 3. a, c, d; 4. b; 5. b; 6. a.

ASCENT PROCEDURES

There are two potentially hazardous conditions related to a diver's ascent that you're already familiar with from your Open Water Diver course: lung overexpansion injuries and decompression sickness. Ascent recommendations help you avoid these. So far as decompression theory is concerned, an ascent procedure consists of three parts: 1) no decompression limit, 2) rate of ascent and 3) safety stop.

No Decompression Limit

From a theoretical point of view, the no decompression limit dictates when you'll start to ascend. This component of ascent has no bearing on lung overexpansion injuries.

Rate

The ascent rate for The Wheel has been established at a maximum of 18 metres/60 feet per minute based on human tests, though some computers specify slower rates. Ascend no faster than 18 metres/60 feet per minute or at the rate prescribed by the table or computer you are using, whichever is slower. Using The Wheel (or Table) RDP, you may ascend slower than 18 metres/60 feet per minute.

Safety stop

A safety stop is a three minute pause at the 5 metre/15 foot level. Safety stops have been tested to a limited degree, and show significant benefit in reducing the probability of decompression sickness. When analyzed mathematically with a decompression model, the safety stop theoretically also produces a significant reduction in absorbed nitrogen. A safety stop at 5 metres/15 feet also allows you a moment to double-check your depth and time information. In addition, the stop gives you a moment to readjust your buoyancy, so

it may help prevent runaway ascents through the last few metres/several feet of water, and thereby minimize the possibility of lung overexpansion injuries. It's with these reasons in mind that you want to make safety stops on virtually all dives.

Key CONCEPT

Underline/highlight the answers to this question as you read:

1. Why should a dive requiring emergency decompression be the last, and preferably only dive of the day?

EMERGENCY DECOMPRESSION

Within the scope of recreational diving, decompression diving is exclusively an emergency procedure. However there's an important aspect to note about combining a dive that requires emergency decompression with a repetitive dive: It's a bad idea.

A 1986 U.S. Navy test revealed an unacceptable rate of decompression sickness resulting from repetitive decompression dives, despite table predictions. Furthermore, anecdotal reports from recompression chamber facilities indicate many cases of decompression sickness result from combining decompression diving with repetitive diving. Apparently, even if only one dive in the series is a decompression dive, the probability of decompression sickness increases.

It seems that in many cases, mathematical decompression models can't adequately predict the combination of a repetitive dive with a decompression dive. For this reason, avoid combining a dive that requires emergency decompression with a repetitive dive. If you make a dive and accidentally end up at an emergency stop, after the stop make that the last dive of the day, even if your computer permits more dives. (The Wheel requires *at least* a six hour surface interval.)

USING YOUR COMPUTER

It's your dive computer that really makes multilevel diving practical. While The Wheel makes it possible without a computer, the primary advantage of using a computer for multilevel diving is that it computes your *exact* dive profile for maximum allowable no stop time. The Wheel helps you understand how a computer calculates, and it's your best option for resuming diving if your computer crashes (it happens), but 99 percent of the time, you'll probably want to use your computer for the convenience and the precision it offers.

 However, as wondrous as your computer is, it's imperative that you make computer-*assisted*, not computer-*controlled* dives. Computers appear almost magical to some people; but they're just highly sophisticated calculators that read the depth and time and then apply the same type decompression model your dive tables use. They're no more or less valid than dive tables, and the same guidelines apply to computer diving as to table diving.

Eight rules for computer diving (some of these apply to tables, too) help you stay within the limits of what has been proven to produce an acceptably minimal probability of decompression sickness.

It's imperative that you make computer-assisted, not computer-controlled dives. Computers are just highly sophisticated calculators that read the depth and time and then apply the same type decompression model dive tables use. They're no more or less valid than dive tables.

1. Don't dive to the no decompression limits and avoid mandatory emergency decompression. Stay well within the computer's (or a table's) limits. You should have ample time before reaching a no stop limit at *all* times during your dive.

2. Topography permitting, make multilevel dives that start deep and work shallower. Avoid "sawtooth" (a.k.a. "reverse") dive profiles with repeated significant shallow and deep depth changes, such as starting a dive at 30 metres/100 feet, then ascending to 18 metres/60 feet and after a while, descending to 28 metres/90 feet. While it's unclear what added risk there may be for this kind of diving, if any, within the realm of no stop diving the vast majority of test data is based on "forward" profiles that start deep and work progressively upward. To stay within the envelope of proved test data, start at the deepest point and progress shallower (minor variations aren't a problem). Your computer may "permit" sawtooth profiles by calculating them, not to encourage this kind of profile, but so you have information if you accidentally do one.

3. Control your rate of ascent to 18 metres/60 feet per minute or slower. Virtually all computers have rate indicators that alert you if you start to go too fast.

4. Take a safety stop at the end of all dives at 5 metres/15 feet for at least 3 minutes.

5. Allow a surface interval of at least 60 minutes with a computer, even if it permits the dive time you want in less time.

6. Limit repetitive dives to 30 metres/100 feet or less. Make your deepest dive first, with subsequent dives progressively shallower.

7. Don't get so caught up in your extended bottom time limit that you neglect your air supply. (Sounds obvious, but on a multilevel dive, you'll usually be limited by air, not by no stop time.)

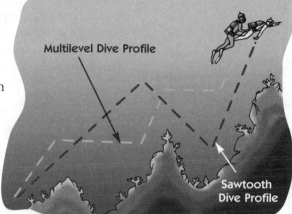

Multilevel Dive Profile

Sawtooth Dive Profile

8. Be aware that no computer or table can account for physiological variations caused by factors such as age, dehydration, alcohol consumption, strenuous exercise, excessive fat tissue, injury or other factors that predispose you toward decompression sickness. The more of these factors that apply, the more conservatively you should use your computer or table. Surprisingly, being conservative doesn't always mean you have to cut your dive short – usually, you can simply move shallower sooner so you always have lots of time before reaching a no decompression limit.

REVIEW

Multilevel 4

1. The primary advantage of using a computer is
   - ☐ a. the ability to make virtually any dive the computer can calculate.
   - ☐ b. that the computer computes your exact profile for maximum allowable no stop time.

2. There's nothing wrong with a multilevel computer dive profile that ascends and descends repeatedly, provided that you don't exceed the no decompression limit.
   - ☐ True   ☐ False

How'd you do?

1. b;   2. False. "Sawtooth" profiles are problems. Avoid them by starting deep and working shallower on a multilevel dive.

MULTILEVEL DIVE EQUIPMENT

Equipment for All Multilevel Dives

Besides the equipment you normally wear in your local dive environment, you want to have three pieces of equipment along for multilevel dives.

The Wheel. As the "table" you can plan multilevel dives with, The Wheel is recommended for two reasons. First, to plan a multilevel dive with or without your computer. The Wheel will give you a rough idea of what your computer will allow as you ascend during the course of a dive. Second, if your computer goes south on you, use The Wheel as a back up that permits multilevel diving – something you'll want especially if all your buddies' computers are still humming along fine. If you're on an exotic dive holiday and your computer quits, you'll kick yourself up and down the dock for leaving your Wheel at home.

Depth gauge and timer. These two pieces of equipment are necessary to back up a dive computer. You'll also need these to multilevel dive with The Wheel without your computer.

Equipment for Computer-assisted Multilevel Dives

When making computer-assisted multilevel dives, you and your buddy should each have your own computers. Multiple divers shouldn't share one computer. Once a diver begins diving with a computer, that diver uses that computer for the entire diving day, or longer if specified by the manufacturer.

The reason for this is that dive computers track your dive profile so closely that even minor variations between you and your buddy affect your allowable dive time. Likewise, the computer tracks nitrogen release between dives, so it's inappropriate to let someone borrow your computer between

Use The Wheel as a back up that permits multilevel diving – something you'll want especially if all your buddies' computers are still humming along fine. If you're on an exotic dive holiday and your computer quits, you'll kick yourself up and down the dock for leaving your Wheel at home.

dives. Never turn off a computer between dives, and always follow the manufacturer's instructions. (You did read them, right?)

When making computer assisted multilevel dives, you and your buddy should each have your own computers. Multiple divers shouldn't share one computer.

KEY CONCEPTS

Underline/highlight the answers to these questions as you read:

1. What are three potential hazards of multilevel diving, and how do you avoid them?

2. What are two common mistakes to avoid when multilevel diving with or without a computer in any environment?

MULTILEVEL DIVE HAZARDS

There are a few potential hazards and mistakes in multilevel diving that you'll need to avoid. No worries – none of these are particularly mysterious or difficult to evade. Just things to watch out for.

Potential Hazards

The three main potential hazards of multilevel diving are not unique to multilevel diving. You can encounter these in almost any diving situation, but we give them special attention here because multilevel dives mean extended bottom times, which means more potential to run into them.

Hypothermia. Extended bottom times increase your exposure to cool water. Your exposure suit that's adequate for a short dive may not be enough for a longer one. Be sure to wear adequate thermal protection. If you begin shivering, end the dive immediately. For more information on hypothermia, see the Dry Suit Diving section.

Running out of air. We touched on this earlier. Your available no stop time on a multilevel dive can easily exceed your air supply. Pay close attention to your air supply and allow plenty for a safe return to boat or shore. A good habit is that when you check your computer, you check your SPG, too.

Pay close attention to your air supply and allow plenty for a safe return to boat or shore. A good habit is that when you check your computer, you check your SPG, too.

Disorientation. A long period underwater means you can go farther, which means more opportunity to get turned around. Use a compass and your other navigational skills so you know where you are and where to exit the water at all times. Take your time and go slower. Just because you can go farther doesn't mean you have to. See the Underwater Navigation section for more information about staying oriented.

Common Mistakes

There are two common mistakes to avoid, both of which we've touched on already:

Sharing a computer. Don't. Computers follow dive profiles too closely to make sharing feasible. The diver not wearing the computer can't be confident in the dive profile, and it would be especially cumbersome if that diver wants to dive with someone else after a surface interval. If you have two divers and one computer, have the computerless diver calculate a multilevel profile with The Wheel. This should provide ample no stop time for both divers to fully enjoy the dive without unnecessary risk or complications.

Sawtooth diving. Because computers and tables are mathematical devices, they calculate any vari-

For more information about...

Hypothermia
See the Physiology of Diving section of the *Encyclopedia of Recreational Diving*, book or Multimedia
Disorientation
See the *Underwater Navigator Manual* and *Underwater Navigation* video

ety of dives, even deep dives following shallow dives or, on multilevel dives, deep levels following shallow levels. These kinds of sawtooth profiles, however, take you outside the body of known test data for reliable diving. It seems that decompression models aren't as reliable in this kind of diving, and in any case, there's been virtually no testing of sawtooth diving.

As stated earlier, avoid this. Make your deepest dive first, with repetitive dives progressively shallower. Multilevel dives should begin at the deepest point and work to progressively shallower levels. Once you've ascended to a shallower depth, don't drop back down. Computers or tables let you calculate it not because it's recommended, but so you've got information if it happens accidentally.

Multilevel 6

1. Three potential hazards of multilevel diving are (check all that apply):
   - ☐ a. hypothermia
   - ☐ b. vertigo
   - ☐ c. oxygen poisoning
   - ☐ d. disorientation
   - ☐ e. running out of air

2. Sawtooth diving, in which the diver moves up and down from shallow levels to deep,
   - ☐ a. is made possible with computers.
   - ☐ b. should be avoided, regardless of the table or computer used.

How'd you do?

1. a, d, e;   2. b.

MULTILEVEL DIVE PLANNING

You're going to find that planning a multilevel dive differs little from planning a single depth dive, making it easy to benefit from extended no stop time at shallower depths.

Considerations

There are three considerations to take into account when planning multilevel dives.

Topography. You need to estimate ascending depth levels when planning your dive. A sloping reef, wall or other moderate rise in the bottom is nearly ideal for multilevel diving because it offers almost any depth level you want. Some "single-depth" sites, such as wrecks or flat reefs have few practical opportunities for making a multilevel dive. At an unfamiliar dive site where you have no information about depth levels, it may be impossible to plan your first visit to the site as a multilevel dive. Of course your computer will extend your no stop time if you do, in fact, find appropriate topography and follow it. Just be sure to include this possibility in your planning.

Air supply. As mentioned in the section on hazards, your no decompression time can be longer than your air supply. Be sure you watch your air when you dive your plan.

Contingency plans. Multilevel dives require contingency planning. If your computer fails, you need to know what to do (discussed in a moment). If intermediate depth levels are deeper than you planned, you need to be ready to skip up a level or revert to a single-depth dive plan, especially if you're using The Wheel without a dive computer.

Multilevel Planning with Computers

If you're diving with a computer, there are a few steps to take for planning. You will get your initial and repetitive dive no decompression limits from your computer, and you can use The Wheel to estimate the time your computer will allow on a multi-

level profile. You also need to know what to do if your computer crashes.

Obtaining no decompression limits. For first and repetitive dives, most dive computers display their no decompression limits for various depths when you activate the scroll mode. Different models activate their scroll modes in different ways, so consult the computer's instruction manual or your instructor.

Using The Wheel to plan computer dives. The Wheel helps estimate your computer's no stop time. For your first dive, simply calculate the multilevel profile you intend to follow; The Wheel will *approximate* the time you can expect at each level.

For repetitive dives, it's necessary to find a pressure group for use on The Wheel. First, set your computer in scroll mode and find your no decompression limit for a repetitive dive to 12 metres/40 feet. Next, set The Wheel's yellow p.g. index for the scrolled time and align it with the NDL mark on the 12 metre/40 foot curve. Now look at where the white p.g. index crosses the 12 metre/40 foot curve to determine your pressure group. (This is similar to setting your Wheel for a minimum surface interval problem.) Use that pressure group on The Wheel to approximate the time your computer will permit on a repetitive multilevel dive.

You will get your initial and repetitive dive no decompression limits from your computer, and you can use The Wheel to estimate the time your computer will allow on a multilevel profile.

In using The Wheel to assist in planning computer dives, remember that dive computers follow your exact profile, and may have different no decompression limits than The Wheel. When diving with a computer, stay within the computer's no stop limits. The computer is your source of no decompression time; The Wheel simply helps you plan the dive.

If your computer fails. If your computer fails between dives, you will have to wait at least 24 hours (longer if recommended by the manufacturer) before resuming diving with another computer or The

Wheel. This is because there's no accurate way to account for the nitrogen in your body. You must wait until the excess nitrogen has left your body for all practical purposes. An exception is if your maximum depths and times fall within the single-depth limits of the RDP (Table or Wheel). In this case, you can calculate the day's dive profile and determine a pressure group for planning another dive. But this is often impossible because multilevel dive times frequently exceed single depth limits, especially if your first level was deeper than 18 metres/60 feet.

If your computer fails while you're diving, make a long stop – perhaps as long as your air supply permits. Do not dive again for 24 hours, or as stipulated by the manufacturer's instructions.

If your computer fails while you're diving, immediately stop the dive and ascend according to the manufacturer's guidelines. If there are none, ascend no faster than 18 metres/60 feet per minute, or the computer's ascent rate, whichever is slower, to 5 metres/15 feet. Make a long stop – perhaps as long as your air supply permits. Do not dive again for 24 hours, or as stipulated by the manufacturer's instructions.

Multilevel 7

1. Considerations when planning a multilevel dive include (check all that apply):
   - ☐ a. topography
   - ☐ b. oxygen decompression
   - ☐ c. air supply
   - ☐ d. contingency plans

2. Most computers display no decompression limits by activating the
   - ☐ a. decompression mode.
   - ☐ b. no decompression mode.
   - ☐ c. scroll mode.

3. Using The Wheel to estimate what a computer will allow on a repetitive multilevel dive is similar to calculating
   - ☐ a. emergency decompression.
   - ☐ b. minimum surface interval.

4. If a computer fails, you should wait _____ before resuming diving with another computer or table.
   - ☐ a. 6 hours, or longer if recommended by the manufacturer
   - ☐ b. 12 hours, or longer if recommended by the manufacturer
   - ☐ c. 24 hours, or longer if recommended by the manufacturer

5. If a computer fails while diving, you should
   - ☐ a. make a normal ascent with a safety stop lasting as long as air supply permits.
   - ☐ b. rely on your buddy's computer.

How'd you do?
1. a, c, d; 2. c; 3. b; 4. c; 5. a.

PADI Multilevel Diver Specialty course

Your Multilevel Adventure Dive may be credited (at the instructor's discretion) toward the PADI Multilevel Diver Specialty certification. In addition to what you've learned in this section and will practice on the Multilevel Adventure Dive, the Multilevel Diver Specialty course includes:

- more about computer performance

- more background on decompression theory

- continuing diving after a computer failure

The PADI Multilevel Diver course is highly recommended for getting the best use from your dive computer, or for using The Wheel for multilevel diving when your – or your buddy's – computer crashes.

Multilevel and Computer Adventure Dive Overview

- Knowledge assessment/ Knowledge Review
- Briefing – Plan dive with The Wheel and (optional) computer
- Gearing up
- Predive safety check (BWRAF)
- Entry
- Descent to deepest depth level
- Ascent to second depth level
- Ascent – safety stop
- Exit
- Debrief
- Log dive – PADI Instructor signs

KNOWLEDGE REVIEW
Multilevel & Computer Diving

1. Describe how no decompression limits are determined.

2. Because people vary in their _____ and susceptibility to decompression sickness, no _____ or _____ can guarantee decompression sickness will never occur, even when diving within its limits.

3. Describe how you should ascend when diving with any table or computer.

4. Why should a dive requiring an emergency decompression stop be the last, and preferably only, dive of the day?

5. List eight rules that apply to computer diving.

1._____

2._____

3._____

4._____

5._____

6._____

7._____

8._____

6. List the three pieces of dive equipment for any multilevel dive (in addition to the regular gear you need for the local environment).

1._____

2._____

3._____

7. List the three potential hazards of multilevel diving.

1._____

2._____

3._____

8. What are the two common mistakes to avoid while multilevel diving, with or without a computer?

1._____

2._____

9. What three considerations do you include in planning a multilevel dive?

1._____

2._____

3._____

10. You can use The Wheel to _____ the time your computer will allow on a first dive and repetitive dives.

11. Describe what to do if your computer fails during a dive.

Student Diver Statement: I've completed this Knowledge Review to the best of my ability and any questions I answered incorrectly or incompletely I've had explained to me, and I understand what I missed.

Signature _____ Date_____

Become a PADI Instructor

The possibilities are endless

Can you imagine a job where you actually look forward to heading off for work in the morning? Or, do you want to lead a life others fantasize about?

Whether you work in a local dive center, at a resort, or on a live aboard dive boat, the adventure of a lifetime is yours for the taking. Contact your local PADI Instructor Development Center, Career Development Center or Course Director for more information.

PADI®
padi.com

Dive More.
Do More!

Join the PADI Diving Society!

Whether you're a dedicated snorkeler or avid diver – beginner or pro – the PADI Diving Society is your passport to the underwater world and the exciting lifestyle diving has to offer.

Take advantage of Society membership and enjoy:

- Equipment Rebates & Incentives
- Exotic Members-only Dive Trips
- Local Society Events & Socials
- Personalized Membership Card
- Savings on Dive Insurance
- Members-only Publication
- Travel Specials

Plus, your membership supports Project AWARE environmental initiatives. The PADI Diving Society makes it easy to dive more and *do more!* Join today at your local PADI Dive Center or Resort, or visit padi.com.

PADI Diving Society®

*PADI Diving Society offices are located in the US and UK. US residents call toll free at 888 333 7234 or +1 386 447 2535. UK residents call 0117 300 7373. Benefits differ in certain regions, please contact your local Society office for a full list of benefits in your area.

NIGHT DIVING

Introduction

Dive at night? Why? If you're new to diving and have never tried it, the idea might seem strange, or even intimidating. What can you see at night that you wouldn't during the day?

Think about a nocturnal stroll through a familiar park. At first it seems a little scary perhaps, but as your eyes adjust to the dark you relax, recognizing the familiar paths and trees. It's the same place you've seen many times during the day, yet somehow different.

Your flashlight illuminates a jasmine blossom that opened at nightfall; you almost didn't recognize it as the same flower you see during the day. The birds that normally flit about are gone, but a different bird – one you're not familiar with – whistles in the darkness. It's the same park, but already you've discovered something new and fascinating about it.

Visiting a favorite, familiar dive site at night can be like visiting a whole new dive site. You may feel a little bit anxious about going underwater in the dark – no worries, that's natural and for some, even a bit of the fun. But, as you explore applying the techniques you'll learn in this section, you'll find curiosity and excitement replacing hesitation and anxiety. Chances are, before the dive ends you'll be fascinated with night diving, already ready for your next.

THE APPEAL OF NIGHT DIVING AND NIGHT DIVING ACTIVITIES

Key CONCEPTS

Underline/highlight the answers to these questions as you read:

1. What five aspects of night diving commonly appeal to divers?

2. What three diving activities does diving at night enhance?

Why Dive At Night

Just as different people dive for different reasons, they have different reasons for night diving. Probably you can find as many reasons for diving at night as there are night divers, but you'll find these five reasons again and again.

Natural curiosity. "Because it is there," justifies night diving just as well as it justifies mountain climbing. You may want to night dive simply for the excitement– to do something you're curious about because it's a bit different and a bit more adventurous than daytime diving. Know what? That's all the reason you need.

To observe aquatic organisms. At dusk, nocturnal animals such as lobsters in salt water or catfish in fresh, become active. Animals that are difficult to approach by day, including many fish, let you get closer at night. Still others that you're quite familiar with look very different at night. Coral polyps open at night to feed, for example, making the reef look "fuzzy" and colorful instead of hard and rocky.

A new look at old sites. The "same old site" takes on new appeal at night. It puts the spark back into visiting dive sites that have lost some of their daytime fascination. Night diving gives you a reason to revisit familiar dive sites, because in the dark, they're not quite so familiar any more.

More chances to dive. You may discover that night diving equates with diving more. While your work schedule might make day diving impossible most days, you may have adequate time to get wet after work.

Colorful dives. As you recall from your entry-level course, water absorbs color so that the deeper you dive, the less colorful the scenery. When night div-

At dusk, nocturnal animals such as lobsters in salt water or catfish in fresh, become active. Animals that are difficult to approach by day, including many fish, let you get closer at night.

ing, however, you take your light with you, and the beam doesn't get filtered through very much water. This means that at night, the colors appear more vibrant and "true" than during the day.

Things To Do at Night

Swimming around exploring at night is interesting, but you'll find that darkness enhances, or adds a new twist to different diving activities. Notably, sightseeing, underwater photography, and wreck diving benefit from night diving.

As mentioned, you'll see aquatic life at night that you seldom see during the day, and you'll observe behaviors and phenomena unique to the after-sunset environment. In the ocean, for example, you may encounter bioluminescence – chemical light flashes microscopic plankton generate when a diver disturbs them. When bioluminescence is present, cover your light and then wave your hand through the water. As you do this, you'll see "sparks" ignite in its wake.

If you're into underwater photography, you'll find that night provides a dramatic black backdrop for striking pictures, plus opportunities to photograph nocturnal creatures and behaviors. In fact, you might find that you prefer night photography to day photography.

Of all the sites that take on new character after dark, it's hard to beat a wreck. At night, wreck diving can be a mysterious experience, with the ship taking on a new dramatic dimension. If you're interested in wreck diving, the Wreck Adventure Dive and the Wreck Diver Specialty course offer guided introductions to visiting sunken ships. Among other things, you learn that on a night dive, you don't enter a shipwreck because there's no natural light to help you find your way out if you become disoriented. Entering a shipwreck (or any other overhead environment, for that matter) requires

If you're into underwater photography, you'll find that night provides a dramatic black backdrop for striking pictures, plus opportunities to photograph nocturnal creatures and behaviors. In fact, you might find that you prefer night photography to day photography.

special training, equipment and techniques; to do so without the proper equipment and training places you in unnecessary and excessive risk.

NIGHT DIVING EQUIPMENT

Ask almost any diver what special equipment you need to night dive, and you'll get the answer, "A dive light or torch." Okay, that's pretty obvious, and we'll focus entirely on dive lights in a moment. But night diving has some other equipment considerations, which we'll cover here – everything other than lights.

Aside from lights, your personal equipment for night diving does not differ much from day diving, but there are a few points worth attention. It's always recommended that your alternate air source be clearly identifiable and secured in the triangle formed by your chin and the lower corners of your rib cage, where you or a buddy can find it easily. For diving at night, if your alternate isn't conspicuously colored already, you might consider adding a bright colored hose protector to make it stand out better in the dark.

It's recommended that your alternate air source be clearly identifiable and secured in the triangle formed by your chin and the lower corners of your rib cage. A conspicuous color and/or a bright colored hose protector make it stand out better in the dark.

Carry a whistle, especially at night so you can make your presence known in the dark if necessary. Attach it to your BCD inflator hose near the mouthpiece, where it's out of the way but ready for immediate use.

Depending upon the environment, it's often wise to protect yourself with an exposure suit, booties and gloves.

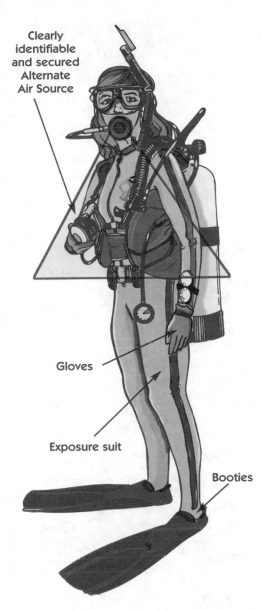

Clearly identifiable and secured Alternate Air Source

Gloves

Exposure suit

Booties

Since you'll have a light in one hand, you'll want one-hand BCD control – which is probably how it's already set. You should have complete instrumentation – depth gauge, timer (or dive computer) and compass – ideally with luminous/illuminated markings for easy reading. A reference line from a boat or buoy will make your ascents/descent easier, and for reliable communication, take your slate. For surface communication, it's a good idea to carry a whistle, especially at night so you can make your presence known in the dark if necessary. Attach it to your BCD inflator hose near the mouthpiece, where it's out of the way but ready for immediate use.

Depending upon the environment, it's often wise to protect yourself with an exposure suit, booties and gloves. It's a bit easier to bump into things in the dark, which can cause some scrapes or cuts if you're unprotected. Remember, though, that just because you're protected from the reef doesn't mean the reef's protected from you. Take extra care at night to avoid blundering into fragile corals or other aquatic life.

It's generally recommended that you avoid using new or unfamiliar equipment at night. You want to work with familiar, comfortable equipment on a night dive (or any other specialized diving activity, for that matter). If you've acquired a new BCD, regulator or other equipment, it's best to become familiar with it during the day under favorable conditions before diving with it at night.

1. Aside from a dive light, there's no difference between night diving and day diving equipment.
   ☐ True   ☐ False

2. Diving with new or unfamiliar equipment at night
   ☐ a. is a good idea so you quickly adapt to using it in the dark.
   ☐ b. generally, isn't recommended.

How'd you do?
1. False. Night diving equipment is generally the same as day diving equipment, but alternate air sources, low pressure inflators, reference lines, communication equipment and exposure suits have some extra considerations. **2.** b.

NIGHT DIVING LIGHTS

Obviously you need a dive light, or dive torch as some call it, at night not just to see the reef, but to read your gauges and to show your buddy where you are. If you're not near an ascent line, without a light it can be tough to make a slow, controlled ascent. Although you'll find modern dive lights tough, reliable and trustworthy, even the best of them fail. That's why you really want to dive with two dive lights – your primary and a backup. Although it sounds a bit paranoid, some divers even carry three or four lights, just to ensure that neither they nor a buddy won't have to end a night dive without one.

Choosing a Dive Light

There are dozens of dive lights that you can choose from, so finding two you like shouldn't be a problem. Generally, you'll buy a big bright, wider beam light as your primary light, and a more compact light as your backup. The primary light will be in your hand, and you clip your backup light to your weight belt or BCD, tuck it in your BCD pocket or carry it some other way.

When selecting dive lights, look for these six features:

Rugged outer case. Most dive lights are made from plastic or aluminum to resist corrosion. Regardless of which, choose the most rugged, tough light in

Underline/highlight the answers to these questions as you read:

1. Why should you carry two underwater lights while night diving?

2. What six features do you look for in a dive light?

3. What are the advantages of rechargeable and non-rechargeable batteries in a dive light?

4. Why shouldn't you turn on some dive lights above water?

5. What are three uses for marker lights, and where do you attach them for those uses?

6. How do you take care of a dive light?

7. How do you care for a flooded dive light?

Dive Lights
See the Dive Equipment section in the *Encyclopedia of Recreational Diving*

your price range. This isn't a license to abuse your lights, but they get banged against other equipment, dropped on decks, and slammed against the bottom despite your best efforts. Choose lights with this in mind.

Dependable switches. The three most popular switches are indirect (magnetic or screw-down lenses), o-ring gland and rubber-boot covered switches. With proper maintenance (discussed shortly) all are reliable. A lock mechanism (which isn't possible with all switch types) prevents accidentally running your batteries down while the light's in your bag, which you may find a nice feature.

O-ring seals. The fewer o-ring sealed openings, the easier the maintenance and the fewer potential leaks. This is one advantage of screw-down lens models. Some lights have two o-rings on one opening for added reliability.

Comfortable handle or mount. You may be holding your light for up to an hour, so be sure it's comfortable. Some smaller lights (usually used in addition to your primary) mount on your mask, on special helmets or on mounting brackets. If you choose these, be sure they're comfortable and don't cause your mask to leak. Also, mount them so they shine somewhat downward, if possible, to reduce their potential for blinding other divers accidentally.

Look for a dive light with a rugged case, dependable switches, a comfortable handle, a wrist lanyard and as few o-ring-sealed openings as possible.

Wrist lanyard. You generally use a lanyard to prevent loss and so you can release your light momentarily to work with your equipment, etc. You can buy wrist lanyards separately at your PADI Dive Center or Resort if your light didn't come with one.

Fresh/recharged batteries. Without power, the best light in the world is no better than the worst. Most light "failures" during a night dive arise from diving with weak batteries. Make sure that you have fresh batteries – new for disposable, or freshly charged for rechargeables.

Besides these six features, you'll want to consider other features based on your preferences. You may decide to buy a disposable battery light so you don't have to deal with recharging when traveling, because disposable batteries last longer before they're replaced than rechargeable batteries last before they're recharged, and/or because disposable battery lights cost less initially. On the other hand, you may opt for rechargeable batteries because they're less expensive in the long run if you use the light a lot, and because Nicad rechargeables hold their voltage until they need charging, so the light doesn't dim as the batteries weaken.

The dive lights typical for night diving may be similar to normal flashlights and use two to four D or C cell batteries (smaller lights in this category make good backup lights), or they may be larger, sealed-beam bulb types that use six-volt batteries or clustered battery packs.

Some underwater lights, especially high power models used for video, or used by serious cave/wreck divers, can only be turned on underwater due to their high heat. If you use one of these out of water, the bulb quickly burns out, but usually not before the heat cooks other components in the light. Most high power lights like these have a separate battery pack and light head. You can use most "typical" dive lights out of water, but if you're not sure, check the manufacturer's instructions.

The dive lights typical for night diving may be similar to normal flashlights and use two to four D or C cell batteries (smaller lights in this category make good backup lights), or they may be larger, sealed-beam bulb types that use six-volt batteries or clustered battery packs.

Other Light Systems

Besides your dive light, you'll find marker lights and underwater flashers (strobes) useful in night diving. Marker lights are small battery powered lights or chemical lights, such as the Cyalume-brand light sticks. The former typically use an AA battery and a small bulb, while the latter produce light from a chemical reaction that you can rely on, even if you have an unlikely failure of both a primary and backup light.

You normally use marker lights as orientation lights for your own and your buddy's location, for marking boats/buoys, and for marking ascent/descent lines. You can attach these to your snorkel or tank valve, to the boat motor, antenna or buoy flag-staff, and string them at intervals along the ascent/descent lines.

Underwater flashers make it easy to find your way back at night. In clear water, you may be able to see these beacons from more than 30 metres/100 feet away.

Underwater flashers make it easy to find your way back at night.

Dive Light Maintenance

After use in salt water, or fresh water that's dirty or has lots of minerals, you should wash your dive lights thoroughly in fresh water along with the rest of your equipment, preferably by immersing them and agitating them for a minute, followed by a soak for 20 minutes to an hour. Then, dry and open each light and remove the batteries, recharge them (if appropriate) and store them separately. Clean, lubricate and inspect the o-rings, replacing any that show nicks, cuts or wear. Clean battery and other electrical contacts with a soft pencil eraser, and then store your lights in a cool place out of direct sunlight.

If your light floods, immediately turn it off (if you're underwater, switch to your backup light). As soon as possible, open and drain the light, and rinse the interior and exterior with fresh water. Discard disposable batteries appropriately. Remove the o-rings and rinse the interior and

rechargeable batteries with iso-propyl alcohol to aid drying. Drain off the alcohol and complete the drying with a hair dryer on mild heat. Return the light to your dive store or the manufacturer for service. Consult the manufacturer's instructions for specific steps to take with your light.

After use in salt water, or fresh water that's dirty or has lots of minerals, you should wash your dive lights thoroughly in fresh water along with the rest of your equipment, preferably by immersing them and agitating them for a minute, followed by a soak for 20 minutes to an hour.

Underwater Organisms
Attracted by Light

In some areas, depending on the season, your dive lights may attract small aquatic organisms. These can range from interesting organisms to those that can sting. Be careful about placing bright lights near surface entry and exit points when there's a possibility of attracting these organisms. If in doubt, check with local divers for more information before using bright surface or underwater lights.

Quick REVIEW

Night 3

1. It's important to carry two underwater lights because
   - ☐ a. even the best dive lights can fail.
   - ☐ b. there are times when you'll need to use two lights at once.

2. Which of these are among the six features you look for in a dive light? (check all that apply):
   - ☐ a. rechargeable batteries
   - ☐ b. wrist lanyard
   - ☐ c. reliable switch
   - ☐ d. rugged case

3. Rechargeable battery lights
   - ☐ a. cost more than disposable battery lights, but are cheaper in the long run if you night dive frequently.
   - ☐ b. are not considered reliable.

4. Some high intensity dive lights should not be switched on above water because they'll burn out and could be damaged.
   - ☐ True   ☐ False

5. One use of marker lights is to mark your own and your buddy's location underwater.
   - ☐ True   ☐ False

6. After each use, a dive light should be
   - ☐ a. rinsed in fresh water.
   - ☐ b. rinsed internally with fresh water, and then isopropyl alcohol.

7. Basic care for a flooded dive light includes:
   - ☐ a. rinsing it externally in fresh water only.
   - ☐ b. rinsing it internally with fresh water and then isopropyl alcohol.

How'd you do?
1. a;   **2.** b, c, d;   **3.** a;   **4.** True;   **5.** True;   **6.** a;   **7.** b.

PLANNING NIGHT DIVES

Rewarding night dives don't just happen. Like all worthwhile dives, they're planned, following the same steps you learned in the Open Water Diver course. You evaluate the dive site and carefully plan your time and depth limits, entry and exit points, and other considerations just as you would during any dive.

Choosing the Dive Site

It's generally recommended that you night dive in places you know. Ideally, diving or at least snorkeling the site during the day before your night dive puts the details fresh in mind for planning the night dive. If you can't dive the site the same day as your night dive, you can consult your log book for dive data, arrive before sunset so you can more easily evaluate the conditions, or go with an experienced guide or buddy who has been there before.

⚠️ As a general rule, night dive when conditions are good. Marginal conditions within your experience and training by day may not be acceptable for a night dive. Especially try to avoid these five conditions at night: heavy surf, strong currents, poor visibility, overhead environments (caverns, caves, thick kelp, the insides of wrecks, etc.) and heavy surge.

Many divers especially enjoy night diving from a boat. Using a boat can simplify night diving by making entries and exits easier than dealing with surf or watching where you're wading. Second, boats make great support platforms where you can gear up, warm up, store equipment and carry emergency/accessory equipment. Third, boats provide comfortable transportation to and from the dive site. Of

Underline/highlight the answers to these questions as you read:

1. What should you consider in evaluating and choosing a potential night diving site?

2. What are five environmental conditions that you should generally avoid when planning a night dive?

3. What are three reasons for conducting night dives from a boat?

4. What are four general night diving planning considerations?

Many divers especially enjoy night diving from a boat. Using a boat can simplify night diving by making entries and exits easier than dealing with surf or watching where you're wading.

course, there are many ideal places for night diving from shore, so don't take this to mean you should only night dive from a boat.

General Night Diving Considerations

Four considerations apply to planning night dives.

Prepare equipment ahead of time. It's easier to put your kit together and check it over in the light, so you may want to set up before nightfall if you won't be working in a well-lit area. When using a chemical light to mark your location, attach it to your snorkel or tank ahead of time, but don't activate it until you begin your dive.

Don't skip a meal. Especially if you've been diving during the day, you can run out of energy during a night dive, especially if you skip dinner in the excitement of getting ready for the night dive. Eat a proper meal before the dive so you have the energy you need for the dive. Diving involves exercise, though, so try to allow enough time between the meal and the dive to avoid stomach discomfort during the dive.

Dive with familiar buddies. With the additional challenges darkness brings, it's best to dive with people you feel comfortable with, either because you've made dives with them before, or based on their diver qualifications.

Bring a nondiver. It's a good idea to have someone at the surface in the boat (in addtion to the boat captain when possible) or on shore. This person tends the lights that help you find your way back and generally lends a hand. It's always good to have someone there in case of a problem.

It's easier to put your kit together and check it over in the light, so you may want to set up before nightfall if you won't be working in a well-lit area.

It's a good idea to have someone at the surface in the boat (in addtion to the boat captain when possible) or on shore. This person tends the lights that help you find your way back and generally lends a hand. It's always good to have someone there in case of a problem.

Night 4

1. Ideally, you should choose a night dive site that you've never visited before.
   ☐ True   ☐ False

2. Environmental conditions to avoid when night diving include (check all that apply):
   ☐ a. heavy surf
   ☐ b. surge
   ☐ c. thermoclines
   ☐ d. overhead environments

3. One reason for conducting night dives from a boat is that it simplifies entries and exits.
   ☐ True   ☐ False

4. When at a dive site during daylight hours, prepare your equipment
   ☐ a. immediately before the dive.
   ☐ b. ahead of time, so you don't have to do it in the dark.

How'd you do?

1. False. Ideally, you should choose a dive site that you're familiar with and have dived during daylight hours; **2.** a, b, d; **3.** True;
4. b.

CONCEPTS

Underline/highlight the answers to these questions as you read:

1. How can you avoid and cope with stress during a night dive?

2. What should you do if your dive light fails during a night dive?

3. What should you do if you and your buddy become separated while night diving?

4. What should you do if you become disoriented or lost while night diving?

NIGHT DIVING STRESS

Back in Neanderthal times, prehumans who didn't fear walking into dark caves became bear food. That's why today, any hesitation you have about darkness is normal; it's part of nature's way of making you cautious when you can't see. The thought of going underwater magnifies this – you may imagine that "something" (probably not a bear) waits just outside the reach of your dive light, and then you can have real concerns such as waves, poor visibility or unfamiliar equipment (which is why you avoid these).

The result is the heightened arousal we call stress. A little stress on your first night dive is normal – in fact, can be an important part of the fun because without some

A little stress on your first night dive is normal – in fact, can be an important part of the fun because without some stress, there's no adventure or challenge.

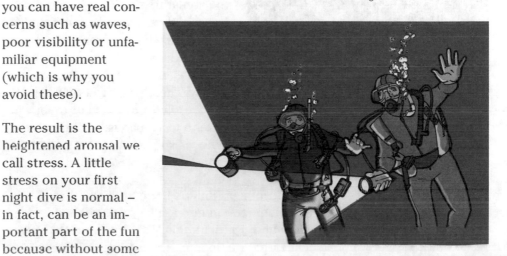

stress, there's no adventure or challenge. But there's a limit. You need to feel confident that you can meet the challenges of night diving so that you have fun and excitement, and not fear or panic.

Coping With Stress

Much of what you've learned so far removes potential night diving stress sources. Diving in a familiar area, with familiar equipment and a familiar buddy helps eliminate them as sources of stress. Avoiding poor environmental conditions helps prevent stress. Completing the Night Adventure Dive and later, the PADI Night Diver Specialty course will also reduce stress by raising your experience and abilities with night diving while supervised by an instructor. And for your first few night dives, you can reduce stress by keeping the dive plan simple. If you're into photography, for instance, you might want to get a couple night dives under your belt before you bring the camera along.

But there will still be at least a little stress, some of which comes from dealing with problems unique to night diving. By knowing what to do, you don't have as much worry before or during the dive. And if one of these problems comes up, you can deal with it.

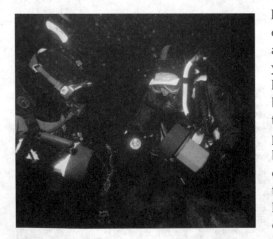

If your light fails, no worries. Stop, switch to your backup light, signal your buddy and head for the boat or shore.

If you have a problem, or simply feel overly anxious, stop, think and then act (if action is called for). Keeping your breathing slow, deep and regular – it's physiologically impossible to breathe slowly and deeply and be tense at the same time. Don't react to problems or fears instinctively and blindly. There's no need to; if you can't resolve a problem or if you continue to feel anxious, end the dive. Diving is something to enjoy, not to endure.

Three problems unique to night diving that you're most likely to run into are light failure, buddy separation and disorientation. They're all pretty easy to deal with.

Underwater light failure. If your light goes out, no worries. That's why you carry a backup. Stop, switch to your backup light, signal your buddy and head for the boat or shore. Keep in mind that backups are there to get you reliably out of the water with a working light – so don't simply continue the dive with it.

In the unlikely event your backup light malfunctions (or was lost), borrow your buddy's backup light. In the even more unlikely event that your buddy's backup light fails, leaving one working light between the two of you, it may be best to immediately ascend if conditions allow. This avoids an ascent in the dark if the last light calls it quits, too.

Buddy separation. Oops. It happens. If you discover your buddy isn't where you thought, look for your buddy's dive light glow. No? Cover your light with your hand (or hold it against your body – avoid switching it on and off, because that's when the bulb's most likely to fail) and look. If that doesn't work, look around for no more than a minute, then surface cautiously – conditions allowing and if that's what you discussed in your dive plan – inflate your BCD and wait for your buddy to do the same.

If you and your buddy separate, cover your light momentarily and look for the glow of your buddy's light.

Agreeing what to do if you get separated when planning the dive helps prevent confusion; after reuniting, you may resume your dive depending upon time and air supply. Be sure to reorient yourself with your exit point before redescending. Keep current and other conditions in mind when you plan what to do if separated – you don't want to drift past the boat in the dark. It may be more appropriate to reunite at the anchor line, for example. If you do suface, keep your light on so you can be seen by your buddy, and by any water craft. Plan what you'll do ahead of time, just in case.

Disorientation. The skills you learn in the Navigation Adventure Dive, head-up ascents and descents and using a line for ascents and descents (more about this shortly) go a long way toward keeping you oriented during a night dive. But you can still get turned around.

If you get disoriented on the bottom, consult your compass and then look for familiar natural references to reestablish your position. If you remain disoriented, surface with your buddy and check your position. Provided you have ample air and time, you can redescend and continue your dive.

If you lose your sense of direction midwater while ascending or descending without a reference line, watch your bubbles to help reestablish your sense of up-and-down. It may help to hug yourself in some instances, or if your buddy agrees, you can also hold on to each other to help regain orientation. Ascend slowly to discontinue your dive, following your bubbles at a rate no faster than 18 metres/60 feet per minute (or the maximum allowed by your computer) if the disorientation doesn't pass.

If you lose your sense of direction midwater while ascending or descending without a reference line, watch your bubbles to help reestablish your sense of up-and-down.

If you get disoriented on the bottom, consult your compass and then look for familiar natural references to reestablish your position. If you remain disoriented, surface with your buddy and check your position. Provided you have ample air and time, you can redescend and continue your dive.

Ascending Without Light

Carry a backup light and a night ascent without a light should almost never occur — you'd have to have your primary light fail, your backup light fail and lose your buddy, all at the same time. If you maintain buddy contact, four lights would have to fail at the same time. Not too likely.

But suppose it does. Are you without an option? No, you can ascend safely in the dark. If you're near a reference line, follow it up slowly, using one hand to maintain line contact and the other to vent air from your BCD and to protect you from overhead objects (like boats).

Without a reference line, you'll have to ascend using your bubbles as a reference. If you're with your buddy, grab each other's arms to maintain contact. Allow your eyes to adjust to the dark — you may be surprised how much light there is underwater at night, depending on the visibility — and then slowly and carefully follow your bubbles to the surface at a rate not exceeding 18 metres/60 feet per minute, or your dive computer's maximum rate. If you have luminescent gauges or a marker light, you may be able to read your depth gauge to help guide your ascent. Many computers beep if you go too fast, which can also help you keep your ascent at the right speed.

Night 5

1. If a problem occurs during a night dive, you should cope with stress by
   ☐ a. trusting your instincts and acting accordingly.
   ☐ b. stopping, thinking and then acting.

2. If your primary light fails during a night dive, you should
   ☐ a. share your buddy's light and abort the dive.
   ☐ b. switch to your backup light and continue the dive.
   ☐ c. switch to your backup light and abort the dive.

3. If you and your buddy become separated and you don't relocate each other within one minute you should
   ☐ a. reunite on the surface, or as you and your buddy planned.
   ☐ b. continue the dive until your buddy locates you.

4. If you become disoriented during a night dive and cannot reorient yourself by consulting your compass and natural references, you should
   ☐ a. swim in a straight direction until you know where you are.
   ☐ b. surface with your buddy and reestablish your position.

How'd you do?

1. b;   2. c;   3. a;   4. b.

NIGHT DIVING TECHNIQUES

Night Diving Entries

Night diving entries apply the same procedures that you use during the day, but with a few accommodations to the darkness. Evaluate the conditions just as you always would, being sure to watch for waves and offshore objects if you're diving from shore. Next, plan your dive and then go through your Predive Safety Check (Begin With Review And Friend), being extra-careful to check equipment adjustments that would be difficult to change later in the dark. Check that both your lights are working, secure your backup light and secure the primary light's lanyard around your wrist. You're now ready to enter the water.

From a boat. Check the entry area, using your light if necessary. Turn the light on (so you can find it if you lose it during the entry) and enter as usual. Signal "OK" (assuming you are, of course), clear the area and wait for your buddy.

Key CONCEPTS

Underline/highlight the answers to these questions as you read:

1. How do you enter the water from a boat, and from shore while night diving?

2. How do you relocate a dive site while night diving?

3. How should you descend and ascend while night diving to avoid disorientation?

4. How do you use signals for communication during a night dive?

5. How do you avoid contact with bottom-dwelling organisms during a night dive?

6. What natural and compass navigation techniques do you use to avoid disorientation and loss of direction while night diving?

From shore. Turn your light on and check the entry area. Enter the water either holding on to your buddy, or staying within reach of each other. If you're diving through mild surf, move as quickly as possible through the surf zone. When night diving from shore, be cautious about slipping or stepping on sharp objects, rocks or aquatic life. Begin swimming as soon as the water's deep enough, while maintaining contact with your buddy.

Navigating to an Offshore Dive Site

When night diving from a boat, you usually anchor right over your dive site, but when diving from shore, you may have to swim on the surface to the site and then descend. A few techniques and your navigation skills make it easier to find your spot, even in the dark.

After entering, let your eyes adjust to the dark while staying within reach of your buddy so you don't get separated. If you've been there before, the easiest way to find the dive site is to follow a compass heading and distance established during the day. If necessary, use your light to look for offshore rocks or other bearings. Moonlight/permanent shore lights may also help you relocate an offshore dive site. Be careful that you don't try to use moveable lights (cars, for example) or lights that can be turned off (houses and some street lights) for navigation.

Descend slowly, with a head-up orientation to prevent disorientation, while pointing your light downward frequently to watch for the bottom. Check your gauges as you go so you don't accidentally descend deeper than planned.

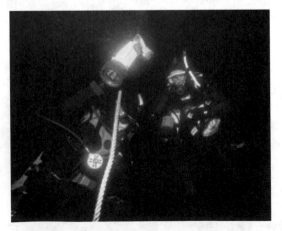

Descents and Ascents at Night

Because it's harder to see the bottom and other references you're used to during the day, you'll find it much easier to become disoriented during night ascents and descents. To eliminate this, use a reference line from the boat or a float/buoy or, the anchor line from a boat. From shore, swim out and back along the bottom to provide a reference.

Descents. Turn on your light before you descend, check the time and set a compass bearing for the shore or boat. Check that your buddy's ready to go and descend next to the reference line. Hang on to the line during the descent for tactile reference, and to keep from drifting in a current. Descend slowly, with a head-up orientation to prevent disorientation, while pointing your light downward frequently to watch for the bottom. Check your gauges as you go so you don't accidentally descend deeper than planned. You may want to mark your descent line with lights or chemical light sticks, which can help your orientation and help you gauge your descent rate.

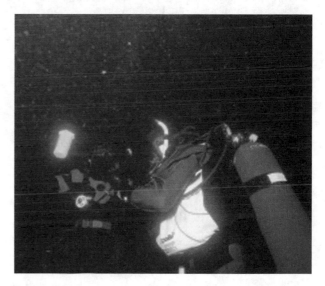

Ascents. Try to plan your dive so you return to the reference line without having to search for it. When you're ready, signal your buddy, note your bottom time and start up the line at 18 metres/60 feet per minute, or as stipulated by your computer if you're using one. Ascending in the dark, it's a good idea to keep your BCD deflator above your head to vent air from your BCD and to protect you from overhead objects. Keep your right hand on the line if necessary, and point your light up to watch overhead. Make a safety stop at 5 metres/15 feet as usual, then finish your ascent watching above. (As you can probably tell from this emphasis on looking up, it's easier to accidentally run into things overhead in the dark.) After you surface, establish buoyancy and if you need to, point your light down to let your eyes readjust to the dark for the swim back to the boat or shore. Again, marking the line with lights before the dive can help your orientation.

If you can't relocate the reference line, air and topography allowing, you may be able to swim to-

You can ascend without a reference line if necessary by using your depth gauge (or computer) and bubbles as a reference so that you ascend no faster than 18 metres/60 feet per minute (or as permitted by your computer).

ward your exit along an ascending bottom. But that's not always an option, so you might also ascend using your depth gauge (or computer) and bubbles as a reference so that you ascend no faster than 18 metres/60 feet per minute (or as permitted by your computer). Since the dark may reduce the visual cues that help you gauge ascent speed, check your depth frequently, and try to control your buoyancy closely. Using your BCD and gauges, make your safety stop at 5 metres/15 feet while hovering, and then ascend checking for boats or other overhead objects.

Ascending and descending at night isn't particularly complex. Just keep in mind that in the dark, you have to be more deliberate in watching where you're going, controlling your buoyancy, and gauging your ascent/descent speed.

Night Communication

When you first learned to dive, you adapted to communication by using (primarily) hand signals. Night diving takes this a bit further – not only do you use signals, but you have to take steps to be sure your buddy can see them.

"Okay" signal with dive light.

"Emergency Attention" signal with dive light.

Like always, the first step in communicating is to get your buddy's attention. Rapping on your tank and gently touching work, of course, and on a night dive, waving your light slowly up and down is an attention signal. But, a rapid side-to-side light wave is considered an emergency attention signal.

Use hand signals by shining your light on your hands in a manner that avoids blinding your buddy. Holding your hand at waist level or to one side

while you shine your light on it with the other works well. When trying to see your buddy's face (to "read" expressions), point your light at foot level; enough stray light will illuminate the mask without pointing your light there.

You can also signal with your light – making a large circle means "everything's OK." When swimming, you can signal "okay" by making a circle on the bottom with your light where your buddy will see it. Your buddy returns the "okay" by making a circle where you made yours. This way you can maintain communication without having to stop as much.

Use hand signals by shining your light on your hands in a manner that avoids blinding your buddy. Holding your hand at waist level or to one side while you shine your light on it with the other works well.

At the surface, you can use your whistle to gain attention, or wave your light back-and-forth, which means "emergency – help." And, holding the light overhead so that it points down on your head means "everything OK" to someone at a distance. Night diving signals aren't all universal, so it's a good idea to review them before diving.

Avoiding Bottom-dwelling Organisms

Responsible divers carry out their dives without killing or injuring aquatic organisms, and likewise you'll want to dive without them stinging you. The easiest way to meet both goals is to watch what you're doing and where you put your hands, feet and knees. During entries, exits and descents, look above and below, and keep an eye on where you step. Stay neutrally buoyant and never touch anything or put your hands or feet anywhere without checking with your light first.

Holding the light overhead so that it points down on your head means "everything OK" to someone at a distance.

Keep in mind that many aquatic organisms, such as coral polyps, are more vulnerable at night.

Night Navigation

From what you've learned so far, it's easy to see how capable navigation makes night diving easier and helps eliminate stress. During the Night Dive, you'll use both natural navigation and compass navigation skills, like you learned during the Navigation Dive. If you'll make the Night Dive first, read through the Navigation chapter so you're familiar with the techniques, which build upon what you learned in the Open Water Diver course.

You should consider a compass standard equipment for all night dives. Before descending, take a compass heading to shore or back to the boat so that you can navigate to your exit underwater, or at the surface when you can't see exactly where you are.

Natural navigation. The natural navigation references you use during the day are just as usable at night, especially at a familiar dive site. This is one reason why it's best to dive the site the same day as the night dive, to review your dive log for natural navigation references, or to go with someone who knows the site.

Compass navigation. You should consider a compass standard equipment for all night dives. Before descending, take a compass heading to shore or back to the boat so that you can navigate to your exit underwater, or at the surface when you can't see exactly where you are. Keep navigation patterns simple on a night dive and stay close to your entry/exit and reference line. In less familiar areas, it's often best to follow a heading out a short distance, then return on the reciprocal heading and relocate your reference line. If you still have plenty of air, explore a short distance on another short heading and return. This way, you stay close to your reference line, entry/exit point and don't become disoriented.

Navigating back to shore. Exiting the water after a shore night dive is usually a simple matter of swimming back to shore, but if you have to pass through a narrow channel or surface obstructions (like kelp or coral in some areas), you'll need to plan ahead.

For more information about...

Night Navigation
See the *Underwater Navigator Manual,* and *Underwater Navigation* video

Before the dive, place two lights on the beach aligned with the channel you'll return through. Preferably, use two distinct lights (flashing and/or colored – but check local regulations to be sure they won't be confused with local boat navigation signals), and separate them as far as possible. Elevate the light farthest from shore, and preferably leave someone to tend the lights so that no one moves them. When you exit, simply swim parallel to shore until the lights align, and then swim toward them keeping them aligned. This should bring you in through the narrow channel.

REVIEW

Night 6

1. When making a night entry from a shore or boat, leave your light off during the entire entry.
   ☐ True   ☐ False

2. The easiest way to relocate an offshore dive site while night diving is to follow a compass heading established during the day.
   ☐ True   ☐ False

3. To help avoid disorientation during ascents and descents a_____is highly recommended.
   ☐ a. compass
   ☐ b. reference line
   ☐ c. backup light

4. Hand signals cannot be used during a night dive because you can't see them in the dark.
   ☐ True   ☐ False

5. The best way to avoid contact with bottom-dwelling organisms during a night dive is
   ☐ a. maintain neutral buoyancy and keep an eye out for them.
   ☐ b. to flail your feet and scare them out of your path.

6. Natural and compass navigation techniques used during the day
   ☐ a. are nearly useless at night.
   ☐ b. are an important part of night diving.

How'd you do?

1. False. Turn the light on so that you can find it if you accidentally lose it.   2. True;   3. b;   4. False. Use hand signals in the dark by shining your light on your hand signal at waist level or to one side   5. a;   6. b.

PADI Night Diver Specialty

At your instructor's discretion, your Night Adventure Dive may be credited as the first dive in the PADI Night Diver Specialty course. The Night Diver course gives you more opportunities to apply and practice the skills and techniques covered in this section in a variety of situations.

Night Adventure Dive Overview

- Knowledge assessment/ Knowledge Review
- Briefing
- Gearing up
- Predive safety check (BWRAF)
- Entry
- Descent

- Getting used to the dark on bottom
- Navigation exercise
- Tour
- Ascent – safety stop
- Exit
- Debrief
- Log dive – PADI Instructor signs

PEAK PERFORMANCE BUOYANCY

Introduction

Ask any dive professional what skill separates the upper and lower echelons of dive proficiency, and you'll almost always get the same answer: buoyancy control. Bet you already knew that, and it's easy to see why. Divers who master buoyancy control move through the water gracefully. They seem to ascend, stop, hover and descend at will with hardly a fin flick or hand wave – as if they think it, and it happens. By contrast, those without such control constantly kick, scull or wave to stay off the bottom. They constantly adjust their BCDs, and visibly expend effort with every depth change – they may dive safely and effectively, but not efficiently.

Few skills can do as much for you as peak performance buoyancy. It's a skill that reaches into every dive, no matter where or what you're doing. It saves you air, it saves you energy and it makes your diving more fun. It helps you avoid damage to the environment, and it distinguishes you as a diver. If you could only make one Adventure Dive, many instructors would suggest that this is the one.

Peak Performancy Buoyancy
See the *Peak Performance Buoyancy* video

BUOYANCY CHECK

In your Open Water Diver course, you learned the fundamentals of buoyancy control, which form the foundation for Peak Performance Buoyancy. To take the next step, let's take a moment to find out where you are. Answer the following questions about yourself:

Key CONCEPTS

Underline/highlight the answers to these questions as you read:

1. Under what three circumstances should you conduct a buoyancy check before diving?

2. Based on basic weighting guidelines, how much weight do you need for the Peak Performance Buoyancy Adventure Dive?

3. What five steps will help you conduct a buoyancy check at the surface?

4. How does your buoyancy change due to consuming the air in your cylinder?

YES	NO	**Buoyancy Check**
☐	☐	1. I stay in shape for diving, helping me avoid getting out of breath while underwater. This improves my breath control and allows me to fine-tune my buoyancy more efficiently.
☐	☐	2. When I need to establish comfortable breathing and relax, I use visualization to help attain Peak Performance Buoyancy.
☐	☐	3. Before I dive, I adjust the position and distribution of my weight to match the type of dive I'm making.
☐	☐	4. I check my buoyancy at the beginning of any dive each time I change dive equipment, dive environment or haven't been diving in a while.
☐	☐	5. When I haven't been diving for awhile, or when using new gear, I warm up my buoyancy skills at the beginning of my dive.
☐	☐	6. When wearing a wet suit or dry suit, I need only add small amounts of air to my BCD (or dry suit) to remain neutrally buoyant. When not wearing an exposure suit (or a skin suit), I rarely need to add air to my BCD to remain neutrally buoyant.
☐	☐	7. I can adjust my buoyancy using breath control.
☐	☐	8. I'm streamlined in the water with all hoses and gear secure and tucked close to my body. Nothing hangs away from my body more than a few centimetres/inches in any position.
☐	☐	9. I rarely touch the bottom accidentally while diving.
☐	☐	10. I can hover comfortably at 5 metres/15 feet for a safety stop at the end of the dive.

Okay, be honest. How'd you do? If you answered "no" to a lot of these, then you'll gain a lot during the Peak Performance Buoyancy Adventure Dive. If you said "yes" to almost everything, great. You're well on you way, and the dive will help put the finishing polish on your already well-developed skills.

Estimating Your Weight Needs

Rule One for Peak Performance Buoyancy is that *you don't wear more weight than you need.* Your BCD may be able to offset a bit of excess weight, but every gram you wear that you don't need adds to your drag and magnifies the adjustments you have to make throughout your dive.

How do you know how much weight to wear? Easy – you perform a buoyancy check in the water. There's absolutely no other way to precisely figure it out. For Peak Performance Buoyancy, you check your buoyancy: 1. Any time you change your dive gear configuration. 2. Any time you change dive environments (especially fresh water to salt or vice-versa) and 3. Any time you haven't been diving for a while.

We'll look at the five steps for checking your buoyancy in a moment, but what if you have no idea of how much weight you need with a specific gear set up? To make your actual buoyancy check go quickly, you want to estimate the weight you need so you only need to make minor adjustments. Use the following guidelines to get you in the ballpark:

Basic Weight Guidelines

These guidelines assume an average build individual in salt water. Decrease the weight somewhat for lean individuals, and increase it for heavier individuals.

Exposure Suit Type	Start With
Swimsuit/dive skin	.5 - 2 kg/1 - 4 lbs
3 mm/1/16 in. one piece wet suit, shorties, jump suits	5 % of your body weight
5 mm/3/16 in. two piece wet suit	10% of your body weight
7 mm/1/4 in wet suit w/ hood & gloves	10% of your body weight, + 1.5 - 3 kg/3 -5 lbs
Neoprene dry suit	10% of your body weight, + 3 - 5 kg/7 - 10 lbs
Shell dry suit, light undergarment	10% of your body weight, + 1.5 - 3 kg/3 -5 lbs
Shell dry suit, heavy undergarment	10% of your body weight, + 3 - 7 kg/7 -14 lbs

Salt/Fresh Water Change

Body Weight	Add (going to salt) or subtract (going to fresh)
45 - 56 kg/ 100 - 125 lbs	2 kg/4 lb
57-70 kg/ 126 - 155 lbs	2.3 kg/5 lb
71-85 kg/156 - 186 lbs	3 kg/6 lb
86-99 kg/ 187 - 217 lbs	3.2 kg/7 lb

cylinder

Your cylinder's buoyancy characteristics affect these calculations. With the popular 12 litre/80 cubic foot aluminum cylinder, add two kg/five pounds to the above. This is due to the fact that the tank becomes more buoyant as you breathe air from it. You may not need to add anything with other cylinders. In fact with steel cylinders, you may need to remove weight from your system.

For example, suppose you weigh 70 kg/155 lbs and you plan to dive in a 5 mm/3/16 inch two piece wet suit using a 12 l/80 cf aluminum cylinder in salt water. You'd start your buoyancy check with 7 kg/15 lbs weight in salt water, plus 2 kg/5 lbs for the cylinder for 9 kg/20 lbs total. This probably gets you close. However, always perform a buoyancy check prior to descent with new equipment.

Five Step Buoyancy Check

Okay, you've estimated your weight, now you're ready to check it. Here's what to do.

1. Enter the water fully equipped for the dive.

2. Go to water too deep to stand in (or at least deep enough that you can easily raise your feet off the bottom) and completely deflate your BCD. If you're using your dry suit, open the automatic exhaust valve all the way.

3. Hang vertical and motionless holding a normal breath.

4. Add/subtract weight until you float at eye level while holding a normal breath.

5. As your final check, you should slowly sink when you exhale.

With proper weighting, you should float at eye level with an empty BCD and holding a normal breath. If you check with a full cylinder, then add a bit of weight to offset the air you use during the dive.

It may take a few tries to get your weight exact. With practice, you'll have a good feel for how much to add or subtract based on how much you float/sink.

Buoyancy Change Due to Air Consumption

During the dive, you use air from your tank, which makes it lighter. Although different cylinders have different buoyancy characteristics by themselves, the cylinder and its volume become part of your total mass and displacement when you gear up, so your buoyancy **will** increase as you consume your air, *no matter what type of tank you're using.*

Consuming the air from a typical cylinder, from full to reserve pressure, will usually increase your buoyancy about two kg/five lbs. You need to account for this so that you're properly weighted at the end of the dive and can maintain a safety stop without struggling.

Ideally, check your buoyancy and set your weight with a near-empty cylinder, then switch to the same type cylinder, full, for the dive. This isn't always practical, so the alternative is to set your weight as you just learned with a full cylinder, then add about two kg/five lbs. If you'll be making several dives, you may want to recheck your buoyancy at the end of the dive while you're wearing a near-empty tank.

Buoyancy 1

1. Check your buoyancy before diving when (check all that apply):
   ☐ a. you change your gear.
   ☐ b. you go from fresh to salt water or vice versa.
   ☐ c. you haven't been diving for awhile.

2. When conducting a buoyancy check at the surface, perform the check with a small "puff" in your BCD or dry suit.
   ☐ True   ☐ False

3. For Peak Performance Buoyancy, you need to account for buoyancy change due to air consumption
   ☐ a. only with light weight cylinders.
   ☐ b. with any cylinder.

How'd you do?

1. a, b, c; 2. False. Perform the check with your BCD or dry suit completely deflated; 3. b

FINE TUNING YOUR BUOYANCY

Underline/highlight the answers to these questions as you read:

1. What three variables require you to adjust your buoyancy as needed?

2. When should you use your BCD to adjust your buoyancy?

3. How do you control your buoyancy when using a dry suit?

4. How does your lung volume affect buoyancy, and how do you use it to fine-tune your buoyancy?

When you're properly weighted and wearing only a dive skin or swim suit, you'll rarely need to adjust your buoyancy. About the only adjustment you'll need is to release a bit of air from your BCD to compensate for the air you use. If you're making frequent buoyancy changes, you're probably overweighted.

When wearing a wet suit or dry suit, you'll need to adjust your buoyancy throughout the dive to account for three variables. First, you'll need to adjust as you use air from your tank (as just stated). Second, you'll need to adjust for lost buoyancy as you descend as pressure compresses your wet suit or the air in your dry suit. Third, you'll need to adjust for increased buoyancy as you ascend as your wet suit/dry suit air reexpands.

If you're wearing a skin suit, you'll need much less weight than if you dive in a wet or dry suit, and your buoyancy won't change much throughout the dive.

You should only need to adjust your BCD for these three variables, and to float comfortably on the surface. Put air in your BCD as you descend to remain neutral; let it out as you come up to do the same. One tenet of Peak Performance Buoyancy is that you don't use your BCD as an elevator. To ascend, you just start to swim up. To descend, you just exhale. If you need to add or release air for these, you're not controlling your buoyancy closely.

Keep in mind that if you're diving in a dry suit, you primarily use your dry suit to control your buoyancy – not your BCD. The exception is at the surface, where it's more comfortable to float using your BCD.

Keep in mind that if you're diving in a dry suit, you primarily use your dry suit to control your buoyancy – not your BCD. The exception is at the surface, where it's more comfortable to float using your BCD. Controlling with your dry suit avoids suit squeeze, and it simplifies buoyancy control because you're not trying to control your BCD and your dry suit. See the dry suit section for more about buoyancy control while wearing one.

Breath Control

Your BCD (or dry suit) gives you coarse buoyancy control; you use your lung volume to fine-tune it. When you inhale, you increase your displacement and buoyancy, and tend to rise slightly. When you exhale you tend to sink. Once you're neutrally buoyant with your BCD or dry suit, you make minor buoyancy changes by timing your breathing and breathing with somewhat full or somewhat empty lungs as you need to – but never holding your breath. With practice, this becomes automatic and you do it without thinking. That's the first mark of mastering Peak Performance Buoyancy.

Buoyancy 2

1. With Peak Performance Buoyancy, variables that require you to adjust your buoyancy include (check all that apply):
   - ☐ a. the weight you're wearing.
   - ☐ b. using air from your cylinder.
   - ☐ c. reduced buoyancy while descending.

2. You should use your BCD to adjust your buoyancy (check all that apply):
   - ☐ a. to float on the surface.
   - ☐ b. to begin an ascent.
   - ☐ c. to offset wet suit compression.

3. When diving with a dry suit, you don't control buoyancy with your BCD, except at the surface.
   - ☐ True   ☐ False

4. You use lung volume to fine-tune buoyancy by holding your breath with full or empty lungs as needed.
   - ☐ True   ☐ False

How'd you do?
1. b, c; 2. a, c; 3. True; 4. False. You never hold your breath.

Underline/highlight the answers to this question as you read:

1. How do you distribute weight for better attitude and position control underwater?

WEIGHT DISTRIBUTION

It's one thing to wear the right amount of weight, and another to distribute it for optimum performance. Not only does weight distribution vary from one diver to the next, but you'll find it varies from one dive to the next for the same diver. For example, if you're taking pictures along a wall you may prefer a head up position, but during a search for a small object over silty bottom, you may prefer a head down position. Setting your weight accordingly saves your energy and lets you focus on the task at hand.

Typically, though, you want to distribute weight so you swim as horizontally as possible. This minimizes drag as you swim, saving you energy and keeping your feet off the bottom.

As a rule of thumb, you want your weight forward, toward your sides and stomach, which helps you maintain a neutral swimming position. Especially when you're using a heavy cylinder, distributing more weight on your back and around your tank tends to make you "turn turtle" (belly up), which most divers find uncomfortable and fatiguing.

Typically, you want to distribute weight so you swim as horizontally as possible. This minimizes drag as you swim, saving you energy and keeping your feet off the bottom.

To find out what your "trim" is (how your weight distribution orients you), become neutrally buoyant and hover in shallow water and then relax completely. Just let your body turn however it will. You may end up on your back or upside down. It doesn't matter – you're trying to find out how to redistribute weight for maximum comfort and minimum fatigue.

To adjust for being feet low, adjust weight toward your head. This can include sliding your cylinder up in the BCD a bit, especially if it's a steel one. To bring your feet down, shift weight down. If you have extreme leg buoyancy, you can use ankle weights or switch to heavier fins.

If you're wearing a lot of weight, such as with a full wet suit or dry suit, you may opt for multiple weight systems, such as a weight integrated BCD and weight belt, or a weight integrated BCD and weight harness. This gives you more options in

If you're wearing a lot of weight, such as with a full wet suit or dry suit, you may opt for multiple weight systems, such as a weight integrated BCD and weight belt, or a weight integrated BCD and weight harness. This gives you more options in weight distribution, and eliminates a single, massive, hard to handle system.

weight distribution, and eliminates a single, massive, hard to handle system.

If you use multiple weight systems, distribute the weight so you can expect ample buoyancy in an emergency by ditching only one. One of the advantages of multiple weight systems is that in an emergency you don't have to dump everything, which reduces the likelihood of a hazardous runaway ascent.

Key CONCEPTS

Underline/highlight the answers to these questions as you read:

1. What are four reasons for being streamlined?

2. How do you look when you're streamlined underwater?

STREAMLINING

Your weight's correct and properly distributed, so now performance lies in the details. You can have the best buoyancy in the world, but it amounts to nothing if your equipment pokes out, hangs and drags. For Peak Performance Buoyancy, you need to be tight and streamlined. Streamlining makes your kicks more efficient, and it makes you comfortable because everything's where it belongs. You use less energy as you swim, and you minimize damage to the environment because you're not dragging gear across sensitive aquatic life.

Here's what you look like when you're streamlined:

1. You're not overweighted (you've probably got this down by now). When you're overweighted, you have to fill your BCD to compensate, which increases drag.

2. You swim horizontally. You don't have excess weight pushing your legs down, and you distribute weight properly.

3. Every hose, gauge and accessory stays in place, stowed in pockets or clipped close to your body, as appropriate for the item. Nothing swings out (clipped or not) when you change position.

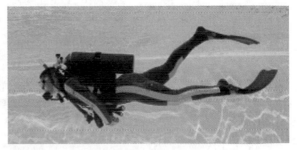

Proper streamlining: Not overweighted and swimming horizontally because no excess weight drags down the hips. All hoses, gauges and accessories in place so nothing dangles.

CONCEPTS

Underline/highlight the answers to these questions as you read:

1. How does visualization help you relax, breathe comfortably and swim gracefully?

2. How do you use visualization to achieve Peak Performance Buoyancy?

VISUALIZATION

It might sound like New Age hype, but you can enhance your performance of any motor skill – including Peak Performance Buoyancy – through visualization. To do this, you mentally rehearse the performance you want, and see yourself doing it well in your mind's eye. Multiple studies show that mental practice improves performance because in essence, your mind programs your body to do it right.

Still sound like New Age hype? Okay, here's the deal. Try it. You don't have to tell anyone you're doing it, and we won't either.

Before diving, take a moment to relax. See yourself underwater, swimming in your gear, streamlined, horizontal, with the right weight properly distributed. Now go inside your imagined self. Feel yourself moving through the water. Feel the buoyancy changes. Feel yourself adjust through your breathing. Now hover. Feel yourself suspended; feel your gear; feel yourself slightly rise and sink as you breathe with perfect buoyancy control.

Now, go make the dive you just saw. During the dive, think back to your visualized dive. Make your buoyancy on your real dive meet the dive in your mind's eye.

After the dive, visualize what you did and compare it with your mental rehearsal. Adjust your mental rehearsal, if necessary, to further improve your performance. Remember this for programming your mind for your next dive.

Before diving, take a moment to relax. See yourself underwater, swimming in your gear, streamlined, horizontal, with the right weight properly distributed. Go inside your imagined self. Feel yourself moving through the water. Feel the buoyancy changes. Feel yourself adjust through your breathing. Now hover. Feel yourself suspended; feel your gear; feel yourself slightly rise and sink as you breathe with perfect buoyancy control. Now make the dive you just saw.

Buoyancy 5

1. You use visualization to improve performance by
   ☐ a. mentally picturing yourself doing everything right.
   ☐ b. mentally picturing yourself doing everything you hope to avoid.

2. To achieve Peak Performance Buoyancy, visualize (check all that apply):
   ☐ a. before the dive.
   ☐ b. after the dive.
   ☐ c. during the dive.

How'd you do?
1. a; 2. a, b, c.

PHYSICAL FITNESS

Underline/highlight the answers to this question as you read:

1. How does physical fitness fit into Peak Performance Buoyancy?

You might not think of physical fitness as part of mastering buoyancy control, but actually, they go hand-in-hand. The more fit you are, the easier it is to control your buoyancy and trim.

When you're physically fit, you have more stamina and more muscle power. You cruise through the water well within your physical limitations rather than pushing them. You're not overexerted and you have the reserves you need to handle problems.

Since you're not overexerted, you don't breathe hard. An exhausted diver who huffs and puffs loses the ability to control buoyancy through breath control. The more stamina you have, the harder you can exert yourself when necessary without losing breath control.

Diving is like any physical activity. The better shape you're in, the more you get out of it and the better you do it. You don't have to be an athlete, but proper fitness goes a long way to making your diving more enjoyable.

Lean mass sinks; fat tissue floats. When you're fit, you have more lean mass and less fat tissue, and therefore require less weight, which not only means less to lug around, but less problem distributing it effectively. It's easier for a fit diver to trim for an effortless, horizontal swimming position.

When you're fit, you're sleeker and more naturally streamlined. Your body presents minimum drag. An out of shape diver tends to be fatter, which means more drag. It also means a larger exposure suit, which adds buoyancy beyond the fat tissue's buoyancy. So, all else being the same, the out of shape diver tends to need more weight than the fit diver.

The bottom line is that diving is like any physical activity. The better shape you're in, the more you get out of it and the better you do it. You don't have to be an athlete, but you don't want to be a couch slug, either.

PADI Peak Performance Buoyancy course

Your Peak Performance Buoyancy Adventure Dive may credit (at the instructor's discretion) toward the Peak Performance Buoyancy Specialty certification. In addition to what you've learned in this section and will practice on the Peak Performance Buoyancy Adventure Dive, the Peak Performance Buoyancy course provides added experience applying and practicing these principles. Mastering Peak Performance Buoyancy comes only with time and effort. But, the more you practice under instructor guidance, the more efficiently you spend this time and effort, and the faster you master these skills.

The Trusted Name in Dive Travel™

We Can Get You There...
Ask Us How!

PADI Travel Network has dive travel packages to over 200 resorts in more than 90 top dive destinations around the world. Working in partnership with PADI Dive Centers and Resorts, PADI Travel Network is a one-stop resource for all your diving needs – wherever you want to go – PADI Travel Network's experienced staff of di____ ___ get you there!

Visit your local PADI Dive Center or Resort or padi.com for more information.

SEARCH AND RECOVERY

Introduction

If you've not done it yet, you will. – Lean over the side, and . . . oops! There go your prescription sunglasses. Or:

> "Here, let me hold your
>   mask for you."
> "Thanks. Got it?"
> "Nope."
> "Me neither."

Oops. Hang around water, and search and recovery is inevitable. Whether it's something a friend drops from a boat, losing your fin in the surf or a friend-of-a-friend's fiancee's bracelet that bounced off a dock, eventually you'll need to or will be asked to search for something underwater. But that's one of the cool things about being a diver: provided the object isn't too deep, too big or in a hazardous environment, it's not gone. It's just wet.

Besides the practical advantages, one of the most gratifying experiences in recreational diving is setting out to find and recover a lost object – and succeed-

ing. In this section, you'll begin learning the skills and techniques that can help you do this.

CONCEPTS

Underline/highlight the answers to these questions as you read:

1. What are three reasons for learning search and recovery?

2. What's the difference between recreational and professional search and recovery?

THE SEARCH AND RECOVERY DIVER

Ask five divers why they enjoy search and recovery and you get five answers. There are as many reasons to learn search and recovery as there are divers and objects to bring up. But, you can usually group every answer you get into one of three general reasons to learn search and recovery skills.

Hang around water, and search and recovery is inevitable. Eventually you'll need to or will be asked to search for something underwater.

First, sooner or later, you'll need them. Everyone who spends time near the water loses something in it, and that's especially true of divers. Second, it's fun. It's hard to match the challenge and reward of a successful search and a recovery. Third, you may be interested in earning "hobby" money and getting more familiar with what professional divers do for a living.

This brings up the important distinctions between recreational search and recovery and professional search and recovery. In search and recovery, recreational divers learn how to use simple equipment to find small (10 kg/25 lbs or less) to medium (up to 45 kg/100 lbs) objects within recreational depths and environments. Professionals use sophisticated equipment in virtually all water environments and to extreme depths to locate objects as large as ships. Recreational divers look for objects with relatively little value, whereas professionals look for objects that have great value, that involve crimes, or even missing persons. Leave professional jobs to the professional divers trained to handle them. If your interest lies beyond recreational search and recovery, complete training with an appropriate professional/commercial dive school.

Search and Recovery
See the *Search and Recovery Manual,* and the *Search and Recovery* video.

REVIEW

TWO TYPES OF SEARCH AND RECOVERY

Underline/highlight the answers to this question as you read:

1. What are the two types of search and recovery, and how do they differ?

"Search and recovery" really describes two closely related activities: searching for a specific object that you know someone lost in the vicinity, and bottom-combing, i.e., searching for no specific object, but perhaps a type of object, such as jewelry, golf balls, etc., that you suspect you might find in the search area.

When you're searching for a specific lost object, you know there's something to find there, somewhere. The dive ends when you find it, or when you reach another limit such as your air supply or no decompression limit. This type search requires the most careful planning and search techniques. The search patterns you'll practice in the Search and Recovery Adventure Dive apply to these types of searches.

Searching for nonspecific objects is exciting because you never know what you'll find – maybe nothing, maybe something interesting, maybe lots – but until you look, you don't know what you'll find. Your dive doesn't necessarily end when you find something; rather, you keep going until you're low on air or reach some other limit. The recovery skills you practice in the Search and Recovery Adventure Dive help you get what you find to the surface, whether you're making a specific or a nonspecific search.

When you're searching for a specific lost object, you know there's something to find there, somewhere. The dive ends when you find it, or when you reach another limit such as your air supply or no decompression limit.

Search & Recovery 2

1. Your friend calls and asks for help locating a titanium golf putter that "slipped out of my hand" and "accidentally" flung into a pond. (Yeah, right.) This would be an example of
   □ a. searching for a specific object.
   □ b. searching for nonspecific objects.

   How'd you do?

   1. a.

THE SEARCH AND RECOVERY ENVIRONMENT

In many types of diving, you choose the diving environment, but in search and recovery, the environment often chooses you. That is, you don't decide
where someone loses something, and sometimes
the only reason you'd dive in a particular area is to
search for and recover something lost there.

Besides dictating where you dive, the environment's *bottom topography* – its contour, shape, obstructions and composition – dictates the search
techniques you use. For instance, a flat, open bottom allows you to use ropes and scan large areas
quickly, but also makes it easier for water flow to
move the object. By contrast, an irregular, ob-
structed bottom is more difficult to search, but
more likely to keep the search object from being
swept away. These call for differing search techniques.

Water movement affects search and recovery more
than by moving the object. Tides, surge and currents can bury an object and inter-
fere in your search by making it
hard to maintain an accurate
search pattern. Water movement
can also help. In a current, for example, you can fan away silt and
dirt, letting the water carry it away
as you work.

Environment will also affect visibility, whether you have boat traffic
to contend with, and potential hazards you need to avoid. (More
about these next.) If you're unfamiliar with the environment, if possible, get an area orientation from
a diver experienced with diving
there. You might want to make
some acclimation dives before beginning a search.

Besides dictating where you
dive, the environment's bottom
topography – its contour,
shape, obstructions and composition – dictates the search
techniques you use. For instance, a flat, open bottom allows you to use ropes and scan
large areas quickly, but also
makes it easier for water flow to
move the object.

Underline/highlight the answers to this question as you read:

1. What are the six potential hazards of search and recovery diving?

POTENTIAL HAZARDS

⚠ Search and recovery sometimes takes you into some unusual dive environments, so you face potential hazards that don't exist, or are not as common with other types of diving. Once you're aware of them, none are particularly extreme or difficult to avoid, provided you stay alert.

Sharp Objects and Debris

If you're looking for something small, you may grope around a bit on nonsensitive bottom. But, that's where mud and silt can hide broken glass, wire, rusted metal and other sharp objects that can cut the unwary diver. When swimming close to the bottom, or pulling yourself along, or in poor visibility, always wear an exposure suit and heavy-duty gloves for protection. Watch where you put your hands, feet and knees, and move cautiously. It's not a bad precaution to keep your tetanus immunizations current, too.

Always wear an exposure suit and heavy-duty gloves for protection, especially in poor visibility.

Entanglement

Some search and some recovery techniques involve ropes, and when you have rope, you have potential entanglement. Handle lines carefully and store slack on a reel. Around piers and when diving on irregular bottoms, watch for monofilament line and fishing nets that can also cause entanglement. Carry a sharp dive knife or dive tool as a precaution against severe entanglement.

Low Visibility

If the water were air-clear, chances are you wouldn't need a search to find what you lost. Less-than-ideal visibility goes hand-in-hand with search and recovery most of the time, which can add stress caused by disorientation and buddy separation. If the viz is too poor for your comfort, don't dive – remember, this is supposed to be a fun challenge. If you dive, take care not to kick up the bottom and make the visibility worse, and pay close attention to navigation and buddy contact. A short line between you and your buddy (buddy line) may help you stay together.

Currents

The concern with currents is being swept away from the dive boat, your exit or the search area. Plan the dive with currents in mind, consulting local dive professionals or divers about them if you're not familiar with the environment. Try to search into the current away from your exit point and be prepared to abort your dive if it's stronger than anticipated. When searching rivers and other environments where strong currents are inevitable, use the search techniques developed for currents. If a current is so strong as to present an unreasonable hazard, leave searches in that environment to professionals.

Sinking Recovered Objects

When recovering an object with a lift bag, a poorly tied knot or improper lifting poses a hazard if what you're recovering slips and sinks. Not good. During your Search and Recovery Adventure Dive, you'll practice recovering objects using techniques that make dropping the recovered object unlikely. And, assuming your best intentions go awry, you'll also learn how to be out of an object's way if it does sink back to the bottom.

Boat Traffic

Since you can count on boaters to drop things overboard from time to time, it follows that search and recovery frequently takes place near boat traffic. To minimize boat hazard, mark your position with a locally recognized dive flag, and preferably, mark off your entire search position (if you can do so without obstructing the traffic) with dive flags. If possible, have someone at the surface to watch and warn off boats encroaching on the search area.

To minimize boat hazard, mark your position with a locally recognized dive flag, and preferably, mark off your entire search position (if you can do so without obstructing the traffic) with dive flags. If possible, have someone at the surface to watch and warn off boats encroaching on the search area.

Quick REVIEW

Search & Recovery 4

1. Potential hazards in search and recovery diving include (check all that apply):
    ☐ a. falling recovered objects
    ☐ b. sharp objects
    ☐ c. boat traffic
    ☐ d. equipment loss

How'd you do?
1. a, b, c.

Key CONCEPTS

Underline/highlight the answers to these questions as you read:

1. What are two reasons for planning search and recovery dives?

2. What are the five general steps in planning a search and recovery dive?

PLANNING SEARCH AND RECOVERY DIVES

As with diving in general, the uppermost concern during search and recovery dives is for *safety*, which (as you'd expect) takes priority over the search itself. A thorough dive plan accounts for potential hazards, air supply, depth and the usual considerations. But for search and recovery, a second reason is for success. Haphazard searches rarely result in finding what you're looking for; success lies with a good dive plan and proper technique.

The environment, the object being recovered and diver skill all create variables that dictate your dive plan. In addition to normal dive plan concerns, you plan your search and recovery dive (or dives) following five general steps.

1. Define the objective. Decide specifically what you're looking for, and what you're trying to accomplish. Be realistic in planning within your capabilities and equipment. For instance, when looking for a small object in a large area, you may plan to search only part of the area in a single dive.

2. Collect and analyze information. When looking for a lost object, find out as much as you can before you start. Where was it lost? Interview anyone who witnessed the loss. Determine how big and heavy the object is and what equipment, if any, you'll need to recover it. Learn what you can about the environment, including bottom topography, surface conditions, probable depths and potential hazards.

3. Choose scuba or snorkel. Do you need to use scuba? Maybe not if you're looking for a large object in shallow, clear calm water. You may be surprised how often you can at least search for, if not recover, something by snorkeling.

4. Select a buddy or team. Your buddy should be someone trained and experienced in search and recovery, such as a PADI Search and Recovery Diver. When the plan calls for several divers, choose people with the appropriate skills and who can work as a team guided by a single person organizing the search.

5. Briefing. When multiple buddy teams search together, a briefing is crucial to avoid confusion and gaps in the search. Each diver should have and understand a specific responsibility. It's usually most effective to select a single divemaster or supervisor to coordinate and control the search.

CONCEPTS

Underline/highlight the answers to these questions as you read:

1. How do you establish a search area?

2. When do you use an expanding square compass search pattern and a U search pattern and how do you execute them?

3. When do you use circular and jackstay rope search patterns, and how do you execute them?

UNDERWATER SEARCHES

When someone points to the water and says, "It sank right there," you can be almost certain the object is anywhere but right there. Witnesses to a loss can get you in the ballpark, but it's a pretty big park and their recollections seldom put you much closer. And, if by chance they do point to exactly where something went under, it may not sink straight down, but move some distance due to surge, currents or waves, depending on the object's shape and weight.

As a result, you establish a search area that you systematically go over until locating the object. The search area should be large enough to minimize doubt about whether the object is in it, but not so large as to make the search longer than necessary. It also helps you organize your search if you can establish distinct boundaries in a rectangular/square search area by using natural boundaries such as piers, jetties, banks and the shoreline.

Using Search Patterns

After establishing the search area, you're ready to search using the simplest search pattern appropriate for the environment and object you're looking for. Mark your start point (varies with the search pattern you use – hang on, we're coming to patterns next) with an anchored buoy and then start the search, preferably using a cardinal compass point (north, south, east or west) to simplify navigation.

As you and your buddy swim the pattern, it usually works best if one of you navigates while the other looks for the object. The "navigator" can track your position on a slate or NavFinder and note submerged landmarks to aid in navigation, and use the other techniques in the Underwater Navigation section. Swim above the bottom to avoid contact and stirring up the silt, and if boat traffic is heavy, it may be wise to tow a dive flag and float.

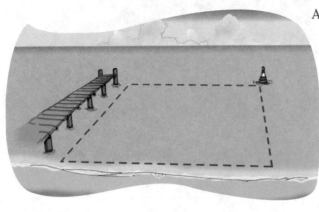

The search area should be large enough to minimize doubt about whether the object is in it, but not so large as to make the search longer than necessary.

Ropeless Search Patterns

The simplest search patterns are those requiring no special equipment. You can use these patterns to easily plan and execute the search, but they may lack some of the precision of rope search patterns. Ropeless patterns make your best choice over irregular topography that tangles ropes. The two most common ropeless search patterns are the *U search* and the *expanding square*.

U search. The U search is suitable for finding small or larger objects primarily in calm water over relatively flat, unobstructed bottoms. However, you can use the U search under less ideal conditions when you're looking for a medium-sized or larger object in a large area and you don't have any special search equipment.

To execute the U search, begin in one corner of the search area and swim a straight line to the end of the area. Turn 90 degrees toward the search area for a short length and then turn 90 degrees again,

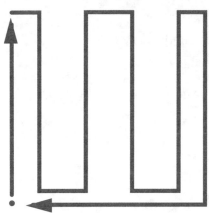

U-PATTERN

To execute the U search, begin in one corner of the search area and swim a straight line to the end of the area. Turn 90 degrees toward the search area for a short length and then turn 90 degrees again, swimming back to the other side of the search area. Repeat the process, so that two right turns alternate with two lefts, resulting in a series of U shapes with close overlap.

swimming back to the other side of the search area. Repeat the process, so that two right turns alternate with two lefts, resulting in a series of U shapes with close overlap. Establish the distance between the short legs (the short length between turns) based on the visibility, and spaced so there's some overlap.

In executing a U search, use a compass to maintain a straight line, and orient the long legs parallel to the current if one is present (if you can). This will help keep the current from interfering with your navigation.

Expanding square. The expanding square is well-suited for finding medium-sized objects in rough terrain in reasonably calm water. It is especially useful when the search area isn't large.

Start the expanding square at the center of the search area, which is generally about where someone saw the search object go down. Swim a short distance, turn 90 degrees and swim a slightly longer distance, turn 90 degrees in the same direction and swim a distance slightly longer than that. Repeat this so that you're swimming in the pattern of a straight-sided spiral. You set the "tightness" of the spiral based on the visibility, again planned with some overlap as you swim each square.

Rope Search Patterns

Rope search patterns sometimes require a bit more planning than ropeless patterns, but they are more accurate, especially when dealing with water movement and when searching for small objects. One aspect of using ropes is that in low visibility, divers may have to communicate with rope signals. Signals might be:

EXPANDING SQUARE

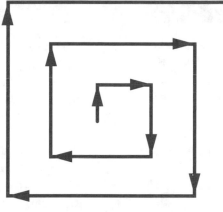

Start the expanding square at the center of the search area, which is generally about where someone saw the search object go down. Swim a short distance, turn 90 degrees and swim a slightly longer distance, turn 90 degrees in the same direction and swim a distance slightly longer than that. Repeat this so that you're swimming in the pattern of a straight-sided spiral.

One pull	=	Attention, or Begin search.
Two pulls	=	OK? or OK!
Three pulls	=	I've finished the sweep/length.
Four pulls	=	Come here or Let's meet.
Continuous	=	I need your assistance immediately.

You may develop your own signals, depending upon your dive plan and search technique. Rope pull signals aren't standard like common hand signals, so be sure to review them with your buddy before diving.

Rope search patterns sometimes require a bit more planning than rope-less patterns, but they are more accurate, especially when dealing with water movement and when searching for small objects.

Circular Search Pattern. Use this pattern for finding a small object in a small area. Although it requires a relatively flat and unobstructed bottom, it is a good pattern for currents, since the line keeps your position well-marked.

CIRCULAR SEARCH

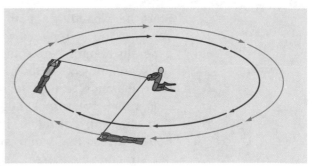

To execute a circular search, one buddy stays in the center of the search pattern acting as a pivot for one end of the rope. The searcher takes the other end on a reel, and swims a circle around the pivot using the line to maintain an even circle. Not found? The searcher plays out some line (length depending upon object size and visibility, allowing some overlap to assure no search gaps) and circles again, repeating this until finding the object or reaching a dive limit (time, air, temperature). You can accomplish the same pattern by attaching the pivot end to an anchor, post or other solid object that you won't pull free, and in some instances, the pivot diver may control the reel.

To execute a circular search, one buddy stays in the center of the search pattern acting as a pivot for one end of the rope. The searcher takes the other end on a reel, and swims a circle around the pivot using the line to maintain an even circle.

Jackstay search pattern. Use the jackstay search to cover a large area with a relatively flat bottom and no more than a moderate current. There are actually several "jackstay patterns," but the following is one of the most useful.

Start by establishing one edge of the search area as the baseline, along which the search will progress. Stretch a rope out perpendicular to the baseline with you at one end and your buddy at the other. Anchor the rope ends (weights work well), and then on signal (line pull or tank rap), swim down opposite sides of the rope (determined before hand) searching. You pass each other and continue until reaching the rope ends. If no luck, on signal, you both pick up the ends and move it along the baseline a short distance (determined by the visibility and object size), reanchor the ends and swim the length searching. Do this until you find the object or reach a dive limit.

JACKSTAY SEARCH

Use the jackstay search to cover a large area with a relatively flat bottom and no more than a moderate current.

REVIEW

Search & Recovery 6

1. When establishing a search area (check all that apply):
   - ☐ a. use natural boundaries.
   - ☐ b. make it as large as possible.
   - ☐ c. try to form a rectangle/square.
   - ☐ d. cover an area the object's almost certainly in.

2. A U search is best used to search for an object in a large area, in relatively calm water.
   ☐ True   ☐ False

3. The advantage of the circular search is that you can conduct it without special equipment.
   ☐ True   ☐ False

How'd you do?

1. a, c, d; **2.** True; **3.** False. The circular search requires a rope. Its advantage is that it is accurate in a current.

RECOVERY PROCEDURES

Underline/highlight the answers to these questions as you read:

1. Why shouldn't you use your BCD as a lifting device to recover underwater objects?

2. At about what weight does a lift bag become mandatory to recover an underwater object?

3. What are three reasons to use commercially made lift bags for recovering underwater objects?

4. How can you make a homemade lift bag if a commercially made one isn't available?

5. Why do you select a lift bag based on the weight of the object being lifted?

6. How do you tie a bowline, two-half-hitches and a sheet bend, and under what conditions should you be able to tie them?

7. Where should you position yourself when a lift bag is ascending?

8. Which air source should you use to fill a lift bag?

Once you locate your search object, you need to bring it up. For a small item, like a wallet, fin, mask or something, you just grab it and bring it along. But when an object weighs more than you can swim up comfortably – about 4 kg/10 lbs as rule of thumb – it's too heavy to raise that way. Yes, your BCD probably has enough buoyancy to raise objects weighing more than that, **but you never use your BCD for lifting**. If you were doing so and the object broke free, or you dropped it, you'd be overly buoyant and facing a hazardous runaway ascent, with a high risk of decompression illness. Since you don't want that, when an object weighs more than 4 kgs/10 lbs, consider a lift bag (or other appropriate lifting device) mandatory for the job.

Lift Bags

Lift bags are the most common recovery tool, and you can find a wide selection. Generally speaking, use a commercially-made lift bag rather than an improvised one for three reasons. First, you can rely on commercial bags, which are typically constructed from heavy-duty materials, to withstand the stress of raising a heavy object. Second, most lift bags have exhaust valves that allow you to control ascents. Third, commercial lift bags have loops, slings and other convenient locations for rigging and securing the recovery object.

Lift bags are the most common recovery tool, and you can find a wide selection. Generally speaking, it's best to use a commercially-made lift bag rather than an improvised one.

On occasion, you may be forced to improvise. This might happen at a remote location where you weren't planning a recovery, but the need came up. Oops. You can build a homemade lift bag out of almost any strong, heavy duty bag capable of holding air. A mesh goodie bag or a duffel bag lined with a plastic trash bag or an inner tube with a side cut out and a line through it are just two examples. Note, however, that a plastic bag can tear and that homemade lift bags don't have vents for releasing expanding air. Don't use homemade bags unless you really need to, and then with caution. You can avoid this need, by the way, by keeping a moderate-sized commercial bag in your gearbag at all times. Then when you need one, you have it.

Whether commercial or homemade, try to pick one just large enough to handle the object's weight. Air in a lift bag expands during ascent, so if the bag is nearly full before you start, the expanding air simply spills out. But if the bag is large and you only partially fill it to start ascending, it retains expanding air as you go, gaining buoyancy and speed. You need to control a lift bag when ascending, and matching lift bag size to object weight minimizes the likelihood of a runaway lift bag.

On occasion, you may be forced to improvise a lift bag. This might happen at a remote location where you weren't planning a recovery, but the need came up.

Rigging the lift bag

Before you can raise an object, you have to tie it to the lift bag. Prestretched nylon rope makes an ideal rigging rope; avoid polypropylene, which tends to slip loose more easily. To tie the line, you'll find three knots most useful for rigging and tying. The first is the *bowline*, which you normally use to tie line directly to an object. It is a strong, dependable knot that unties easily. You use the *sheet bend* to tie two lines of different diameter together (it works for same diameter lines, too), and two half-hitches for a quick way to attach line to an object.

TWO HALF HITCHES

BOWLINE

SHEET BEND

With low visibility a common situation in search and recovery, learn to tie all three knots wearing gloves and with both eyes closed. Practice the knots above water until you can tie them easily. Then put on your gloves and close your eyes. Not so easy, huh? Keep going until you can.

Lifting Procedures

Once you've rigged the object and you're ready to raise it, attach a marker line if you haven't already so that if it sinks again while raising, you can relocate it without another search. Then use your alternate air source – not your primary second stage – to put just enough air in the bag to make it stand off the bottom. You'll always use your alternate for putting air in the bag, taking care to not tangle it in the rigging.

Attach a marker line to the search object so that if it sinks again while raising, you can relocate it without another search.

Check the rigging. If it looks secure, add a little more air to put some strain on the knots. Check them for slippage. Still okay? All systems go.

Use the bag to make the object neutrally buoyant – not positively buoyant. Add a small amount of air, pause, and then pull up on the rigging to see if you can raise the object. If not, repeat the process, a small burst each time, until you can. You may have to overcome suction from mud on some bottoms, so go slowly and pull up firmly after each air burst.

Use the bag to make the object neutrally buoyant – not positively buoyant. Add a small amount of air, pause, and then pull up on the rigging to see if you can raise the object.

At this point, if you need to move the object horizontally (to a dock, for example), you may wish to swim it along the bottom, which is easier than towing it at the surface if you don't have a boat or something to do it. But, this usually depends on having a fairly level, unobstructed bottom.

When ready to take the object up, simply pull upward – don't add air. The expanding air will increase its buoyancy naturally as you start up. Depending upon the situation, you may either accompany the bag to the surface, or you may allow it to rise independently. In either case, position yourself so that you are *not*

under the lift bag and object. This way you avoid being hit if the object slips loose or the lift bag spills.

If you ascend with the bag, control its ascent by exhausting air periodically through the exhaust valve. Be cautious not to exceed 18 metres/60 feet per minute or whatever your computer dictates. If you have difficulties and the lift bag begins to take off on you, don't fight it – it'll just drag you along. Let it go and pour on the steam, getting out from under it in case it topples at the surface and sinks. Remember, your safety is more important than anything you may be recovering – even a chest full of rubies.

If you ascend with the bag, control its ascent by exhausting air periodically through the exhaust valve. Be cautious not to exceed 18 metres/60 feet per minute or whatever your computer dictates.

Search & Recovery 7

1. You shouldn't use your BCD as a lifting device because
   - ☐ a. it won't have enough buoyancy.
   - ☐ b. it can cause a hazardous runaway ascent.

2. A lift bag is mandatory for recovering objects heavier than about
   - ☐ a. 2 kg/5 lbs.
   - ☐ b. 4 kg/10 lbs.
   - ☐ c. 8 kg/ 20 lbs.

3. Commercial lift bags are preferable to homemade ones because they are made from stronger materials, have exhaust valves and are easier to rig.
   - ☐ True   ☐ False

4. You can improvise a homemade lift bag from a heavy duty bag capable of holding air.
   - ☐ True   ☐ False

5. Select a lift bag based on object weight to
   - ☐ a. ensure ample excess lift is available.
   - ☐ b. simplify controlling the ascent.

6. You should be able to tie a bowline, sheet bend and two half-hitches
   - ☐ a. with gloves on and your eyes closed.
   - ☐ b. with the aid of your buddy.
   - ☐ c. with both hands tied behind your back.

7. When a lift bag is ascending, you should position yourself
   - ☐ a. out from under it.
   - ☐ b. directly beneath it.

8. Use your primary regulator to fill a lift bag because you don't have to unsecure it.
   - ☐ True   ☐ False

How'd you do?
1. b; 2. b; 3. True; 4. True; 5. b; 6. a; 7. a; 8. False. Use your alternate air source for filling a lift bag.

PADI Search and Recovery Specialty Course

Your Search and Recovery Adventure Dive may credit (at the instructor's discretion) toward the Search and Recovery Specialty certification. In addition to what you've learned in this section and will practice on the Search and Recovery Adventure Dive, the Search and Recovery course covers:

• pinpointing lost objects from the surface

• boat and surface controlled searches

• semicircular and alternate jackstay searches

• practicing four different search patterns

• practice raising larger objects

KNOWLEDGE REVIEW
Search & Recovery

1. Describe a recreational search and recovery diver as compared to a professional one.

2. List the six potential hazards of search and recovery diving.

   1._____

   2._____

   3._____

   4._____

   5._____

   6._____

3. List the five general steps in planning a search and recovery dive.

   1._____

   2._____

   3._____

   4._____

   5._____

4. Briefly describe when to use an expanding square and a U search pattern.

5. Briefly describe when to use and how to execute a circular rope search.

6. Explain why you shouldn't use your BCD as a lifting device.

7. At approximately what object weight does using a lift bag become mandatory?

8. List three reasons why it's preferable to use commercially made lift bags for object recovery.

   1._____

   2._____

   3._____

9. Explain the procedures for rigging, lifting and controlling an object while using a lift bag.

10. Which air source should you use to fill a lift bag?

Student Diver Statement: I've completed this Knowledge Review to the best of my ability and any questions I answered incorrectly or incompletely I've had explained to me, and I understand what I missed.

Signature _____ Date_____

Search and Recovery Adventure Dive Overview

- Knowledge assessment/ Knowledge Review
- Briefing
- Practice search patterns topside
- Practice rigging topside
- Gearing up
- Predive safety check (BWRAF)
- Entry

- Descent
- Small area search
- Large area search
- Rigging and lifting object – ascent and safety stop
- Exit
- Debrief
- Log dive – PADI Instructor signs

UNDERWATER NATURALIST

Introduction

By definition, a "naturalist" is someone versed in natural history (not to be confused with a "naturist," who is someone who sunbathes naked), so by definition, someone versed in aquatic natural history is an "underwater naturalist." To some extent, then, you're already a naturalist – whether you realize it or not.

Think about your diving experiences. Whether you've made only a few dives or hundreds, or whether you dive in salt water or fresh, you've seen and become familiar with aquatic organisms and some of their characteristics. Even if you don't know them by name, you know how they behave or where they "belong," so that you recognize where to expect them. For example, if you've previously encountered octopus in holes in your favorite reef, you might think to look for octopus in similar holes on a similar reef. In this sense you're already an underwater naturalist.

This section takes your experiences and builds upon them. You'll understand more about the animals and plants you see underwater and learn how the environment dictates their form and behavior. You'll learn to put aside conclusions drawn from land organisms, and instead comprehend underwater plants and animals in light of their aquatic environment. Most importantly, this section shows you how you fit in, how your actions affect organisms that you interact with, and how to visit the aquatic world in a responsible manner.

INTRODUCTION TO THE AQUATIC REALM

Underline/highlight the answers to these questions as you read:

1. How do you define "ecology" and "ecosystem"?

2. What are at least three physical/structural differences between the land environment and the underwater environment?

Imagine walking into the living room of someone you've never met. Glance around the room, you spot an expensive stereo and classical music compact disks. In the corner stands a piano and next to it a cello. Immediately you conclude that for this person, music is very important, and not just any music, but classical music. In a rudimentary sense, this person's environment tells you about the person who lives there. Similarly, underwater naturalists observe the aquatic environment to understand the organisms that live there.

With this in mind, a study of underwater life begins with ecology, which is "the study of the interrelationship of living things and their environment." Ecology examines not just organisms and their relationships with their environments, but also ecosystems, which are "the complex of living things and their environment functioning as a unit."

An ecosystem can be large and general, or small and specific, depending upon your context. The earth is an ecosystem, but so is a vegetable garden or a puddle of rainwater. Underwater naturalists focus on aquatic (underwater), rather than terrestrial (land) ecosystems, so comparing the physical and structural differences between the two environments lays the foundation for understanding the differences between the organisms that live in water versus on land.

An ecosystem can be large and general, or small and specific, depending upon your context. The earth is an ecosystem, but so is a lake, or vegetable garden or a puddle of rainwater.

Terrestrial and Aquatic Environments – Physical Characteristics

You don't have to be a diver to realize that the big difference between terrestrial and aquatic environments is that on land, organisms are surrounded by air, and underwater they're surrounded by water. But you do have to be a diver to experience firsthand how existence differs from one environment to other.

Density. Water is 800 times denser than air, which is in fact, the main cause for most of the differences between terrestrial and aquatic environments. Water density restricts motion, so that fast-moving animals (primarily fish) have streamlined shapes to minimize water resistance. Only terrestrial animals that move fast enough to encounter significant air resistance, such as birds, show comparable streamlining. The cheetah, for example, runs faster than many fish swim, yet has far less streamlining by comparison.

Gravity. Water exerts far more buoyancy than air, so for practical purposes, aquatic organisms can exist in a nearly "weightless" environment. While land organisms must have a rigid structure to resist gravity, some aquatic organisms such as the jellyfish grow quite large with virtually no rigid structure at all. This makes it possible for some aquatic organisms to live their entire life floating in the water column, never or rarely touching the bottom; many fish species have a special organ – the air bladder – specifically for controlling "weightlessness." By contrast in the terrestrial environment gravity is ever-present; even birds spend a significant amount of their lives perched.

Even among aquatic animals with rigid structure, the absence of gravity often affects energy use and potential size. A 225 kg/500 lb fish barely flicks a fin to hover motionlessly, but a tiny hummingbird beats its wings at a blur to accomplish the same – and no 225 kg/500 lb terrestrial animal can hover in air at all. Even the smaller whales dwarf the largest terrestrial animal, the elephant. Dinosaurs, which were the largest terrestrial animals that ever lived, are small compared to the great whales (especially the blue whale). The potential for large size is greater when organisms are not restrained by gravity.

It's worth noting that while buoyancy practically negates gravity underwater, the aquatic world isn't truly weightless in the sense of being in outer space. Aquatic organisms feel and respond to gravity, as demonstrated by fish swimming "right side up." In true weightlessness, no reference to up or down exists.

Movement. Air has wind, water has currents and both affect their respective ecosystems. You're probably familiar with seeds that drift in the breeze, small spiders that ride web "balloons" or other organisms that drift with the wind, but these are insignificant compared to analogous underwater organisms that drift "weightless" in currents. Plankton (which means "wanderers") is a community of microorganisms that drifts through the aquatic realm. The abundance of plankton is such that many aquatic animals don't have to forage to feed – sponges, tube worms, corals and other organisms spend their entire lives attached to one spot, straining the plankton they eat from the water.

While a few terrestrial plants use the wind to aid reproduction, the majority of aquatic invertebrates and many vertebrates release their larvae into the water, where they float long distances to new habitats. Many aquatic animals release sperm and eggs into the water, permitting fertilization outside the parents' bodies.

Light. Life gets most of its energy from the sun. Plants use light directly, whereas animals use it indirectly either by eating plants or other animals that eat plants. For practical purposes, air doesn't affect the life-providing light spectrum, making land the ideal environment for plants. Water absorbs light (and therefore color) unevenly, first absorbing red in shallow depths, then orange, yellow, green, blue, indigo and violet. In the clearest water, light cannot reach deeper than about 180 metres/600 feet, and in many aquatic environments it cannot even penetrate a tenth that deep. Consequently, plant life survives only at the shallower depths, where, depending on depth, it may have only part of the spectrum available. In contrast, terrestrial plants are limited by temperature, altitude and availability of water.

Oxygen. In air, oxygen is evenly distributed and plentiful, making up about 21 percent of the atmosphere (at altitude, the oxygen pressure is lower, but the distribution is the same 21 percent). In water, oxygen may be unevenly distributed; for example in a lake, the shallows may have more oxygen compared to stagnant bottom waters. Proportionately little oxygen exists in water, requiring aquatic organisms to have gills, which compared to terrestrial lungs are significantly more efficient at gathering oxygen. Other aquatic animals – notably marine mammals, reptiles and amphibians – return to the surface periodically to breathe air.

Terrestrial and Aquatic Environments – Structural Characteristics

The physical differences between terrestrial and aquatic environments explain the differences in the structures of their ecosystems and organisms.

Plants. On land, plants dominate. Their large, rigid structure, which combats gravity, makes them massive and difficult to move. This makes plant ecosystems relatively stable compared to aquatic plant ecosystems. Long-lived plant communities control short-lived animal communities. Terrestrial ecosystems tend to be described in plant-terms: redwood forest, grass prairies, rain forest, etc.

Underwater the majority of plants tend to be small and primarily microscopic. Small aquatic animals easily eat aquatic plants, so that plant-consuming animals play the role of bringing plant-energy into the ecosystem. Animal populations dominate many aquatic ecosystems, which are referred to in animal-terms: coral reef, oyster beds, clam beds, etc.

Food chains. Because large animals eat the stable-population plants directly, terrestrial food chains tend to be shorter than aquatic food chains. For example: grass converts light into chemical energy, grass eaten by antelope, antelope eaten by lion. This is a three-link food chain.

In aquatic environments, small and microscopic animals eat the plant plankton, adding at least one immediate link. For example: Algae converts light into chemical energy, algae eaten by animal plankton is eaten by small fish, small fish are eaten by dolphins. This is a four-link food chain.

Quick REVIEW

Naturalist 1

1. Ecology is the study of interrelationships between living things and their environment.
   ☐ True   ☐ False

2. An ecosystem is
   ☐ a. a single unit composed of an environment and its organisms.
   ☐ b. a method of air-quality control.

3. Significant physical and structural differences between underwater environments and land environments include (check all that apply):
   ☐ a. gravity
   ☐ b. sound
   ☐ c. oxygen
   ☐ d. plant/animal dominance

How'd you do?
1. True; **2.** a; **3.** a, c, d.

HUMAN PERCEPTIONS OF AQUATIC LIFE

CONCEPTS

Underline/highlight the answers to these questions as you read:

1. What is the most common cause of aquatic animal "attacks"?

2. What is an accurate view of potentially dangerous aquatic animals?

3. What are four inaccurate ways people may perceive aquatic organisms?

One way human beings handle unfamiliar situations is by drawing analogies from previous experiences. This is why as you read, you're referred back to your entry-level class or to common experiences, both of which help you learn by drawing upon what you already know.

In the underwater world, you do the same thing consciously or not. For example, when you clear your mask at 18 metres/60 feet, you've made the (obvious) comparison to clearing your mask in a pool and concluded that doing it on a reef or in a quarry doesn't differ significantly. In this case, it helps you react correctly.

On the other hand, suppose you approach a coral reef without knowing anything about coral. How do you interact with coral? Your experience tells you animals move. Coral doesn't. Compared to terrestrial organisms, coral seems to be a plant (or even inanimate rock) rather than an animal. You can stand on many plants (or rock) without harming them, but if you treat coral accordingly, you will kill it. Therefore, your terrestrial experiences with organisms have only limited value in understanding aquatic organisms, because they can lead to misconceptions, such as about "dangerous" marine organisms and about the nature of aquatic organisms in general.

Aquatic Life Mythology

Probably the most wide spread misconception about the underwater world is that some aquatic creatures seek out and attack human beings. There's no denying that some aquatic organisms present potential hazards. But, experience shows that tall tales, fiction and false assumptions fuel our fears.

As a diver learning underwater naturalism, you need to avoid character judgments about an organism based on whether it may sometimes pose a hazard. An organism's form and behavior spring from its survival needs, and nothing more. While you can't ignore potentially hazardous organisms, you can learn to understand the organism and to avoid the hazard. As you probably know, the vast majority of all aquatic life injuries are avoidable.

When you think of "dangerous" aquatic animals, what species come to mind? Usually sharks, barracuda, eels, stingrays, jellyfish, orca, crocodiles and snakes – those that might seem to "attack" by moving or acting in a way that you could interpret as malicious. You know that fire coral, sea urchins and crown-of-thorns sea stars are potentially dangerous, but since they lack intelligence or an obvious ability to move, you're less likely to attribute injuries from them to an "attack." Stepping on a sea urchin with bare feet causes a painful injury, but no one would think the urchin willfully attacked by maneuvering itself under your feet. This brings up three important points regarding "dangerous" aquatic life.

Animals rarely attack unprovoked. The vast majority of "attacks" are defensive reactions. If, without looking first, a diver reaches in a moray eel's hole, the eel will more than likely be terrified (how would you feel if a giant arm suddenly thrust in through your front door and started groping around) and defend itself by biting the diver. The fact the diver intended no harm is irrelevant; the eel reacts according to instinct.

You avoid injuries caused by defensive actions by being able to recognize potentially hazardous animals, by knowing the potential severity of an injury, and by acting in ways that don't threaten them.

Realizing this, you avoid injuries caused by defensive actions by being able to recognize potentially hazardous animals, by knowing the potential severity of an injury, and by acting in ways that don't threaten them. In the case of the eel, this means knowing what an eel looks like, knowing that it can bite, and knowing that reaching into holes is a good way to startle it into

doing so. The same principle applies to a sea urchin or fire coral – recognizing it, realizing that it can stick or sting, and understanding that merely touching it can cause the injury.

Animals do not attack out of malice. Not all injuries from aquatic animals are defensive, but even these can be attributed to natural behavior. Animals don't seek humans out of malice, revenge or anger, which is what makes many fictional portrayals unrealistic. Animals may initiate an attack for one of four reasons: to defend themselves, to defend territory, a mate or young, to obtain food and by mistake.

In the previous discussion, you saw how a diver can provoke a defensive response. Animals such as the black-tip reef shark are known to be territorial and will defend their territory if they perceive a diver as a competitor. Likewise, baleen whales and dolphins, which are normally docile around humans, become quite agitated when they perceive a diver as a threat to offspring. As with avoiding a defensive "attack," you want to know which aquatic animals have territorial behavior or protect their young and mates, and avoid being mistaken as a threat to territory, young or mate.

Animals also attack for food, which rules out divers. You're not natural prey for any aquatic organism. More of a concern, however, is that an aquatic animal may mistake a diver for prey or food. At some dive sites, some animals learn to eat out of divers' hands. If an unfortunate diver's finger resembles food to a nearsighted moray or grouper, an "attack" may result. In other areas, a surfer with arms and legs dangling from a board may look like a turtle or sea lion to a shark below. This may have precipitated attacks from sharks that prey on turtles and sea lions. To avoid these types of "attacks," you must understand what aquatic animals feed on, what triggers feeding

behavior, and how to not accidentally resemble the animal's idea of food.

Underwater animal attacks seem worse than terrestrial animal attacks. Because humans are so vulnerable in the water, aquatic animal attacks cause more sensation and emotional reaction. We understand terrestrial animals better because we're terrestrial, and in many areas, we've killed off or displaced most of those terrestrial animals we fear (not necessarily intentionally).

The reality is, to most aquatic organisms, you're not worth attention. They're too busy going about surviving to give you much notice unless you seem to threaten survival or enhance it as a food source. Because aquatic life behavior is predictable, however, you can avoid unpleasant interactions by obtaining local orientations to aquatic life, by reading about aquatic organisms and by acting on what you learn. For example, if you know sharks frequent an environment, and you realize that bleeding and struggling fish attract them (looking for food), you may want to avoid spearfishing in that area. Likewise, if you're river diving and spot a snapping turtle, you avoid handling it based on the knowledge that it may bite.

Human Perceptions of Aquatic Life

Misconceptions about "dangerous" aquatic animals are just one way people perceive the nature of aquatic organisms. There are four common misperceptions of aquatic life, beginning with one that continues the discussion on "dangerous aquatic life."

As dangerous and harmful. Beliefs that aquatic animals are dangerous may be specific and have some basis in fact (e.g.: All sharks eat humans), or may be widespread and general (There are "things" out in the lake waiting to get you). These perceptions grow from sensationalizing fiction in the print and film media, and also from rumors, distortions and inaccurate impressions. In the excitement of telling a story, the 150 centimetre/5-foot harmless horned shark grows into a 6 metre/20 foot savage beast. When a landed shark happens to flop toward the fisherman, the story may be, "The shark came after me in the boat!" These distortions, plus the previously discussed misunderstandings, lead some people to inaccurately believe that even harmless aquatic animals are dangerous.

As harmless animals similar to domestic/ friendly animals. Some misconceptions lead people to believe aquatic animals are unrealistically harmless instead of dangerous. One might regard hermit crabs, dolphins and whales as harmless, or, in the case of dolphins or whales, as perhaps benevolent and favoring or especially fond of humans. These impressions arise from popular portrayals, or stunts in zoos and marine parks, or because the animal in question (usually a more complex organism with eyes) exhibits complex behaviors that you can relate to, perhaps comparing the animal to a familiar dog or cat.

These misconceptions can at least lead you to misunderstand the animal in question, or to more serious misunderstandings that cause injury. For example, if, after seeing a trainer kiss or pet a sea lion at the zoo, you attempt to pet or kiss a wild sea lion, you could end up bitten severely.

As nonliving, inanimate objects. Organisms that exhibit few obvious behaviors and live attached to something may appear inanimate because they lack the eyes and movement common to the vast majority of terrestrial animals. Sponges, sea squirts, sea stars, sea urchins and others fit in this category, but even very animate creatures can "transform" into "inanimate objects." When a harassed pufferfish inflates, on an emotional level a diver might no longer regard it as an animal (even though logically the diver knows it is), but as a nonliving "thing" to play with like a football.

As an underwater naturalist, recognize that how animate an organism is or is not has nothing to do with its value in the ecosystem. Coral seems extremely inanimate, yet entire ecosystems grow from it and rely on it. Sea urchins feed on algae that would contaminate and kill the coral. In their own ways, all organisms are important to the ecosystem.

As having human characteristics. Some misperceptions arise out of attempts to give animals human characteristics, such as marine shows that have dolphins wearing sunglasses and grass skirts, or (for a terrestrial example) when zoos or films dress chimpanzees in human clothes. These attempts at humor put the animal in an unnatural situation where it cannot behave normally, so conclusions based on these behaviors (like kissing the sea lion) are likely to be inaccurate.

In other instances, the media can create the false impression that some animals can think like humans. Television and media have portrayed dolphins and whales (not to mention dogs, cats and birds) as able to recognize when humans are in trouble and then summon help. This not only presupposes that animals can relate to human problems, but also that they would care enough to do anything about it. While there have been a few verified instances of dolphins aiding swimmers, and certainly instances of dogs rescuing and protecting humans, you're out in left field if you get in trouble and expect a dramatic rescue just because a dolphin swims by.

Presenting animals as imperfect humans impedes recognizing them for what they are, how they behave and where they fit in the environment. It can lead to value judgments based on whether an organism has or lacks human characteristics rather than based on its role in the ecosystem.

Naturalist 2

1. Most "attacks" by aquatic animals are caused by
   ☐ a. malice and revenge.
   ☐ b. a defensive reaction.
   ☐ c. a strong dislike of humans.

2. An accurate view of potentially dangerous aquatic animals would be that aquatic animals behave according to predictable natural behavior, and that through knowledge, understanding and forethought, you can avoid most unpleasant interactions with aquatic animals.
   ☐ True   ☐ False

3. Inaccurate perceptions of aquatic animals include the belief that aquatic animals are (check all that apply):
   ☐ a. dangerous.
   ☐ b. inanimate.
   ☐ c. capable of having human characteristics.
   ☐ d. harmless, like a dog or cat.

How'd you do?
1. b; **2.** True; **3.** a, b, c, d.

RESPONSIBLE INTERACTIONS WITH AQUATIC LIFE

Types of Interactions

As soon as you enter an aquatic environment, you interact with the organisms living there, whether you intend to or not. You may not intend to involve aquatic life at all in your dive plan – such as a search and recovery dive, or aquatic life may be your focus, such as in underwater photo and video, fish feeding, fish watching, shell-collecting or gathering tropical fish for aquariums. Some of these interactions are relatively passive and have little negative effect on aquatic life; others may have tremendous negative effect, such as those that kill the organism. Besides your intent, your awareness can be important because your interaction can kill, injure or terrorize aquatic animals without you being aware that you're doing so. You can classify interactions into several categories, each with varying degrees of negative effect on aquatic life.

Passive interactions. Passive interactions are those with the least effect. Most passive interaction falls into the category of observing aquatic life – organisms themselves, organism interactions, and interactions between divers and organisms. You can learn a great deal about aquatic life by watching it.

Touching and handling aquatic life. Humans are naturally curious, so there's a tendency to want to touch and handle aquatic organisms. For many organisms, this is terrifying and sometimes kills them. For a diver, ignorantly touching the wrong organism can be a painful, or even life-threatening experience. In general, touching and handling aquatic life should be done by those experienced with the particular organism. This action should not harm or disrupt the organism's natural behavior, and doing so should provide some in

Passive interactions are those with the least effect. Most passive interaction falls into the category of observing aquatic life – organisms themselves, organism interactions, and interactions between divers and organisms. You can learn a great deal about aquatic life by watching it.

Underline/highlight the answers to these questions as you read:

1. How do you "passively" interact with aquatic organisms?

2. When and how can you responsibly touch or handle aquatic life?

3. Why should divers avoid riding aquatic animals?

4. How do you responsibly feed fish and other aquatic life?

5. What diving techniques should you use to preserve bottom dwelling organisms and to minimize disturbing all aquatic life?

sights into the organism's natural history without compromising its health. Otherwise, leave it alone.

Riding aquatic life. If you consider your own reaction when an uninvited insect drops on your back, then you can relate to how a manta ray, turtle or manatee feels when an uninvited diver does the same. There are no circumstances in which riding an animal benefits it, and in some cases, (particularly sea turtles since they need to surface for air) doing so may injure it.

Spearfishing and gathering aquatic life. Taking aquatic life, even for human consumption often has a detrimental effect on the aquatic environment. (It certainly has a detrimental effect on the organism.) These practices should only be done within the guidelines established by local law, which exist to help ensure a healthy underwater community and long-term survival of the species you gather. Don't harm aquatic animals that you must measure for minimum size before taking.

Collecting aquatic life for aquariums and collections. As in spearfishing and gathering aquatic life to eat, taking aquatic life for aquariums and collections may have a negative effect because the organism no longer fills its place in the environment. If you collect, do so responsibly, keeping in mind that in many areas it is illegal and/or requires special licensing.

Feeding fish and aquatic life. At first, feeding aquatic animals sounds like an interaction that benefits the aquatic environment. When conducted responsibly, fish feeding can be rewarding and can help you understand animal behaviors, but you need to avoid some practices. First, feed with food you bring on the dive. Don't kill one organism to feed another. Second, feed fish sparingly so you don't seriously interrupt their natural behavior, including normal feeding and mating. These are important in retaining the balance in the local ecosystem. Remember that feeding in the same location again and again may change local animal behaviors, affecting an entire local ecosystem. Those who see such animals won't witness their natural behaviors.

Underwater photography and videography. Underwater imaging, done with forethought and consideration of the environment, gives you a rewarding way to "capture" aquatic life with little negative effect. Provided that you're careful not to damage coral, river grasses or other aquatic life, that you don't capture, chase or harass animals for the sake of your camera and that you apply good buoyancy skills, you can enjoy years of underwater photo and video while causing little damage to the underwater environment. It's perhaps one of the most rewarding interactions you can have underwater. See the sections on underwater photography and videography for more information.

Dive Techniques That Preserve

Compared to acid rain, offshore dumping and other forms of pollution that damage reefs, divers inflict little damage to the underwater world. Of that damage, most is unintentional and can be prevented with a little bit of care and forethought. Although divers probably aren't a major threat to the world's reefs, as the underwater world's ambassadors and advocates, it's our responsibility to

Underwater imaging, done with fore thought and consideration of the environment, gives you a rewarding way to "capture" aquatic life with little negative effect.

set a good example. Here are a few guidelines that will help you swim through your favorite dive site with minimal damage.

Secure dangling equipment. Dangling submersible pressure gauges, alternate air sources and other accessories drag across the bottom and reefs, destroying and killing. Use Velcro-type fasteners, clips, snaps and other holders to keep your equipment and accessories tucked in close to your body and not dragging. This not only helps the environment, but minimizes snags, reduces wear on your equipment and saves energy through streamlining.

Try to glide quietly through the water; you'll disturb the environment less, and you'll see more natural behavior.

Dive carefully. Use good diving techniques. Stay properly weighted, neutrally buoyant and off the bottom. Swim in a horizontal position (not with your feet down). This keeps your fins farther from the bottom so you don't kick (and destroy) aquatic life. Try to glide quietly through the water; you'll disturb the environment less, and you'll see more natural behavior. Also, avoid touching anything on the bottom with your hands. Most bottom dwelling aquatic organisms are very delicate. A simple bump or touch can do harm. If you're a boater, avoid anchoring over delicate reef bottoms. Anchor over sandy areas or better yet, go out of your way to use mooring buoys.

Project AWARE and You

As you better understand the aquatic realm and its inhabitants, you appreciate why divers need to take an active role in preserving the underwater environment. We see this world firsthand and are truly its ambassadors.

Spreading this message is one of the goals of PADI's Project AWARE (Aquatic World Awareness, Responsibility and Education). PADI teaches divers not only to dive safely and competently, but in an environmentally educated manner.

PADI monitors and responds to legislation that could affect divers and the underwater environment, and provides PADI Instructors, Assistant Instructors, Divemasters, Dive Centers and Resorts information so that they can organize and participate in activities such as beach and lake cleanups. PADI also established the Project AWARE Foundation to fund environmental education, study and cleanup.

If you're interested in learning more about Project AWARE, talk to your PADI Instructor, PADI Dive Center or PADI Resort, or visit PADI's website, www.padi.com. PADI Members, you, your fellow PADI Divers – all of us – have a part to play in ensuring that future generations continue to enjoy the wonders of the aquatic world.

PROJECT AWARE

Naturalist 3

1. How do you passively interact with aquatic life?
   - ☐ a. primarily by observing only
   - ☐ b. by adhering to game laws
   - ☐ c. by feeding fish

2. Touching and handling aquatic life should never compromise the health of the organism.
   - ☐ True   ☐ False

3. Divers should not ride wild aquatic animals because
   - ☐ a. it is stressful and doesn't benefit the animal.
   - ☐ b. most aquatic animals swim fast enough to dislodge equipment.

4. Responsibly feeding fish and aquatic life includes (check all that apply):
   - ☐ a. using other organisms in the environment as food.
   - ☐ b. not disrupting natural behavior.
   - ☐ c. not continually feeding the same population of animals.

5. You could summarize the best technique for minimizing damage to the environment as staying streamlined, neutrally buoyant and well off the bottom.
   - ☐ True   ☐ False

How'd you do?
1. a; 2. True; 3. a; 4. b, c; 5. True.

PADI Underwater Naturalist Specialty Course

Your Underwater Naturalist Adventure Dive may be credited (at the instructor's discretion) toward the Underwater Naturalist Specialty certification. In addition to what you've learned in this section and will practice in the Underwater Naturalist Adventure Dive, the Underwater Naturalist Specialty course includes:

- overview of aquatic life taxonomy

- study of aquatic life relationships

- evaluation of human effects on the local diving environment

Underwater Naturalist Adventure Dive Overview

- Knowledge assessment/ Knowledge Review
- Briefing
- Gearing up
- Predive safety check (BWRAF)
- Entry
- Descent
- Identify aquatic plant life
- Identify and observe aquatic invertebrates
- Identify and observe aquatic vertebrates
- Ascent – safety stop
- Exit
- Debrief
- Log dive – PADI Instructor signs

KNOWLEDGE REVIEW Underwater Naturalist

1. Define "ecology" and "ecosystem."

   Ecology:

   Ecosystem:

2. List three physical/structural differences between aquatic and terrestrial ecosystems:

   1._____

   2._____

   3._____

3. What's the most common cause of aquatic animal "attacks"?

4. Describe an accurate view of potentially dangerous aquatic animals.

5. List four inaccurate ways people may perceive aquatic life:

   1._____

   2._____

   3._____

   4._____

6. Explain how to interact passively with aquatic organisms.

7. Explain how and when you can responsibly touch or handle aquatic organisms.

8. Explain why you shouldn't ride aquatic animals.

9. Explain how to responsibly feed fish or other aquatic life.

10. Describe the dive techniques to use to preserve bottom dwelling organisms and to minimize disturbing all aquatic life.

Student Diver Statement: I've completed this Knowledge Review to the best of my ability and any questions I answered incorrectly or incompletely I've had explained to me, and I understand what I missed.

Signature _____ Date_____

UNDERWATER NAVIGATION

Introduction

Remember your first open water dive? More than likely, you were thrilled with your first venture beyond a confined water or pool dive, but perhaps somewhat disoriented. Depending upon the dive site, you might have been surprised to find out that even though you were turned around, your instructor knew exactly where you were all along. Your instructor demonstrated underwater navigation, an important diving fundamental that, as you discovered on your subsequent dives, you learn and apply easily through a few principles and practice. The Navigation Dive in the Adventures in Diving program takes the rudimentary skills you've picked up, and expands them so you can use them with greater accuracy and under wider circumstances.

KEY CONCEPT

Underline/highlight the answers to this question as you read:

1. What are five benefits of mastering underwater navigation?

THERE'S NAVIGATION AND THEN THERE'S NAVIGATION

"Hey, I find my way around. What do I need a "nav" dive for"? Good question. Navigation can be one of those things that you don't recognize the benefits of until you really, really need it, or until you've followed a navigation ace who takes you straight from one place to the next with no wasted effort. Almost any diver can wander around in a general direction and eventually end up in the right place, but you'll find that greater precision brings with it at least five distinct benefits.

Reduces Anxiety and Confusion

If you've ever been completely disoriented underwater, you know it can create anxiety, especially if you're low on air and would prefer to avoid surfacing (due to boat traffic or chop, for example). You don't know which way to go, which can be disquieting because you're not sure where to head if you need to cut the dive short. Or, you may have a general idea of where you are, but be confused about where you're trying to go, which can be irritating as your air supply drops while you search. It's really annoying to find your "hot spot" just in time to leave due to low air.

Navigation eliminates stress and confusion because you will always know where you are, which way to go, and how far you are from the boat or shore.

Avoids Long Surface Swims

If you're not good at underwater navigation and your dive objective is some distance from the boat or shore, the only way to reach it without losing your way is to swim on the surface and then descend. Likewise, if you get turned around during a dive, when you run low on air you have no alternative but to ascend where you are and swim back on the surface. Not only are surface swims more tiring and less interesting than swimming underwater, but also in some areas with high boat traffic, they may be more hazardous.

Increases the Effectiveness of a Dive Plan

Navigation helps make a dive plan effective by eliminating guesswork about the time and air needed to reach your objective and return. For example, if you and your buddy plan to take pictures on a familiar part of a reef, you'll swim straight there rather than waste time searching for it. Navigation means you use more of your time doing what you came to do and less trying to find your way about.

Avoids Buddy Separation

When you and your buddy plan a dive, navigation takes you together along the same path to an agreed-upon destination, minimizing the likelihood that you'll be separated from one another. If you stray apart momentarily, you both know where to look and are more likely to find each other within a minute. This avoids spending time and air reuniting on the surface.

Conserves Air

Anything that saves you time saves you air. Anything that helps you be confident and relax saves you air. More air means more time doing what you like (taking pictures, observing fish, whatever), and makes for a relaxing underwater swim back to the boat or shore instead of a not-so-relaxing surface swim.

Although underwater navigation benefits all diving, it's especially valuable for some specialized activities. For example, underwater navigation helps you avoid disorientation during night dives and it's easier to search for and recover a lost object when you know how to find your way.

REVIEW

Navigation 1
1. Learning underwater navigation is important because it (check all that apply):
   - ☐ a. reduces confusion and anxiety.
   - ☐ b. makes surface swims more enjoyable.
   - ☐ c. increases the effectiveness of a dive plan.
   - ☐ d. extends your no decompression limits.
   - ☐ e. conserves air.

How'd you do?
1. a, c, e.

Key CONCEPT

Underline/highlight the answers to this question as you read:

1. What are five methods for estimating distance underwater, and how do you use them?

DISTANCE ESTIMATION

Although navigation requires some practice and applies several techniques to know where you are and where you're going, you really only need to know two things: which way you're headed, and how far you travel. All navigation techniques accomplish one or the other of these.

Let's look at distance estimation – knowing how far you travel. There are five methods commonly used: kick cycles, elapsed time, tank pressure, arm spans and measured line or tape.

Kick Cycles

One of the most convenient ways to gauge distance is to count kick cycles. A kick cycle is the distance you cover when both of your legs complete one fin

One of the most convenient ways to gauge distance is to count kick cycles. A kick cycle is the distance you cover when both of your legs complete one fin stroke. To track kick cycles, choose either leg and count each time that leg returns to the same position.

stroke. To track kick cycles, choose either leg and count each time that leg returns to the same position.

The distance you travel in one kick cycle is usually consistent. During your navigation dive, you'll count your kick cycles as you swim 30 metres/100 feet. If it takes you 40 kick cycles, you know you travel about .75 metres/2.5 feet with each kick cycle. Then if you were to swim 100 kick cycles, you'd have traveled approximately 75 metres/250 feet.

Gauge your kick cycles by swimming in the same, relaxed pace you use when diving normally. Measure kick cycles while swimming underwater because surface-swimming is slower, and so your kick cycles will differ from your underwater swimming measurements. You'll find that kick cycles are most accurate in calm, still water, though in surge they're also moderately accurate if you maintain a steady pace because the back-and-forth water motion tends to cancel itself out.

Kick cycles are particularly useful for measuring medium to long distances, and have the advantage of allowing you to stop, if necessary, and then resume your distance estimation. However, changes in your gear will affect kick cycles from one dive to the next. The size and stiffness of your fins, drag from a larger tank or accessories like cameras, or diving overweighted will affect the distance you cover with each cycle. If you change fins or anything that alters how streamlined you are, you'll need to remeasure your kick cycles, though they'll still be consistent within the same dive. Current and water motion can affect accuracy, too.

Changes in your gear will affect kick cycles from one dive to the next. For example, drag from accessories like cameras will affect the distance you cover with each cycle.

Elapsed Time

You can also gauge distance underwater by measuring the time it takes to swim a known distance. If you know it takes you 30 seconds to swim about 30 metres/100 feet, you can estimate your travel distance by timing your swim.

In addition to kick cycles, you'll measure how long it takes you to swim 30 metres/100 feet during your underwater navigation dive. As with kick cycles, swim at your normal, relaxed pace. The primary disadvantage of measuring distance with elapsed time is that if you stop or pause, you can throw off the measurements. Current can also reduce your accuracy.

You can gauge distance underwater by measuring the time it takes to swim a known distance. If you know it takes you 30 seconds to swim about 30 metres/100 feet, you can estimate your travel distance by timing your swim.

Tank Pressure

You can use tank pressure to measure distance for navigating patterns like tracking elapsed time. When remaining at approximately the same depth and activity level, your breathing rate is uniform, so you can base your distance covered during a normal swim on the amount of air you use. For example, if you're navigating a square pattern, you could swim in a straight line until you've used 15 bar/200 psi, then turn 90 degrees and swim until you've used another 15 bar/200 psi and so on until you've completed a square.

The advantages of using tank pressure are that it's often simpler than using a watch and that you're constantly monitoring your air supply. It's not very accurate for measuring specific distances, however, if your depth changes significantly or if your breathing rate changes due to increased or reduced activity. But, you commonly use tank pressure as a general distance measure across different depths when you follow a course you'll return on. For instance, if you use 70 bar/1000 psi swimming away from your entry point, assuming little or no current, you can plan to use about the same coming back. Thus, you limit how far you go based on how much you need to return, plus a reserve.

Arm Spans

An accurate way to measure short distances is with arm spans. You measure by reaching forward with one hand, pivoting on it and reaching forward with the other hand, pivoting alternately until you cover the distance. It helps to know your arm span length ahead of time, but a good rule of thumb is that your arm span is about the same as your height.

Measured Line or Tape

The most accurate way to measure distance underwater is with a marked line or tape. Although this becomes unwieldy when you have to measure an extremely long distance or over terrain with obstacles, it is excellent for short to medium distances over relatively flat terrain. Measured lines are used for accurate measurement in wreck diving, underwater archaeology and in search and recovery.

REVIEW

Navigation 2

1. One kick cycle is counted for each kick.
   ☐ True   ☐ False

2. Which is not a commonly used method of estimating distance underwater?
   ☐ a. arm spans
   ☐ b. tank pressure
   ☐ c. wave lengths
   ☐ d. elapsed time

How'd you do?
1. False. One kick cycle is counted for each two kicks (one with each leg).   **2.** c.

NATURAL NAVIGATION UNDERWATER

Key CONCEPTS

Underline/highlight the answers
to these questions as you read:

1. What four predive observations can you make to assist
   with natural navigation?

2. What descent technique
   should you use to assist in
   natural navigation?

3. What six natural references
   do you commonly use to
   navigate underwater?

From your previous dive experience, you've probably already begun to learn natural navigation, even
if you don't know it. Finding direction from patterns in the sand, following the slope of a reef or
swimming against the current are all forms of natural navigation. Any given dive site has features that
you can use as navigational references. It's just a
matter of paying attention to the small details and
environmental features that tell you where you are.

Predive Observations

Natural navigation begins before you dive
by looking at the environment for navigation references. From the surface, you can
usually tell a great deal about what you'll
encounter underwater, and you can use
that information to determine where you
are when you're diving.

Waves, currents and tidal movement. The
direction of waves, currents and tides,
while changeable, usually remain consistent over the length of a dive (though they
will change on you once in a while — especially tides). You can determine wave and
current direction by watching floating debris, and in the case of tides, by consulting
tide tables. Once you know which way the
water flows, you can orient yourself by
swimming relative to the flow. Knowing the tides
avoids having to fight them on the way out and on
the way back.

Sun angle. Before getting in the water, check how
shadows fall and where the sun is in relation to
your planned travel direction. Even in turbid water
you can usually tell where the sun is and use it to
orient yourself.

Offshore objects and formations. It's useful to
note the position of reefs, piers, kelp beds, buoys
and other objects so that you know where you are

Natural navigation begins before you
dive by looking at the environment
for navigation references. From the
surface, you can usually tell a great
deal about what you'll encounter underwater, and you can use that information to determine where you are
when you're diving.

when you encounter them underwater. Waves breaking offshore may indicate a shallow reef or sandbar, giving you reference even if the reef or sandbar does not reach the surface.

Depth finder. If you're diving from a boat with a depth finder, you'll be able to see a "picture" of the bottom. Depth finders can show you bottom contours, wrecks and reefs, and even schools of fish, all of which can be references that tell you where you are during the dive. Well, not schools of fish. They move.

Natural navigation begins with your descent because how you descend can influence your ability to navigate. Ideally, descend in a head-up orientation (feet below head level) to prevent vertigo and disorientation.

Descents and Natural Navigation

Natural navigation begins with your descent because how you descend can influence your ability to navigate. Ideally, descend in a head-up orientation (feet below head level) to prevent vertigo and disorientation. Either you or your buddy should face the direction you intend to go and reach the bottom that way. Note the speed and direction of any current as you descend. These steps will ensure that you begin your dive properly oriented.

Natural References

Once underwater, you orient yourself through a variety of natural references that cue you through sight, touch and sound. The six most common of these are light and shadows, water movement, bottom composition and formations, bottom contours, plants and animals, and noise.

Light and shadows. Noting the sun's angle predive as mentioned, underwater you have a visual reference almost any time of day, but especially in early morning or late afternoon when the sun's lower on the horizon and casts distinct directional shadows. To use the sun and shadows for navigation, note their direction relative to your planned course. For example, at the start of a dive you note that the sun is on your right and/or underwater shadows are to the left. If you get disoriented during the dive, turn so the sun's on your right and shadows are to your left. This faces you in your

To use the sun and shadows for navigation, note their direction relative to your planned course.

original direction. If you turn so the sun's on your left, you face the direction you came from. Changes in light intensity can cue you to unnoticed depth changes.

Water movement. Currents provide one of the surest means of underwater navigation. If you're drift diving (see the Drift Diving section), or diving with the flow of a river, the current naturally navigates for you, carrying you where it will. In most cases, however, you swim against the current with the flow giving a constant bearing. Be aware that currents can shift direction during a dive, especially when tides change. Plan your dive with this in mind, so that the current helps you return to your

exit at the end of the dive. Pay attention to current direction and speed as you descend.

Surge is another reliable reference because the back-and-forth motion swings to and from shore or shallow areas. Because waves passing overhead and then flowing back to sea cause surge, you feel it most strongly in shallow water. However, large swells can make surge quite noticeable in even relatively deep water. When diving in surge, note the water movement to determine the direction toward shore. If you're disoriented to the point that you don't know which "swing" is shoreward, follow the surge in one direction and watch your depth gauge. In the majority of cases, shoreward will be shallower and seaward will be deeper, but it helps to know the dive site before hand.

Bottom composition and formations. Changes in bottom composition are something else to note during a dive. You may find that various areas have distinctly different bottoms, ranging from rock, to sand, mud or reef, depending upon the environment. Plant life (discussed shortly) can vary with the bottom type.

Even when the bottom composition is the same, water movement may create patterns you can use for navigation. Sand ripples are a good example; they form perpendicular to the water flow. In lakes and the ocean near shore, sand ripples always parallel shore; by swimming perpendicular to the ripples you'll head toward or away from shore (easily judged by whether you're getting deeper or shallower).

Bottom contour. The bottom almost always has notable contours suitable for navigation. You can follow a natural slope toward deeper water; rock ridges, coral reefs, kelp beds and in man-made lakes, even lines of felled trees form natural paths you can swim along. To follow contour, simply keep the slope or other reference on your right or left. To reverse your course, turn around and keep the contour on the opposite side.

Plants and animals. Aquatic plants and animals often have specific natural niches or characteristics that provide clues you can use for navigation. Some organisms live only at specific depths, cuing you to deeper or shallower water nearby. Other examples include sea fans, which always grow perpendicular to prevailing currents, and sand dollars (when alive), which typically orient themselves perpendicular to shore. Finding fish in open sand may suggest a reef or habitat near by.

Through careful observation and training, such as offered in the PADI Underwater Naturalist Specialty course and during the Underwater Naturalist Adventure Dive (see the Underwater Naturalist section), you recognize the different organisms that provide information about your location underwater. Note how these organisms lie relative to your position and travel direction at the start of your dive, and you can use them as a reference to maintain your direction or reorient yourself. But schools of fish move, so forget those.

Noise. As you learned in your Open Water Diver course, it's difficult to determine sound direction. But, you can still use sound as a navigation aid by paying attention to its strength and your relative distance from it. Organisms on reefs sometimes click or crackle, telling you you're approaching or leaving it. The sound of a boat compressor or generator, the clanking of an anchor chain or rocks tumbling in the surf can all provide reliable information about your distance from the boat or shore.

USING UNDERWATER PATTERNS

Underline/highlight the answers to these questions as you read:

1. What four patterns do divers use for underwater navigation?

2. What are six ways you can use an underwater pattern effectively?

It's much easier to know where you are and where you're going if you follow a predetermined pattern instead of swimming about randomly. This might sound restrictive, but you actually explore more of the dive site than you would by wandering aimlessly. You use your limited air and bottom time more effectively when you use a pattern suited to the dive site. Out-and-back-lines, squares/rectangles, triangles and circles are commonly used navigation patterns, each with its own characteristics.

Out-and-Back Lines

The simplest pattern is a straight line out, then reverse course and return to your exit. This works well along long narrow formations that form the line you follow. The edge of a reef or a wall may mark your line, or you may use a compass heading. Using a compass heading, watch for cross currents, which can push you off your intended path.

START

TURN

FINISH

The simplest pattern is a straight line out, then reverse course and return to your exit.

Square/Rectangle

Squares and rectangles cover more area than a line. You can make 90 degree turns easily whether or not you use your compass, so they're suitable patterns for either natural or compass navigation. A typical rectangle pattern might be to swim out from shore, turn 90 degrees and swim parallel to shore (perhaps following a reef), then turn 90 degrees and swim toward shore. In shallow water you might turn 90 degrees again to swim (perhaps at safety stop depth) parallel to shore to your exit.

Triangles

You don't commonly use triangles in natural navigation, but more so when using a compass. A triangle covers a wider area than a straight line and may be useful in areas where a rectangle or square is impractical, but again, it's difficult to navigate a triangle using only natural navigation. Triangle patterns without a compass usually happen when underwater features create a triangle that you can follow conveniently.

Circles

It's nearly impossible to swim in an accurate circle with either natural or compass navigation. For this reason, you use circles primarily for underwater searches with a line. One diver holds the line while the other pivots around in a circular search pattern. You can learn more about using circular patterns in the Search and Recovery Adventure Dive and in the PADI Search and Recovery Specialty course.

Effective Pattern Use

There are six ways you can use underwater patterns more effectively. First, discuss and agree on a pattern with your buddy as part of your dive plan. This helps prevent confusion and buddy separation. Second, try to visualize the pattern both before and during the dive, so that you'll have a

Look Ma, No Compass!

Natural Navigation 90 Degree Turns

It's easy to make a 90 degree underwater turn, even without using your compass for reference.

1. Swim in a straight line until you're ready to turn. Stop at your turn point, but keep facing your original travel direction.

2. Point your arm straight out to your side, right or left (whichever way you want to turn) so that it points along your new travel direction.

3. Keeping your arm stationary relative to the new direction, turn so that you face straight ahead. Your arm should point directly ahead of you, and you should be facing your new direction and ready to continue swimming.

"map" in your mind's eye. Third, use a small pattern and swim slowly along it. Large patterns are more difficult to follow accurately. Fourth, if you leave the pattern to look at something, remember where you were and the general heading so you can resume the pattern. Fifth, have one buddy navigate and follow the pattern. Sixth, if you become disoriented, surface slowly and carefully and check

Try to visualize the pattern both before and during the dive, so that you'll have a "map" in your mind's eye.

Theoretical Dive Pattern

Actual Dive Pattern

Start

your position. If you've deviated from your pattern, you can swim to intercept and resume your original pattern, or you can develop a new navigation plan based on where you are.

Quick REVIEW

Navigation 4

1. Patterns for underwater navigation include (check all that apply):
   - ☐ a. circle
   - ☐ b. rectangle/square
   - ☐ c. triangle
   - ☐ d. pentagon
   - ☐ e. out-and-back line
   - ☐ f. staircase

2. One of the ways to use underwater patterns effectively is to have both buddies share responsibility for following the pattern.
   - ☐ True   ☐ False

How'd you do?

1. a, b, c, e; 2. False. One buddy should navigate the pattern. However, buddies should discuss the pattern to use before the dive.

COMPASS NAVIGATION

You can compare navigating underwater to navigating in the air. In clear weather, a pilot can navigate by following landmarks and roads, but in poor weather, at night, or in the clouds, the pilot relies on instruments. Similarly, while you use natural references for much underwater navigation, when you navigate in poor visibility, at night, or in midwater where you can't see the bottom, you'll rely on your compass. Let's review and build upon what you learned about compasses and compass use in your Open Water Diver course.

Compass Features

The first step in underwater compass navigation is to invest in one suitable for the job. The ideal underwater compass has all of the following features:

Liquid filled. A liquid-filled compass withstands pressure and dampens needle movement so it's easier to read.

Free-swinging needle. Choose a compass with a needle (or compass card – a disk with the needle printed on it) that rotates even if the compass isn't perfectly level (which is frequently the case underwater).

Numerical degree markings. You need degree numbers, rather than just north, south, east and west markings, to navigate patterns and when noting bearings in your dive log.

Luminous features. Glow-in-the-dark markings and needle will help at night and in low visibility because you won't have to point your light at the compass and try to use it at the same time.

Lubber line/direct sight and bezel. As you learned in your Open Water Diver course, you normally use your compass by swimming along an imaginary line

Key CONCEPTS

Underline/highlight the answers to these questions as you read:

1. What features are essential in a good underwater compass?

2. How do you hold and use a compass to maintain an accurate heading while swimming?

3. How do you set a compass heading? a reciprocal heading? headings to navigate a square or rectangle? headings to navigate a triangle?

4. What are several useful hints for navigating underwater with a compass?

Emerging Navigational Technologies

Electronics has touched almost every aspect of our lives, including navigation. GPS (Global Positioning System) receivers guide hikers, cars, airplanes and practically anything else that moves from point to point, with accuracy as close as 10 metres/30 feet.

At this writing there are no mass marketed similar devices for underwater use (GPS signals are too weak to receive easily underwater), but they're in development and may be available by the time you read this. It's an exciting direction for finding your direction underwater; before too long, divers may be using the underwater equivalent of GPS instead of compasses.

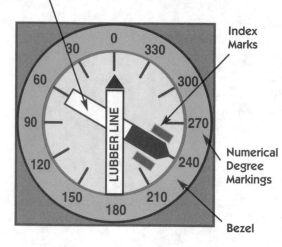

Magnetic North Needle

Index Marks

Numerical Degree Markings

Bezel

LUBBER LINE

straight through the center of the compass. A lubber line is a marked line bisecting the compass face (or along the compass side) that you use to align yourself with your travel direction. A direct sight compass has no lubber line, but uses a sight over the compass face to accomplish the same purpose. You use the movable bezel to set your desired heading.

A few new electronic compasses accomplish the same tasks with digital readouts. Some models display the heading you're facing, while others display a compass face similar to a standard compass. Features for setting headings while navigating vary greatly from one electronic compass to the next — see the manufacturer literature for specifics.

If you carry your compass in a console, hold the console with both hands centered in front of you, with your elbows tucked into your sides so the lubber line aligns with your body centerline.

Holding the Compass

A compass is no more accurate than the person using it, and accuracy starts with how you hold it. Holding it incorrectly probably accounts for the vast majority of compass navigation errors divers experience. To hold a compass correctly, whether you wear it on your arm or carry it in your instrument console, align the lubber line with the center line of your body.

If you wear the compass on your arm (let's assume your left), hold your right arm straight ahead and grasp it with your left hand so that your middle finger rests in the depression behind your right elbow. This should put your compass squarely in front of you. If not, adjust your grip and/or the compass position until it does. If you carry your compass in a console, hold the console with both hands centered in front of you, with your elbows

If you wear the compass on your arm (e.g. your left), hold your right arm straight ahead and grasp it with your left hand to put the compass squarely in front of you.

tucked into your sides, again so the lubber line aligns with your body centerline.

Swimming With the Compass

Holding the compass properly, you swim with the compass lubber line centered with your body's centerline, looking over (not down on) the compass face. Keep the compass as level as possible so the needle doesn't lock, and keep the needle inside the index marks on the bezel (more about setting the bezel in a moment). With practice, you'll be able to swim in a very straight line.

Setting the Compass

Setting the compass is based on two points: First, the compass needle always points to the magnetic north pole. If you find the needle no longer within the compass index marks when you're navigating, either you've turned off course or the north pole moved thousands of kilometres. (Guess which is most likely. Actually, the magnetic north pole *does* move, but so slowly it requires decades to affect your readings. This movement causes magnetic declination, which is a difference between true north and magnetic north. This difference has no practical effect on basic underwater compass use.) Second, you *always* travel along the lubber line. The bezel and index marks help you maintain the relative angle of the lubber line (direction of travel) to the needle (north) so that you swim in a straight line.

Setting a heading. To set a heading, point the lubber line in your desired travel direction. Next, rotate the bezel to set the index marks over the compass needle (it's a good habit to note the degree heading, too). Now swim along the lubber line as you just learned, keeping the needle between the index marks. If the

To set a heading, point the lubber line in your desired travel direction. Then, rotate the bezel to set the index marks over the compass needle.

Step 1
Aim Compass

Step 2
Align Index Marks

Direction
of
Travel

needle leaves the marks, you're off course. Turn until you return the needle within the marks, and resume swimming.

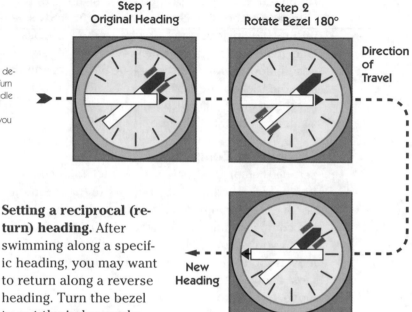

Step 1
Original Heading

Step 2
Rotate Bezel 180°

Direction of Travel

For a reciprocal heading, turn the bezel to put the index marks 180 degrees from the original heading. Turn until you center the compass needle between the index marks; you should be facing back to where you came from.

New Heading

Step 3
Turn to Recenter Compass Needle

Setting a reciprocal (return) heading. After swimming along a specific heading, you may want to return along a reverse heading. Turn the bezel to put the index marks 180 degrees from the original heading. Turn until you center the compass needle between the index marks; you should be facing back to where you came from. Return by swimming along the reciprocal heading.

Navigating a square/rectangle. To compass navigate a square or a rectangle, begin by setting a heading for the first side and swimming the desired distance (use your distance estimation techniques to measure). Rotate the bezel 90 degrees and turn to realign the needle with the index marks. Add 90 degrees for a right turn, or subtract 90 degrees for a left. (When adding, due North is 0 degrees; when subtracting it is 360 degrees.)

Swim along the new heading the desired length and then rotate the bezel another 90 degrees in the same direction (right or left) for the next turn. Repeat the process until you complete the pattern.

To compass navigate a square or a rectangle, begin by setting a heading for the first side and swimming the desired distance. Rotate the bezel 90 degrees and turn to realign the needle with the index marks.

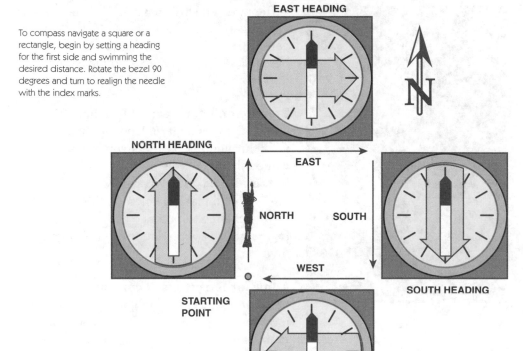

EAST HEADING

NORTH HEADING

EAST

NORTH   SOUTH

WEST

SOUTH HEADING

STARTING POINT

WEST HEADING

Using your compass in a triangular pattern is the same as with a square or rectangle, except that you turn the bezel 120 degrees for each turn.

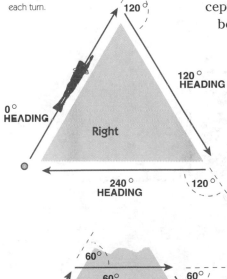

120°

120° HEADING

0° HEADING

Right

240° HEADING

120°

60°

60° HEADING

60°

Wrong

120° HEADING

0° HEADING

Navigating a triangle. Using your compass in a triangular pattern is the same as with a square or rectangle, except that you turn the bezel 120 degrees for each turn. (Note: A compass measures the outside of each turn, which is why triangle pattern turns are 120 degrees rather than 60. Make five 60 degree turns if you want to navigate a hexagon.)

Useful Hints for Compass Use

Here are a few pointers that will make using a compass easier and more accurate.

Trust your compass. Sometimes it feels like your compass is "wrong," but the compass works based on basic laws of physics, whereas your sense of direction is based on the same intuition you use to predict the weather. Go with the compass.

Use natural references. The combination of natural navigation with compass navigation is the most effective navigation. The compass closes gaps where you can't effectively navigate with landmarks, and natural navigation helps offsets any mistakes you make using your compass.

Practice on land. Become familiar with your compass by using it on land. Set headings and walk through the patterns you intend to use while relying entirely on your compass (but watch where you're going so you don't step into an open manhole or something). You'll have a chance to practice with your instructor before making your Underwater Navigation dive.

Allow for the effects of currents. A compass helps you swim in a straight line, but water movement such as currents or surge can carry you off course. If currents are common in your local area, your instructor may teach you how to navigate accordingly.

Be prepared to navigate around obstacles. This is usually accomplished with four 90 degree turns detouring the obstacle. The first and last legs of the detour should be the same length.

Become familiar with your compass by using it on land. Set headings and walk through the patterns you intend to use while relying entirely on your compass (but watch where you're going so you don't step into an open manhole or something).

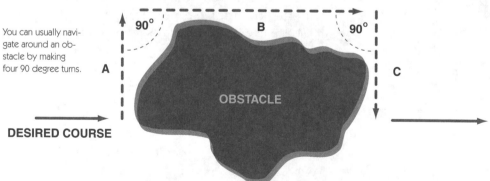

You can usually navigate around an obstacle by making four 90 degree turns.

90°   90°

A   B   C

OBSTACLE

DESIRED COURSE

Share responsibilities midwater. If you're navigating in midwater, have one buddy read the compass and the other monitor depth. The depth buddy can hold the compass buddy's arm to keep the team together while watching instruments.

Use intentional error on long distances. If you're looking for a small, specific destination a long distance away, chances are you're going to miss. Sorry, but even the best underwater navigation just isn't that precise when you start swimming hundreds of metres/feet. So, aim for slightly to the right or left of your target. If you miss your mark (probably), you know which way to search.

Use compass aids for accuracy. A compass board extends the compass lubber line, thus increasing your accuracy. Heading calculators like the Nav-Finder let you map irregular courses, and show you compass headings for patterns without having to calculate in your head.

Heading calculators like the Nav-Finder let you map irregular courses, and show you compass headings for patterns without having to calculate in your head.

If you're navigating in midwater, have one buddy read the compass and the other monitor depth. The depth buddy can hold the compass buddy's arm to keep the team together while watching instruments.

Understand the limits. Underwater navigation, with or without a compass, is useful in relatively small areas. If you need to cover a long distance, you may be better off swimming on the surface or surfacing periodically to check your location. Plan your dive within the reasonable limits of underwater navigation.

Take your time. Effective navigation relies on taking your time, relaxing and paying attention to your compass and other navigational clues. The more you hurry toward a destination, the more likely you are to end up somewhere else.

PADI Underwater Navigator Specialty

At your instructor's discretion, your Underwater Navigation Adventure Dive may be credited as the first dive in the PADI Underwater Navigator Specialty course. The Underwater Navigator course gives you more opportunities to apply and practice the skills and techniques covered in this section in a variety of situations.

Navigation 5

1. Which features are important in an underwater compass (check all that apply)?
   - ☐ a. lubber line
   - ☐ b. compass board
   - ☐ c. liquid filled
   - ☐ d. wrist lanyard

2. A compass should be held
   - ☐ a. level so the needle doesn't lock.
   - ☐ b. tipped toward you for good visibility.

3. When setting a compass heading, the_____points in the direction of travel and you turn the_____ so the index marks are over the _____.
   - ☐ a. compass needle, bezel, lubber line
   - ☐ b. lubber line, compass needle, bezel
   - ☐ c. lubber line, bezel, compass needle

4. The hints for compass navigation include knowing that your compass is an unreliable instrument that you should ignore based on your sense of direction.
   - ☐ True   ☐ False

How'd you do?

1. a, c; **2.** a; **3.** c; **4.** False. You should trust your compass, even when you feel disoriented.

Buoyancy and Navigation

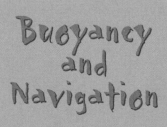

When you're focusing on swimming accurately, you don't want to complicate your task with awkward buoyancy control. Maintaining neutral buoyancy is important for keeping depth changes under control, for staying off the bottom and for avoiding damage to sensitive aquatic life. The Peak Performance Buoyancy Adventure Dive shows you how to raise your buoyancy skills to proficiency.

As you learn new skills in the Advanced Open Water program, don't neglect to make buoyancy checks before each Adventure Dive. Diving properly weighted is not only important for safety, but also for the environment and for learning.

Both Point the Right Way

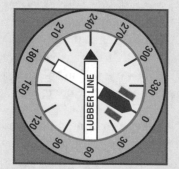

Direct Reading Compass

Dive compasses come in various models and sizes, including direct or indirect reading compasses. What's the difference? Move the bezel on a compass – if the degree headings move with the bezel, you're holding a direct reading compass. If the headings don't move, you're holding an indirect reading compass. On a direct reading compass the numbers count upward clockwise around the dial, whereas with an indirect, they count upward anti-clockwise. It doesn't matter which you get – both do the same job – but the way you set each for a particular degree heading differs.

Setting a heading: Suppose you want to set a heading for 240 degrees. With a direct reading compass, rotate the bezel to put 240 at the end of the lubber line. Now turn to put the compass needle between the index marks; you're on a 240 degree heading.

With an indirect reading compass, rotate the bezel until the index marks sit at 240. Turn to put the compass needle between the index marks and you'll be on a 240 degree heading.

Taking a bearing: To get a bearing (such as the heading from one object to another), point the lubber line in the desired direction, then rotate the bezel to place the index marks over the needle. With a direct reading compass your bearing is the number at the end of the lubber line. With an indirect, it's the number by the index marks. Here's a tip: If you always get 0, you're using direct compass methods with an indirect compass, or vice-versa.

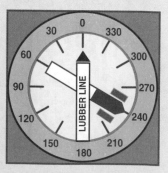

Indirect Reading Compass

UNDERWATER PHOTOGRAPHY

Introduction

It's hard to imagine activities more versatile than underwater imaging: underwater photography and underwater videography. Whether snorkeling, exploring amid reefs, under ice, at altitude, or on wrecks, if there's something worth seeing, there's something worth photographing or videoing. This makes underwater photography a pursuit that mixes well with your other diving activities, and one that permits you to share the underwater world with nondivers.

Not that long ago, only those with patience, extensive photographic expertise and a mountain of cash to invest in obscure and elaborate equipment took pictures underwater. Today, however, if you're interested, underwater photography lies within your reach and ability. New cameras and camera systems cost less and apply technology that makes it far easier to take a sharp, properly exposed photo. Digital cameras (electronic imaging) as well as conventional film cameras offer a new picture-taking option above and below the surface. Perhaps interesting most divers, casual picture taking with submersible point-and-shoot cameras give you underwater snapshots as easily as the nonsubmersible models do in air. For more serious photography, you have sophisticated technology in underwater camera systems at affordable prices. The world of underwater photography is wide open – all you have to do is start.

ACCOMMODATING **YOUR** INTEREST IN PHOTOGRAPHY

Now let's jump into the fascinating world of f-stops, shutter speeds, film grain, reciprocity failure and depth of . . . Right about now, about half the people who read this are saying, "Skip that, I just want to take pictures. Let me do that and then if I'm interested, I'll come back to that stuff."

Okay, no worries. That's what we'll do. About now the other readers are saying, "Hey, wait, what about me? I've already been taking underwater snapshots and I want to learn about f-shutter thingees or whatever they're called. That's why I'm making this Adventure Dive."

Again, no problem. This section and the Underwater Photography Adventure Dive accommodate both needs. (Not often you get to have your cake and eat it, too.)

1. If you're mainly interested in getting some decent snapshots with minimal concern for the "art" and "science" of photography, keep going into the next subsection, The Underwater Photo Fast Track. We'll take you through a good, all-round set up that will give you acceptable pictures the majority of the time. You'll learn what to do without long explanations as to why. (But we'll tell you where to look if you decide you want to know.)

2. If you're interested in learning more about the principles and details of photography (even if you plan to use a snapshot-type camera), you can skip ahead to Underwater Photography and the Aquatic Environment. Or, you can read through the Underwater Photo Fast Track to review the basics, and then continue into Underwater Photography and the Aquatic Environment.

Underwater Photography
See the *Underwater Photographer Manual* and *Underwater Photography* video

THE UNDERWATER PHOTO FAST TRACK

Underwater Snapshot Camera Setups and Film

Key CONCEPTS

Underline/highlight the answers to these questions as you read:

1. What kind of camera gear and film are ideal for underwater snapshots?

2. How do you set up your camera for underwater photography?

3. How do you set your camera (and strobe if it has one) for automatic underwater pictures?

4. How do you set and hold your camera for sharp pictures?

5. What can you do to make your pictures as colorful as possible?

6. What's the "good underwater pictures guideline"?

7. What do you need to do after a dive to take care of your photo gear?

If your primary interest in underwater pictures is some interesting snaps you can show friends, you've never had it easier. Today there are more easy-to-operate, yet versatile automatic underwater cameras than ever before. It seems that with each passing day, these cameras become more compact and easier to use. Likewise, film has become increasingly sophisticated (if you need film at all – there are more and more filmless digital cameras) so that you get useable pictures in surprisingly difficult lighting conditions. Between the two, today almost anyone can take decent underwater photos on the first try.

Virtually all point-and-shoot cameras automatically adjust the exposure (amount of light coming into the camera) and either focus automatically for a sharp picture, or don't need to be focused.

Camera gear. In selecting your submersible point-and-shoot camera, it's hard to go wrong. Virtually all of those available automatically adjust the exposure (amount of light coming into the camera) and either focus automatically for a sharp picture, or don't need to be focused. The one feature to look for is a *strobe* (electronic flash). Although you can get acceptable pictures without one, by having a strobe you'll get much more colorful pictures. (See Understanding Light for Underwater Photography for background information.) Underwater, a strobe that attaches to one side is generally preferable to one that's built right into the camera, but those with it built into the camera still give good pictures and are more compact.

Most popular snapshot cameras are 35mm cameras (that's the film size that you ask for), though a growing number are digital and don't need film.

Underwater, a strobe that attaches to one side is generally preferable to one that's built right into the camera, but those with it built into the camera still give good pictures and are more compact.

For underwater snaps with a 35mm camera, ask for 100 ISO film, 36 exposures.

Film. You can get all kinds of film, but for underwater snapshots your best bet is *100 speed color print film*. This film gives you good color, and it's very forgiving if the lighting isn't right-on. You can buy this in different length rolls; in 35 mm you'll normally find 12, 24 and 36 exposure (picture) lengths. Since you can't change film underwater, you'll probably want to use the longest roll you can get. If you have a 35 mm snapshot camera, you'd ask for "35 mm 100 speed color print film, 36 exposures." (See Film and Underwater Photography for background information.)

If you're using a digital camera, the "film" is built in, so you obviously don't need to choose any.

Setting Up Your Camera

Ready to set up your camera and strobe? Good. You want to do this in a dry, clean environment, away from wet divers and confusion. You should be dry, too, because while the outside of a submersible camera can get wet, water on the inside – even only a drop or two – can destroy it.

 Here's what you're going to need:

• the manufacturer instruction book

• a roll of film (except for digital cameras)

• fresh batteries

• silicone grease, cotton swabs and a clean, lint-free cloth

Step One: Clean the o-rings. Your camera and strobe can go underwater because they have watertight o-ring seals. You need to maintain the o-rings or your camera/strobe may leak. You need to remove and clean all user-accessible o-rings, which usually include the camera back where you load the film, and the battery compartment(s). Check the manufacturer instructions for your gear to be sure you take care of all the o-rings you need to.

Remove the o-ring from its groove by pinching it with your finger or lifting it with a blunt, soft instrument like the edge of a credit card. Do not use sharp objects such as dental tools that can damage the o-ring, or worse, the o-ring groove.

First, remove the o-ring from its groove by pinching it with your finger or lifting it with a blunt, soft instrument like the edge of a credit card. Do not use sharp objects such as dental tools that can damage the o-ring, or worse, the o-ring groove.

Next, wipe the o-ring clean by gently pulling it through the soft cloth, while inspecting for nicks or damage. Avoid stretching the o-ring as much as possible. If you find any damage, replace the o-ring – using a damaged o-ring will probably result in a flooded camera or strobe.

After cleaning, lubricate the o-ring by applying a thin coat of silicone grease. The o-ring should appear wet, but not have globs or excess residue of grease, which will not help the seal, but attract dirt that can make it leak.

After cleaning, lubricate the o-ring by applying a thin coat of silicone grease. The o-ring should appear wet, but not have globs or excess residue of grease, which will not help the seal, but attract dirt that can make it leak.

Set the o-ring aside on a clean surface for a moment, and use a cotton swab to wipe old grease and dirt from the o-ring groove. Be sure the groove is completely clean. Also clean the area the o-ring seals against. If dirt remains, you can't rely on the seal. A single hair is all you need to get a leak. Then reseat the o-ring carefully with your fingers.

Step Two: Put in fresh batteries. There's nothing more irritating than having your batteries quit halfway through a dive. Put in fresh batteries (or recharge rechargeables) according to the manufacturer guidelines. With some systems your camera and strobe run off a single set of batteries, and with others you use a set for each. Be sure to use alkaline batteries (if using disposables) because nonalkaline don't hold up well to the power demands of underwater photography.

Step Three: Load the film or clear the memory. Put in your film according to the manufacturer's guidelines. This may include "telling" the camera that you're using 100 speed film by setting it on the camera; other cameras read the film speed automatically.

If you're using a digital camera, you may need to clear the memory of previous pictures so you can take more. Depending on your camera, you may need to download any you want to save to a computer, disk or memory card.

Step Four: Seal the camera. Making sure all o-rings haven't picked up any debris, hair or dirt, close the back and any other open compartments (like the battery compartments). Make sure everything is sealed according to the manufacturer specifications.

Step Five: Set the autoexposure. This will vary somewhat from camera to camera, but will generally be pretty simple. On most cameras and strobes, you set the camera on "Automatic" or "A" for automatic; the camera and strobe will automatically control the exposure for a good picture. With some, you'll set an exposure range, such as whether you're taking pictures in broad daylight, or underwater near dusk. Your strobe will usually be automatic, too, though you may have some simple settings depending on lighting conditions, or how far you are from what you're taking a picture of.

Set the camera for autoexposure. Some cameras are permanently set for autoexposure – see the manufacturer instructions.

Most cameras will have a warning light or other indicator that tells you if there's not enough light to take a picture. With a strobe you can even take pictures on a night dive, but remember to stay within the range of your strobe. See the manufacturer literature for specifics on how to set your camera, strobe and your strobe range.

Step Six: Set the focus. You can have one of three systems: autofocus, focus free or estimated focus. Turn on autofocus according to the manufacturer instructions. For focus free, there's nothing to set – everything from a specific distance (usually about a metre/three feet) and beyond is in focus. For estimated focus, you judge the distance by eye and set the camera accordingly (don't worry – there's plenty of room for error).

An important point here – remember that everything looks closer than it really is underwater. Set estimated focus for the apparent distance – not the real distance – because the camera sees it like you do. (See Understanding Light for Underwater Photography for background information.)

Step Seven: Attach a wrist lanyard or clip. If your system doesn't have one, put on a clip, wrist lanyard or something that lets you have both hands free when you want. This makes it much easier if you're adjusting buoyancy while descending on a line, repositioning a weight belt, or something like that.

You can have one of three systems: autofocus, focus free or estimated focus. Set the focus according to the manufacturer instructions.

Taking Pictures Underwater

When you take pictures underwater, you want to end up with photos that are sharp, colorful and have a pleasing look (composition).

For sharp pictures: Setting the focus properly was the first step for sharp pictures, but you can blur pictures by moving the camera. Try to hold the camera as steady as possible, exhaling steadily and gently as you squeeze the shutter button – don't hold your breath. You can sometimes get blurred pictures if you try to take snaps when there's not enough light, so follow the manufacturer guidelines regarding low-light indicators. (See Photographic Composition for background information.)

For colorful pictures: You get the best color by staying in shallow water, by staying as close to your subject as possible, and by using your strobe. You'll get the best color by staying above about 10 metres/30 feet, and by being no farther from your subject than about one and a half metres/five feet.

For good composition: You want your subject to stand out clearly in a photo for the best look. Underwater, the easiest way to do this is to be slightly

If your system doesn't have one, put on a clip, wrist lanyard or something that lets you have both hands free when you want. This makes it much easier if you're adjusting buoyancy while descending on a line, clearing your mask, or something like that.

lower than the subject, shooting at an upward angle. (See Understanding Lens Openings and Shutter Speeds for background information.)

Applying these three principles at once, you get the "good underwater pictures guideline," which says, get close, get low, shoot upward and use a strobe.

For the sake of you and the environment. Remember when you're taking pictures to pay attention to your buoyancy control and the environment

around you. Don't concentrate on your photography so much that you bang into sensitive reef, or kick up a silt cloud. In some places underwater photographers have a bad reputation because they let photography get in the way of protecting the very world they're photographing – don't become part of that stigma yourself.

And, while you're keeping the environment safe, keep yourself safe. Don't neglect checking your SPG, dive computer, watch, etc. as you take pictures. A good habit is to check your instruments, location and buddy after every picture.

The good underwater pictures guideline: Get close, get low, shoot upward and use a strobe.

Taking Care of Your Photo Gear

The most important step in caring for your camera is washing it in cool, fresh water immediately after the dive. If you can't wash it immediately, keep it wet (salt or fresh water) until you can. *Don't* let it dry out; because once salt crystallizes it is very difficult to remove, causing the most long-term damage and wear to your equipment.

Leave everything assembled and immerse it in cool, fresh water, gently swishing back and forth for at least the first 60 seconds, then allow it to soak for at least 30 minutes. This gets most of the salt and minerals out.

After soaking, gently towel-dry it, and then open it in an environment where spray, splashes and moisture aren't a threat. Dry your hair or wear a hat so you don't drip into it when taking it apart. Remove the film and care for the o-rings as described above.

Although you take care of the main o-rings, you need to have most underwater cameras serviced annually by a specialist who can replace o-rings and other seals that you can't reach. Follow any maintenance as prescribed by the equipment's instruction manual, and your camera and strobe will last many, many years.

Rinse your camera thoroughly after using it.

Photography 1

1. The ideal camera gear and film for underwater snapshots include (check all that apply):
   ☐ a. automatic exposure.
   ☐ b. 100 speed print film.
   ☐ c. manual override of all controls.
   ☐ d. a strobe.

2. Setting up your camera for underwater photography includes (check all that apply):
   ☐ a. cleaning the o-rings.
   ☐ b. putting in fresh batteries.
   ☐ c. attaching a clip or lanyard.
   ☐ d. setting the focus.

3. You want to set your snapshot camera
   ☐ a. for automatic exposure according to manufacturer instructions.
   ☐ b. for manual exposure.

4. For sharp pictures underwater, push the shutter button sharply and rapidly.
   ☐ True   ☐ False

5. For the best color, (check all that apply):
   ☐ a. stay as shallow as possible.
   ☐ b. stay close to your subject.
   ☐ c. avoid using your strobe.

6. The "good underwater pictures guideline" is to get close, get low, shoot upward and use a strobe.
   ☐ True   ☐ False

7. If you can't rinse your camera gear immediately after a dive, your best bet is to dry it as much as possible until you can.
   ☐ True   ☐ False

How'd you do?
1. a, b, d. 2. a, b, c, d. 3. a. 4. False. Squeeze the shutter button gently. 5. a, b. 6. True. 7. False. Keep your camera gear sealed and wet until you can rinse it properly.

You're about ready for the Fast Track version of the Underwater Photography Adventure Dive. Go to the Knowledge Review and complete these questions: No. 4 (second part), No. 9 and No. 10.

UNDERWATER PHOTOGRAPHY AND THE AQUATIC ENVIRONMENT

Divers have been taking cameras underwater since the 1800s, but it wasn't until the 1950s that submersing photo equipment became routine rather than a complicated scientific experiment. The reason is that the underwater environment and photography don't mix well. Two immediate challenges face you as an underwater photographer: equipment corrosion and suspended particles.

Equipment Corrosion

Dissolved salts in water – particularly sea water – severely corrodes photographic equipment quickly. It destroys electronics beyond repair almost instantly. The corrosion destroys metals and electronics so quickly that even equipment specifically designed to get wet needs care to prevent corrosion. To prevent corrosion, you keep sensitive photo equipment and electronics apart from water, and properly wash what can get wet in fresh water after a dive. We'll discuss proper washing procedures in more detail in a bit.

Dissolved salts in water – particularly sea water – severely corrodes photographic equipment quickly. It destroys electronics beyond repair almost instantly. The corrosion destroys metals and electronics so quickly that even equipment specifically designed to get wet needs care to prevent corrosion.

Suspended Particles

Some divers compare underwater photography to taking pictures above water in fog; while that exaggerates it to some extent (at least in clear water), there's a lot of truth to it. Even in clear water, suspended particles – stirred sediment, microscopic organisms or other debris – float between your camera and your photo subject. These cause scattering, which deflects light off its normal path. Scattering creates a foggy effect that makes your photos less sharp, and blocks the amount of light reaching the camera.

To minimize suspended particle problems, you learn to get as close to your photo subject as possible to reduce the water – and therefore particles – between it and the camera. A good rule of thumb

Underline/highlight the answers to this question as you read:

1. How do underwater photographers deal with underwater particles and corrosion?

is that you should be no farther from the subject than one-fourth the water visibility distance. Proper camera and strobe (electronic flash) angles also help reduce suspended particle problems. Paying attention to your fins and body attitude minimizes how much silt you kick up, which exaggerates the problem. You'll learn more about these in a few moments.

Photography 2

1. Avoiding corrosion is a matter of (check all that apply):
   ☐ a. keeping sensitive equipment apart from water.
   ☐ b. getting close to your subject.
   ☐ c. using a flash.
   ☐ d. choosing the right gear.

How'd you do?

1. a.

UNDERSTANDING LIGHT FOR UNDERWATER PHOTOGRAPHY

When you first learned to dive, your instructor explained that water absorbs light, one color after another, making the underwater world darker and less colorful. You also learned that objects appear closer and larger than they really are. These properties of light affect what your camera sees just as they affect what you see.

Overcoming Light Loss

You overcome the loss of light underwater six ways as an underwater photographer:

Take natural light pictures with the sun overhead. If you're not using a strobe, try to take pictures between 10 a.m. and 2 p.m. when the sun's

Underline/highlight the answers to these questions as you read:

1. What are six ways to overcome light loss underwater?

2. What are four ways to overcome color loss underwater?

3. What happens when light bends passing through water, then glass and air?

4. How does your underwater camera focus on real and apparent distances to the subject?

directly overhead. Even when you do use a strobe, these hours give you the maximum light to work with. Similarly, a calm surface reflects less light away than a rough one.

Take natural light pictures when it's clear and bright above water. If you're not using a strobe, don't expect much from your pictures when it's overcast.

If you're not using a strobe, try to take pictures between 10 a.m. and 2 p.m. when the sun's directly overhead.

Use a strobe. The best overall solution to low light is to add light with a strobe, which as you'll see in a second, has other benefits relating to color.

Use high-speed films (or computer chip). "High-speed" or "fast" films have more sensitivity and require relatively less light than "slower" film. For digital cameras, some are more sensitive than others, or you can set the sensitivity higher.

Stay shallow. The shallower the water, the less distance light travels through the water, so the less of it the water absorbs.

Get close to your subject. The less water between you and your subject, the less light water absorbs as it travels from the subject to your camera.

Overcoming Color Loss

You use four techniques for keeping your photos colorful. Note that you use three of them for overcoming light loss in general.

Get close to your subject. The closer you are, the less water there is between you and your subject to absorb color.

Stay shallow. At shallower depths, less color has been absorbed by the water.

Use a color-correcting filter. Filters cannot restore lost colors, but they can help balance the colors that remain so the picture isn't too blue.

Use a strobe. The best overall solution is to use a strobe to put the color back. This is why you see underwater photographers using strobes even on bright days.

These two photos show that if you stay shallow, use a strobe to replace lost color and get close to your subject you can prevent color loss. The photo on the left was taken in shallow water, close to the subject but without a strobe. In the photo on the right, taken with a strobe, notice the reds and the more natural skin tones.

The Bending of Light

Light bends as it passes from one medium to another, such as when it passes from water, through glass, into air. As you're no doubt aware, this bending, or *refraction*, causes objects underwater to appear approximately 25 percent larger and/or closer (depending on your perspective) than they really are.

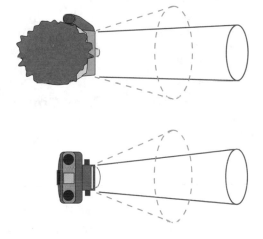

For practical purposes, a camera "sees" just like you do; to it, photographic subjects appear approximately 25 percent closer than they really are. For this reason, you always set a camera's focus distance for the *apparent* distance. If you set it or the actual distance, your picture won't be in focus.

Photography 3

1. Which of the following is not a method for over-coming light loss for underwater photography?
   ☐ a. take pictures between 10 a.m. and 2 p.m.
   ☐ b. use a strobe
   ☐ c. use a diver's light
   ☐ d. get close to your subject

2. A color correcting filter can help restore lost color underwater.
   ☐ True   ☐ False

3. Light bending as it travels from water to air makes objects appear approximately _____ than they really are.
   ☐ a. 25% farther away
   ☐ b. 25% closer
   ☐ c. 15% closer
   ☐ d. 15% farther away

4. You should set your camera focus on the _____ distance to your subject.
   ☐ a. actual
   ☐ b. apparent

How'd you do?
1. c;   **2.** False. Color correcting filters can help correct color balance, but they cannot restore lost color.   **3.** b;   **4.** b.

CONCEPTS

Underline/highlight the answers to these questions as you read:

1. When comparing two f/stops, which one allows the most amount of light through the lens?

2. When comparing two shutter speeds, which one allows the most amount of light to strike the film or computer chip?

UNDERSTANDING LENS OPENINGS AND SHUTTER SPEEDS

Regardless of how much light you have for your underwater pictures, for a properly exposed (not too bright nor too dark) photo you have to control the light coming into your camera. The lens opening and the shutter speed control how much light enters your camera and reaches the film or computer chip.

Lens Opening

The lens opening, or aperture controls the amount of light entering the camera. It's a hole in the middle of the lens that, depending upon the camera, you set manually or the camera sets automatically.

Aperture settings are marked in standard f/stops that indicate how much light passes through the opening. A typical manually controlled lens would be marked f/2.8, f/4, f/5.6, f/8, f/11, f/16, f/22. The higher the f/stop number, the smaller the aperture and the less light it admits into the camera. For example, f/22 lets in very little light and f/2.8 lets in a lot.

Aperture Settings

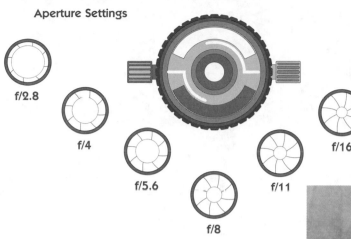

f/2.8

f/4

f/5.6

f/8

f/11

f/16

f/22

f-stop Numbers

Aperture settings are marked in standard f/stops that indicate how much light passes through the opening. A typical manually controlled lens would be marked f/2.8, f/4, f/5.6, f/8, f/11, f/16, f/22. The higher the f/stop number, the smaller the aperture and the less light it admits into the camera.

Shutter Speeds

The camera's shutter controls how long light enters the camera. Typically, shutter settings are in a standard series of fractions of a second, such as 1/30, 1/60, 1/125, 1/250, 1/500, 1/1000 (on the camera, the 1/ is usually omitted, and the dial reads 30, 60, 125, 250 etc.). The shorter the fraction (higher number under the 1/), the faster the shutter speed.

Slow shutter speeds, such as 1/30 or below, keep the camera open a long time and allow a lot of light to reach the film or chip. However, a slow shutter speed may allow camera or subject movement to blur the photo. Generally, don't set a speed slower than 1/60 for underwater photography.

Fast shutter speeds, such as 1/250 and above, keep the camera open a short time and let little light reach the film or chip. A fast shutter speed is better for stopping action in bright light.

Shutter Speeds

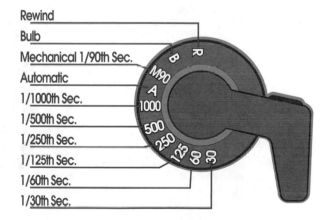

Rewind

Bulb

Mechanical 1/90th Sec.

Automatic

1/1000th Sec.

1/500th Sec.

1/250th Sec.

1/125th Sec.

1/60th Sec.

1/30th Sec.

REVIEW

Photography 4

1. Check the f/stop that allows more light to pass through the camera lens.
   ☐ a. f/16
   ☐ b. f/11

2. Check the shutter speed that allows more light to strike the film or chip.
   ☐ a. 1/125
   ☐ b. 1/60

How'd you do?
1. b; **2.** b.

APERTURE AND DEPTH OF FIELD

Underline/highlight the answers to these questions as you read:

1. What is the purpose of the camera lens?

2. What is "depth of field," and how does aperture size affect it?

Besides controlling the amount of light entering the camera, the lens aperture affects the camera's focus. The primary purpose of the lens is to focus light onto the film or chip for a sharp image. As the aperture changes, the range of sharp focus, or *depth of field* changes with it.

Depth of field is how much of the scene, from front to back, is in focus. The smaller the aperture (high f/number), the greater the depth of field. The larger the aperture (low f/number), the less the depth of field.

Depth of field is how much of the scene, from front to back, is in focus. The smaller the aperture (high f/number), the greater the depth of field. The larger the aperture (low f/number), the less the depth of field.

Underwater, you will typically try to get the greatest depth of field by using the smallest aperture (highest f/number) possible for a correct exposure. Many cameras/lenses have indicators that help you judge the depth of field.

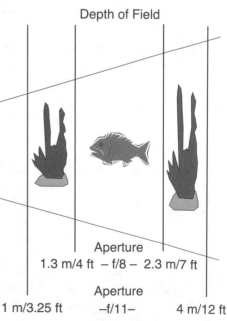

Depth of Field

Aperture
1.3 m/4 ft – f/8 – 2.3 m/7 ft

Aperture
–f/11–

1 m/3.25 ft   4 m/12 ft

Key CONCEPTS

GETTING THE RIGHT EXPOSURE

The Relationship of Aperture and Shutter Speed

As you have learned, the amount of light hitting the film or chip is controlled by the aperture (amount) and shutter speed (time). The relationship of aperture and shutter speed is critical to proper exposure. Exposure is the total amount of light that reaches the film or chip through the combination of aperture and shutter speed.

When you change a shutter speed or aperture one position, you either double or halve the light reaching the film. For example, changing the aperture from f/8 to f/11 halves the light that enters the lens, and changing the shutter speed from 1/60 to 1/30 doubles how long the shutter stays open. By controlling both shutter speed and aperture, you control the exposure.

If you change either aperture or shutter speed, you can balance change and maintain the same exposure by changing the other. For example, a setting of f/4 at

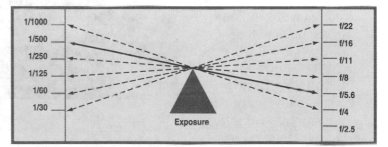

If you change either aperture or shutter speed, you can balance change and maintain the same exposure by changing the other. In this illustration, a setting of f/4 at 1/1000 equals f/5.6 at 1/500, because f/5.6 admits only half the light of f/4 while 1/500 admits twice the light of 1/1000. In the same manner, f/5.6 at 1/500 equals f/8 at 1/250 and so on.

1/1000 equals f/5.6 at 1/500, because f/5.6 admits only half the light of f/4 while 1/500 admits twice the light of 1/1000. In the same manner, f/5.6 at 1/500 equals f/8 at 1/250 and so on.

Setting a Manual Light Meter

You use a light meter to determine the correct combination of aperture and shutter speed. A light meter can be built into a camera, or it can be a separate hand-held instrument. Refer to the camera/meter's instructions for exact directions, but generally the steps are:

1. Set the film's ISO number (found on the film package – more about ISO later) on the camera or meter.

2. Set the shutter speed or f/stop you want and point the camera/meter at the subject.

3. The next step depends on the camera or meter, but you'll either match the meter needle with the appropriate corresponding f/stop or shutter speed, or read the f/stop or shutter speed number from the digital display. See the instruction manual for the meter or camera for exact operation details.

Once you determine one combination of aperture and shutter speed, you can change aperture/shutter speed combinations while maintaining the correct exposure as you learned in the previous section. You set your camera with one of these combinations.

Programming an Automatic Camera

Cameras that automatically control exposure vary in operation (see your camera's instructions for exact directions), but in general the

Cameras that automatically control exposure vary in operation but in general you set the film's ISO number and set the shutter speed dial or f/stop ring to A for "automatic" or P for "programmed."

steps for setting an automatic camera are:

1. Set the film's ISO number on the camera. Some cameras read the film ISO automatically from the film cartridge. You don't have to set an ISO on a digital camera.

2. Set the shutter speed dial or f/stop ring to A for "automatic." On some cameras, you may set both to A; others may have P for "programmed." Newer electronic cameras use a digital display and may offer you a variety of automatic programs for different picture taking situations.

3. On automatic or program, the camera constantly varies the shutter speed or aperture, or both, depending upon the light available.

Bracketing

Although you use a light meter and properly set the camera, you may not get the ideal exposure due to unusual lighting conditions. To help ensure a good picture, you use *bracketing*. Bracketing means taking the same picture at settings that let in more and less light, as well as the exposure indicated by the meter. Generally, you take three pictures: one at the indicated exposure, one with one f/stop or shutter speed less than the indicated exposure, and one with one f/stop or shutter speed more than the indicated exposure.

Nonautomatic cameras. On manual cameras, you accomplish bracketing by varying shutter speeds or apertures. If you're using a manual strobe, you can also bracket by moving the strobe closer and farther away from your subject or by varying aperture. However, changing shutter speeds cannot be used to bracket when using a strobe (we'll discuss proper exposure with strobes later).

Automatic cameras. Many automatic cameras have controls for bracketing. See the camera instructions for their use. If your camera doesn't have such controls and you can't set it on manual, but you can still bracket by changing the ISO setting. Set the ISO number to twice the real ISO for a picture with one f/stop or shutter speed less light. Set the ISO number to half the real ISO number for a picture with one f/stop or shutter speed more light. Don't forget to reset to the correct ISO number when through bracketing.

Whether you're using a manual or an automatic camera, it's a good idea to shoot a roll of film on land to practice using your exposure controls and bracketing before trying it underwater. Your instructor will help you learn to set the correct exposure on your camera.

Photography 6

1. The amount of light striking the film is controlled by
   □ a. shutter speed and aperture.
   □ b. focus and film speed.

2. f/5.6 at 1/60 equals
   □ a. f/8 at 1/30
   □ b. f/8 at 1/125

3. The first step in setting a nonautomatic light meter is to
   □ a. set it for the film's ISO number.
   □ b. select a shutter speed.

4. Automatic cameras control _____, and should be set according to the camera's instruction guide.
   □ a. the shutter speed
   □ b. the aperture
   □ c. either shutter speed, or aperture, or both, depending on the camera

5. There is no way to bracket with an automatic camera.
   □ True   □ False

How'd you do?
1. a;   2. a;   3. a;   4. c;   5. False. You can bracket with an automatic camera by varying the ISO setting.

FILM AND UNDERWATER PHOTOGRAPHY

CONCEPTS

Underline/highlight the answers
to these questions as you read:

1. What are three basic considerations when selecting film?

2. What is meant by a "slow"
   film, and what would be an
   example of its ISO number?

3. What is meant by a "fast"
   film, and what would be an
   example of its ISO number?

4. What are the three attributes
   of a "typical" film selected
   for underwater photography?

If you have a digital camera, your camera comes with its "film" – the computer chip – built in, so there's nothing to select. If you're using a conventional camera, however, there's an almost overwhelming choice. Let's look at what different options you have, and how they'll help you take pictures underwater.

Film Selection

Earlier, you read about "fast" or "high-speed" films and the "ISO number." These relate to the light sensitivity of the film you select. There are essentially three concerns when choosing film: the film type, the number of exposures and the film speed.

Film type. Depending upon whether you want slides or prints, you can choose from color reversal (slide) film or color negative (print) film. In either type, you should choose *daylight* film, which means it renders the correct colors in sunlight or with your strobe. (You'll find the vast majority of films are daylight films.)

Number of exposures. Lengths of 12, 20, 24 or 36 exposures per roll are available for most type film. Since you can't change rolls diving, you'll generally want the longest roll available.

Film speed. Film speed is how sensitive a film is to light. The speed is expressed by the ISO number (formerly called "ASA," which you'll still hear – the number's the same); the higher the number, the more sensitive or "faster" the film and the less light it needs for a correct exposure. Generally, a film with an ISO rating of 200, 400 or higher is considered a "fast" or "high-speed" film, and one with an ISO of 64 or 50 is considered "slow." You trade film speed for quality; faster films tend to have less resolution, sharpness and more graininess than slower films.

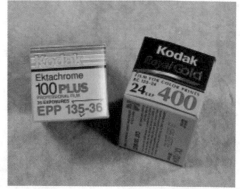

You choose film based on whether you want prints or slides, the size required for your camera, the ISO number and the number of exposures.

Typical Film for Underwater Photography

For general underwater photography, pick a slower color reversal (slide) film (ISO 50 – 125) with 36 exposures. Slower film produces better quality pictures, and with a strobe, its lower ISO isn't a concern. Slides are easy to show to large groups and examine for exposure and sharpness; you can have prints made from slides if you desire. Thirty-six exposure rolls give you the most pictures possible while underwater (in 35 mm film).

It's best to select one film and stick with it until you're thoroughly familiar with its characteristics.

Photography 7

1. "Color reversal film" means
   ☐ a. film for slides.
   ☐ b. film for prints.

2. An example of an ISO for a slow film would be
   ☐ a. ISO 64.
   ☐ b. ISO 400.

3. An example of an ISO for a fast film would be
   ☐ a. ISO 64.
   ☐ b. ISO 400.

4. Typically, for underwater photography you want
   ☐ a. fast film.
   ☐ b. slow film.

How'd you do?

1. a;   2. a;   3. b;   4. b.

USING UNDERWATER STROBES

In the section on understanding light, you learned that strobes replace lost light and color underwater. You'll probably take most of your underwater pictures with a strobe, so it's important to understand the different types, how to aim them to avoid backscatter and how to set your camera for proper exposure with them.

Strobe Types

The two most popular underwater strobes in use today are TTL (Through The Lens) automatic strobes and manual strobes.

Underline/highlight the answers to these questions as you read:

1. What is the difference between a TTL automatic strobe and a manual strobe?

2. How do you aim a strobe to avoid backscatter?

3. How do you set a camera for proper exposure with TTL and manual strobes?

TTL Automatic Strobes. These strobes couple with the camera's electronics for automatic exposures. When you take a picture, a camera sensor controls the flash; the camera typically confirms a proper exposure by flashing a light in the viewfinder.

Light from Strobe

TTL Signal to Strobe

Film

Light Reflected
from Subject

TTL Sensor

You'll find TTL strobes the easiest to use, though you do have to have one intended for your specific camera (not all cameras can use TTL strobes). When on the A (automatic) setting, most cameras that accept TTL strobes set themselves automatically for flash exposure when you turn the strobe on.

Manual Strobes. Manual strobes cost less than TTL strobes. Because they have no automation, an experienced photographer may get better results with a manual strobe in unusual lighting conditions (Note: You can set virtually all TTL strobes manually for this reason). Manual strobes may have variable power settings for more versatility.

If you're using a manual strobe, you must set your camera for correct exposure. The shutter speed must be set on the *synchronization speed*, which is usually 1/60 or 1/90 for most cameras. If you're not on this speed, the shutter may not be open, or only partly open, when the strobe fires, ruining your picture. This is why you can't use the shutter speed to bracket when you use a strobe.

With a manual strobe, you determine the proper f/stop from the strobe's exposure guide, which tells you what f/number to use depending upon how far you are from your subject. Although most strobes come with exposure guides, it's best to develop your own by taking a test roll at various exposures and subject distances.

Whether you're using a TTL or manual strobe, your instructor will assist you in setting your camera for correct exposure.

Strobe Handling

Starting out, you'll probably find it best to attach your strobe to the camera on a bracket. Ideally, you should be able to position the strobe so that it's off to the side and aimed at your subject from a 45 degree angle. Alternatively, if you have a very wide angle strobe, you put it off to the side and aim it straight ahead.

To avoid backscatter, hold or mount the strobe away from the lens at approximately 45 degrees at or slightly above camera level.

With wide beam strobes, have the strobe off to the camera's side, with the strobe face pointing straight ahead, parallel with the lens.

The position of this strobe will produce backscatter.

These positions help eliminate backscatter, which is haze and glare caused by suspended particles reflecting the flash back into the camera lens. To avoid backscatter, try to light your subject while not lighting the water between your camera and the subject.

When using your flash, remember to get as close as possible to your subject so there's less water to absorb color. In aiming the strobe, don't forget that your subject looks closer than it really is; aim behind it a little to compensate.

Underline/highlight the answers to these questions as you read:

1. How do you frame the entire subject using a camera?

2. How do you correct for viewfinder parallax error?

3. How do you hold a camera underwater so you avoid unnecessary camera movement?

4. How do you control buoyancy and fin movement while taking pictures underwater?

5. What's the best general camera angle in underwater photography?

BASIC UNDERWATER PHOTOGRAPHY TECHNIQUES

Besides focus and exposure, successful underwater photography requires some techniques in properly framing a subject, in holding the camera steady, in buoyancy control and in choosing an angle for a good picture.

Framing Subjects

The proper framing technique varies from camera to camera and with the type of photography.

Framing system. Options include a sportsfinder on top of the camera, an optical viewfinder, through-the-lens (single lens reflex) viewing, or (for macro photography) a wire frame. Check your camera's instruction guide or ask your instructor for assistance in the proper use of your camera's framing system.

Parallax. When using a sportsfinder or an optical viewfinder, you have to be careful to prevent *parallax error* (usually called just "parallax" for short). Parallax causes you to cut off the top of your photo subject in the picture, and is caused by a slight difference between what the viewfinder sees and what the camera lens sees (parallax is not a problem with through-the-lens SLR viewing or macro framers. Most digital cameras have through the lens viewing, too.). This is a problem primarily at close distances.

Most optical viewfinders have lines that assist you in adjusting your aim to correct parallax. This is the easiest method for correcting the problem. If your camera has no parallax correction lines, remember to aim slightly higher than normal when taking pictures closer than about 1.2 metres/4 feet.

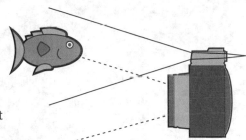

Parallax causes you to cut off the top of your photo subject in the picture, and is caused by a slight difference between what the viewfinder sees and what the camera lens sees.

Steadying the Camera

The most common cause for blurry pictures isn't focusing errors, but failure to hold the camera steady. When ready to take a picture, steady the camera – preferably with both hands – and squeeze the trigger slowly and steadily. Concentrate on holding the camera still.

Buoyancy and Fin Control

Buoyancy and fin control are important for a steady camera, for preventing environmental damage and to keep from kicking up the bottom.

If you're over a bottom that you can rest on without damaging aquatic life, plant yourself firmly on the bottom (one of the few times you'll want to be slightly negatively buoyant). Avoid stirring up the bottom.

If you're midwater or over a sensitive bottom, adjust for neutral buoyancy. Don't kick with your fins, because this can damage the reef or stir up the bottom. Avoid killing coral and other life by inadvertently kicking the reef, or dragging your alternate air source, gauges or camera or attachments across it. Remember, no picture is worth destroying aquatic life. Check out the Peak Performance Buoyancy section for tips on professional-level buoyancy control.

Angle

As you gain experience with underwater photography, you'll experiment with different angles. For

now, remember that an upward angle, pointed slightly toward the surface is the most useful all-around angle. This angle helps keep the subject from becoming "lost" in the picture by making it stand out from a blue background. When taking underwater photos, remember to get close, get low and shoot up.

When taking underwater photos, remember to get close, get low and shoot up. Note also that the photographer is over insensitive bottom and avoids damage to sensitive aquatic life while shooting.

 REVIEW

Photography 9

1. Underwater cameras use a universal framing system.
   ☐ True   ☐ False

2. On some cameras, you most easily avoid parallax by using correcting lines in the camera viewfinder.
   ☐ True   ☐ False

3. When taking a picture underwater, you should
   ☐ a. put both hands on the camera, if possible.
   ☐ b. always keep one hand free for buoyancy control.

4. While taking pictures near the bottom, you should
   ☐ a. avoid fin movement.
   ☐ b. use your fins to maintain a steady position.

5. For most types of underwater photography, your best angle is
   ☐ a. upward.
   ☐ b. horizontal.

How'd you do?
1. False. There are various framing systems, depending upon the camera. **2.** True; **3.** a; **4.** a; **5.** a.

PHOTOGRAPHIC COMPOSITION

As you start out in underwater photography, you're primarily concerned with getting sharp, properly exposed pictures. However, you can improve even your first photos by paying attention to six simple principles of photographic composition.

What is Photographic Composition?

Photographic composition is the arrangement of objects in a photograph. The idea is to create a pleasing, interesting or mood-rendering arrangement. Composition is somewhat subjective – you may like a photo and another person may not. (What do they know, anyway?) Nonetheless, you can apply some basics that create a generally pleasing image.

Six Basics for Better Composition

Image completeness. Avoid cutting off part of an image so the viewer feels that something's missing. For example, cutting off one leg of a starfish at the picture's edge.

Clear foreground. It's generally best to avoid distractions in front of your subject. It's okay to have something in the foreground – it adds depth to your shot – but your subject should not have to compete for attention.

Clear background. In the same way, avoid distractions behind the subject.

Subject direction. Place subjects so their natural direction leads into the photo. For example, a fish should face into a photo.

Subject position. The center isn't necessarily the best place for your subject. Experiment through the viewfinder until you find the best place for your subject. A good rule of thumb is to divide the frame mentally into thirds vertically and horizontally, and place your subject on the lines, particularly where they intersect.

Contrast generally helps, such as having a dark subject against a light background or vice-versa. Look for bright colors that stand out against each other.

Complementary colors. Contrast generally helps, such as having a dark subject against a light background or vice-versa. Look for bright colors that stand out against each other.

REVIEW

Photography 10
1. Photographic composition is best defined as a list of all the subjects found in a particular photo.
   ☐ True   ☐ False

2. The background of a photo should generally be
   ☐ a. free of distractions so the main subject shows clearly.
   ☐ b. full of secondary objects for added interest.

How'd you do?
1. False. Photographic composition is arrangement of objects in a photograph.;
2. a.

CONCEPTS

Underline/highlight the answers to these questions as you read:

1. What is the recommended five-step process for removing, inspecting, cleaning and lubricating an o-ring?

2. What four equipment checks should you make before an underwater photography dive?

3. What is basic postdive care for underwater photography equipment?

UNDERWATER PHOTO EQUIPMENT CARE

As mentioned in the first section, you need to care for photo equipment properly if you expect it to survive the underwater environment. Besides washing and drying, it requires you to have the right tools and follow the correct procedures. Your instructor will provide the necessary tools and assist you in caring for your camera; the care steps described here are those necessary for the purposes of the Underwater Photography Adventure Dive, and you'll learn more in the PADI Underwater Photographer Specialty course.

O-ring Care and Maintenance

To a large extent, it's the o-ring, which is the first easily maintained reliable submersible seal, that makes underwater photography possible. You need to remove and clean all user-accessible o-rings in your camera and strobe system before and after each use to ensure reliable seals. Use this five-step procedure:

1. Remove o-ring. Lift the o-ring from its groove by pinching it with your finger or lifting it with a blunt, soft instrument like the edge of a credit card. Do not use sharp objects such as dental tools or needles that can damage the o-ring, or worse, the o-ring groove.

Lift the o-ring from its groove by pinching it with your finger or lifting it with a blunt, soft instrument like the edge of a credit card.

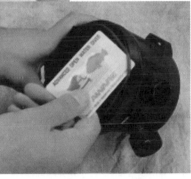

2. Wipe o-ring clean. Use a soft cloth to gently clean the o-ring, while inspecting for nicks or damage. Avoid stretching the o-ring as much as possible. If you find any damage, replace the o-ring – using a damaged o-ring will probably result in a flooded camera or strobe.

3. Lubricate o-ring. Use your fingers to apply a thin coat of silicone grease. The o-ring should appear wet, but not have globs or excess residue of grease, which will not help the seal, but attract dirt that can compromise the seal.

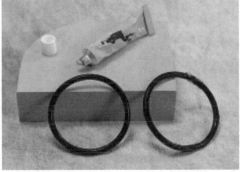

The o-ring should appear wet, like the one on the left. Grease globs or excess residue, like the one on the right, will not help the seal but will attract dirt that can compromise the seal.

4. Clean the o-ring groove. Use a cotton swab or lint-free cloth to wipe old grease and dirt from the o-ring groove. Be sure the groove is completely clean. Also clean the area the o-ring seals against. If dirt remains, you can't rely on the seal. A single hair is all you need to get a leak.

5. Reseat the o-ring carefully. Again, use no sharp instruments. You should be able to replace the o-ring gently with your fingers.

Predive Equipment Check

Before taking your camera underwater, there are four basic checks to ensure successful picture taking.

1. **Camera battery check** – Make sure your camera batteries are good by checking the meter and using the battery check.

2. **Electronics check** – If your camera has automatic systems, check that they work normally by test-firing the system.

3. **Lens check** – Check the focus and aperture settings, and clean the front and rear of lens with photographic lens tissue if necessary.

4. **Strobe check** – Be sure the strobe has fresh batteries, that it charges properly, that the camera connections are correct and that the strobe fires when you trip the camera shutter.

The most important step in caring for underwater photo equipment is to wash it in cool, fresh water immediately after the dive. If you can't wash the camera immediately, keep it wet (salt or fresh water) until you can.

Basic Postdive Photo Equipment Care

The most important step in caring for underwater photo equipment is to wash it in cool, fresh water immediately after the dive. If you can't wash the camera immediately, keep it wet (salt or fresh water) until you can. Do not let it dry out; once salt crystallizes it is very difficult to remove, causing the most long-term damage and wear to your equipment.

When washing the equipment, leave it assembled and immerse it in cool, fresh water. Gently swish the camera and strobe back and forth for at least the first 60 seconds, then allow it to soak for at least 30 minutes. After soaking, gently towel-dry it, and then open it in an environment where spray, splashes and moisture aren't a threat. Dry your hair or wear a hat so you don't drip into it when taking it apart. Remove the film and care for the o-rings as described above. Follow any other maintenance as prescribed by the equipment's instruction manual.

Most underwater photo equipment should be serviced annually by a specialist who can replace o-rings and other seals that you can't reach.

PADI Underwater Photographer Specialty Course

Your Underwater Photography Adventure Dive may be credited (at the instructor's discretion) toward the PADI Underwater Photographer Specialty certification. In addition to what you've learned in this section and will practice on the Underwater Photography Adventure Dive, the PADI Underwater Photographer Specialty course includes:

- More on photo principles
- Choosing different types of equipment
- More on selecting films
- Strobe selection
- Lighting angles
- Equipment maintenance
- Specific techniques for different types of shots

Underwater Photography Adventure Dive Overview

- Knowledge assessment/ Knowledge Review
- Briefing
- Prepare and assemble underwater camera system
- Gearing up
- Predive safety check (BWRAF)
- Entry
- Descent
- Shoot a roll of film (macro or still-life photos)
- Ascent – safety stop
- Exit
- Debrief
- Post dive equipment maintenance and disassembly
- Log dive – PADI Instructor signs

KNOWLEDGE REVIEW
Underwater Photography

1. List six ways to overcome light loss and four ways to overcome color loss underwater.

   Light loss:

   1._____

   2._____

   3._____

   4._____

   5._____

   6._____

   Color loss:

   1._____

   2._____

   3._____

   4._____

2. Define "depth of field" and explain the relationship between aperture and depth of field.

3. Write three equivalent exposures for the two examples provided:

   f/16 at 1/60 = _____ = _____ = _____

   f/8 at 1/30   = _____ = _____ = _____

4. Describe how to set a nonautomatic light meter and how to program the electronics of an automatic camera for proper exposures.

   Nonautomatic:

   Automatic:

5. Explain how to bracket exposure with nonautomatic and automatic cameras.

Nonautomatic:

Automatic:

6. Describe the difference between a TTL strobe and a manual strobe, and explain how to set a camera for proper exposure with each.

7. Describe the best way to aim a strobe, and how to hold a camera to avoid blurring and parallax error.

8. Define "photographic composition" and describe basic principles for better composition.

9. Describe the recommended five-step procedure for removing, inspecting, cleaning, lubricating and replacing an o-ring.

10. The most important step in caring for underwater photo equipment is to _____ it in cool _____ _____ immediately after a dive.

Student Diver Statement: I've completed this Knowledge Review to the best of my ability and any questions I answered incorrectly or incompletely I've had explained to me, and I understand what I missed.

Signature _____ Date_____

UNDERWATER VIDEOGRAPHY

Introduction

"Hey, that's me, that's me!"

"Where'd you find that emperor angel? I didn't see one the whole dive."

"Back that up, back that up. To the part where you swam through the arch. Look how the school of bait fish shimmers like tinsel."

These reflect only a few reactions your fellow divers have to the underwater video you just shot – your hair isn't even dry yet, and already everyone enjoys your work. One of the fastest growing underwater hobbies, underwater video offers you immediate reward, a way to remember and share diving, and imaging that perhaps best shows nondivers what diving is all about. And with rapidly evolving technology, today's video cameras provide higher quality and more features in a smaller package than ever before – ideal for underwater application.

CONCEPTS

Underline/highlight the answers to these questions as you read:

1. What six basic features should you look for when choosing a video camera for underwater use, and why is each important?

2. What six basic features should you consider in choosing an underwater video housing, and why?

3. What three basic differences should you consider in choosing underwater video lights?

4. What basic functions, in and out of the housing, should you be familiar with on the system you will use on this Adventure Dive?

UNDERWATER VIDEO SYSTEMS

If this were the early 1990s or mid 1980s, we might start this section off with a discussion of video formats (tape types and sizes) and video cameras suited for underwater videography. Today, we can't do that. The technology changes so rapidly that by the time you read this, much of what we wrote here would be obsolete and inaccurate. But that's actually good news because as technology advances, you can do more for less investment than ever before. Today's "amateur" cameras are featherweight and provide images that shame the monster "professional" cameras of fifteen years ago.

Though it's impossible to have the latest and greatest formats and models here, look for this information from your PADI Dive Center, Resort or Instructor, as well as your local video retailer, diving and video magazines and websites. What we'll cover here are the basic features you want in your underwater system, no matter what the most current formats and models.

Basic Camera Features for Underwater Shooting

Okay, say you've got the top four whiz-bang video camcorders (video camera with built in recorder – what you want and just about all you can get nowadays) in your price range sitting in front of you. Which one do you invest in? To answer that, compare them in light of these six features that will be important for underwater use:

1. Size. Generally, the smaller the better. A smaller camera takes a smaller housing, which saves you money, reduces travel bulk and makes it easier to hold and steady. The trend is to smaller cameras, so you probably won't have the slightest problem getting a compact camcorder. But keep some perspective; if you've got huge hands, at some point a camera and housing might be *too* small. Your preferences play a part. Also, you might opt for a little more size to get some features.

2. Housing availability. Shop for camcorder and underwater housings *simultaneously*. Don't assume that you can find a housing for every video camera. This is especially true if you're looking at used equipment. You'll narrow your choices just by eliminating those that you can't get a housing for.

3. Batteries. It's almost moot to mention, thanks to advances in battery technology, but choose a camcorder that lets you get a lot of record time on a single battery. There's nothing more frustrating than having your battery die halfway through the dive. However, as time passes, camcorders need less and less power and their batteries hold more and more power.

4. Wide angle lens. As you'll see shortly, this is *very* important in choosing your camcorder. Get the widest lens you can, or even better, choose a camcorder that lets you add an accessory wide angle lens. Practically speaking, you can't be too wide underwater. The ideal underwater lens would be so wide you'd see your backside while you shoot.

5. Flying erase heads. This is practically standard on new models, but if you're looking at used stuff, check for these. Flying erase heads allow a clean cut if you start and stop recording, or back up the tape and reshoot. Without them, you get picture "noise" or other disturbances, which makes in camera editing difficult (more about in camera editing in a bit).

6. Low light operation. Look for the lowest lux (light) number possible. The lower the number, the less light you need to shoot – an obvious plus underwater.

You'll find lots of other features available, which, having covered the above six requirements, may still leave you some options. Choose these based on the type of shooting you plan to do, your interests, and so on. If in doubt, buy up. That is, buy the camcorder that does more, even if you don't think you'll need the features immediately. If you buy down and find you need those features later, you're looking at investing in a whole new system. If you buy up and find you don't quite need everything, you usually didn't pay that much more anyway.

Choose a camcorder for underwater video considering compactness, housing availability, battery life, lens angle, flying erase heads and low light operation.

Basic Housing Features

You're choosing a housing while choosing your video camera. An excellent option is often to get them as a package from your local dive operation. And, you'll find that you usually have a choice of different housings available for a popular camcorder. It's nice to have choices, but what do you look for in the housing? Glad you asked – consider these six basics:

1. Material. Metal housings are rugged and have excellent handling characteristics. Plastic housings are noncorrosive, and you can see inside better (making it easier to spot leaks). Metal housings are usually more compact for a given camera.

2. Controls. At a minimum, you need to be able to turn your camcorder on and off and control record/pause. Most housings also give you focus control and zoom control.

There are two control types: mechanical and electronic. Mechanical controls use rods, gears and such to manipulate the camera. They're inexpensive and very reliable, but they require more maintenance (o-ring seals) and the controls may have to be in awkward locations. Electronic controls plug into the camcorder's remote control system and operate it electronically. Electronic controls minimize leak points (fewer housing penetrations) and can be put where they're most useful when shooting. However, electronic controls are more expensive, are less reliable and cost more to fix. Also, you may not be able to access all of a camera's features through its electronic control system.

3. Buoyancy. Some video systems sink, others float. That's your preference. What's important is that the housing with camcorder be neither greatly positive or negative, or you'll have trouble keeping it steady.

4. Viewing. You need to be able to see what you're shooting, keeping in mind that you're looking through a mask as well as the housing. A system that provides a big, easy to see view screen is usually worth the extra investment.

5. Dome port. This goes with the wide angle lens. A flat front port narrows the camcorder's field of view, but a dome port allows it to stay wide. This is very important for good color and sharpness. You definitely want a dome port. (More about them later).

In picking a housing, think about the material, type controls, buoyancy, viewing, dome port availablity and accessory compatibility.

6. Accessory compatibility. Be sure the housing accepts any internal or external accessories you may want, such as video lights and color correcting filters.

As with the camcorder itself, you may find you have other features and options available after you've satisfied these. Again, if you're not sure, buy up.

Underwater Video Lights
If you're an underwater photographer or you've read the section on underwater photography, you

For more information about...

Underwater Video Lights
See the *Underwater Photographer Manual*, and *Underwater Photography* video

know that water absorbs color, and you often need to replace that lost color for a good picture. You might expect that to apply to underwater video, and it does, but surprisingly, not as much.

Today's camcorders *white balance* by adjusting their sensitivity to the colors in the light available to render good color. You can enhance this somewhat by using color correcting filters. So if you're not planning to shoot very deep or at night, to some extent video lights are optional.

On the other hand, a video camera can't balance a color that's not there. If virtually all of the color red is gone, the camcorder can't put it back. In low light, you may need video lights, and in any case, properly used, video lights make underwater colors "pop" and make your fellow divers more attractive by lighting their faces inside their masks.

In choosing a lighting system, you consider three features.

1. Light quality. Generally you want wide, even light that covers the area of your wide lens. Otherwise, you have a lit "hot spot" in the center of an unlit rectangle. This is why most lighting systems employ two or more lights.

2. Burn time. There's no point having a camcorder record time of two hours if your lights only run 20 minutes. You want as long a burn time as possible, which is sometimes a trade with light power. The brighter the light, the faster it consumes battery power.

3. Battery location. Light systems tend to have big, bulky batteries. They can be in the camcorder housing, but that makes the whole housing more bulky. A better option is batteries in the lights, or in a separate housing that rides under the video housing or on you.

Before Your Dive

In preparation for the Underwater Videography Adventure Dive, if you're not already familiar with the camcorder and housing you'll be using, sit down with it and, using the manufacturer's instructions and instructor guidance, learn to do the following:

- attach and remove the battery
- power on and off (in and out of housing)
- eject tape
- record and pause (in and out of housing)
- focus/autofocus (in and out of housing)
- playback
- zoom (in and out of housing)

Quick REVIEW

Videography 1
1. Features to look for in a camcorder for underwater use include (check all that apply):
   - ☐ a. small size.
   - ☐ b. housing availability.
   - ☐ c. telephoto lens.
   - ☐ d. low light operation.

2. Features to consider in choosing an underwater video housing include (check all that apply):
   - ☐ a. as negatively buoyant as possible.
   - ☐ b. metal versus plastic.
   - ☐ c. control types.
   - ☐ d. availability of a flat port.

3. In choosing a video light, the most important feature is that the light focuses intensely in the center of the camera's field of view.
   - ☐ True   ☐ False

4. System functions you should be familiar with for the Underwater Video Adventure Dive include (check all that apply):
   - ☐ a. record/pause.
   - ☐ b. power on/off.
   - ☐ c. playback.
   - ☐ d. focus.

How'd you do?
1. a, b, d. **2.** b, c. **3.** False. You want light that spreads evenly over the entire field of view. **4.** a, b, c, d.

Underwater Video Principles

Now let's look at the basic video principles you'll apply with your video system, beginning with how water affects light and color, and continuing on to camera handling and foundational shooting principles. If you're already an underwater photographer, much of this will be familiar, though you'll note that with video, some of the rules are different.

Water's Effect on Sharpness and Color

Light doesn't travel through water as well as it does through air, which creates some of the challenges you face as an underwater videographer. For one, as light travels through water, it hits suspended particles that deflect it somewhat, reducing its apparent sharpness. The further light travels, the more water scatters it and the less apparent sharpness it has.

Likewise, as you've undoubtedly experienced, water absorbs color from light, first red, then orange, yellow, green, and then blue. The more water light travels through, the less reds/oranges/yellows, and the more green/blue your videos look.

What all this means is that for maximum sharpness and color, you want to minimize the water light travels through, which in practical terms means you want to get as close as you can to your subject. That's why you want a wide angle lens and dome port – the wider the lens, the closer you can get and still see your subject. A dome port allows your wide angle lens to retain its full angle of view underwater. (Flat ports are best for ultra close-up videography.) With a dome port/wide angle lens combination, you

Sharpness & Color Underwater
See the Physics of Diving section, in the *Encyclopedia of Recreational Diving*, book and multimedia.

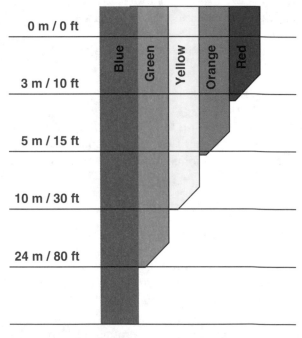

Water absorbs color from light, first red, then orange, yellow, green, and then blue. The more water light travels through, the less reds/oranges/yellows, and the more green/blue your videos look.

0 m / 0 ft

3 m / 10 ft

5 m / 15 ft

10 m / 30 ft

24 m / 80 ft

Blue Green Yellow Orange Red

Underline/highlight the answers to these questions as you read:

1. How does water affect the apparent sharpness of video?

2. How does water affect color?

3. Why does the combination of a dome port and wide angle lens help you with focus, color and sharpness underwater?

4. How do you set the camera focus when using a dome port?

5. What are two ways to improve video color underwater without using lights?

6. How do you position underwater video lights for proper lighting?

7. What are four ways to get maximum effectiveness from underwater video lights?

8. How should you hold a video camera underwater?

9. What is the best general angle and position for shooting underwater?

10. What are four common errors to avoid while shooting videos underwater?

greatly enhance color and sharpness because you minimize how far light has to travel from your subject to your camcorder.

The dome port/wide angle lens has another benefit – extreme depth of field. What this means is that everything from very close to the camera to quite far away will be in focus. This minimizes or eliminates how much you have to focus. It varies with the camcorder and lens, but in reasonably bright conditions, almost everything from about a metre/three feet to infinity can be in focus.

A color correcting filter can't put back color that's not there, but it can rebalance the color for a more natural look. You'll probably want to consider a color correcting filter standard equipment when you're not using video lights.

Dome ports have an optical effect that changes the point of focus to approximately twice the dome's diameter away. With a typical video housing, your camcorder will focus at about .3 metres/1 foot (even though the subject's actually further away). This is not a problem with most video cameras, which can focus quite close, but it's something to check when selecting your system. In practical terms, you simply focus through the viewfinder until your picture is sharp, which will be in the .3 metre/1 foot range (although the subject will actually be much farther away).

A dome port allows your wide angle lens to retain its full angle of view underwater. With a dome port/wide angle lens combination, you greatly enhance color and sharpness because you minimize how far light has to travel from your subject to your camcorder.

Better color without video lights. Besides staying close to your subject by using a wide angle lens and dome port, you can take two other steps for the best color possible. First, stay as shallow as possible. The closer you are to the surface, the less color you lose as light travels down through the water. Second, use a color correcting filter (as mentioned previously). A filter

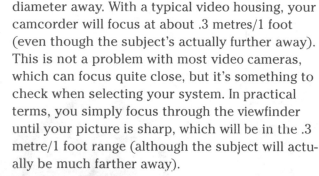

can't put back color that's not there, but it can re-balance the color for a more natural look. You'll probably want to consider a color correcting filter standard equipment when you're not using video lights.

Using video lights. As discussed before, video lights give you the best color because they actually replace lost color. You need to set the lights so they light the subject, but they don't light the water between the camera and the subject. Otherwise, you'll light the suspended particles between your subject and the lens, creating a "snowstorm" effect called backscatter. You also need to set the lights so they cover the area evenly, without creating a bright hot spot.

To avoid backscatter and hot spots, you mount lights well off to the side. Using two lights, you set them so their beams just touch with almost no overlap. If your lights have very wide beams, you point them straight ahead. If they have more narrow beams, you point them in at about 45 degrees, again, minimizing the light that passes between your subject and the dome port.

To avoid backscatter and hot spots, you mount lights well off to the side.

For maximum effectiveness with video lights, try these four tips: First, don't use a color correcting filter with video lights. Second, set the camcorder for indoor or outdoor lighting (if your camcorder has that setting) based on the manufacturer recommendations. If in doubt, your best bet is usually to use outdoor lighting for day shooting and indoor for night. Third, video lights guzzle power, so turn them off when you're not shooting to save power. Note that you can't turn on many underwater video lights out of water; doing so damages them and may cause a fire. Finally, set the lights so they're balanced as well as correctly aimed, so you don't have to strain to keep the system level while shooting.

For maximum effectiveness don't use a color correcting filter with video lights. Set for indoor or outdoor lighting (if your camcorder has that setting) based on the manufacturer recommendations. Turn them off when you're not shooting to save power.

Camera Handling and Basic Shooting Principles

When you go out to shoot with your system, there are some basic principles that go a long way toward making your first efforts better. As you'll see when you complete the entire Underwater Videographer Specialty course, these principles form the foundation you build upon as you expand your shooting skills.

You need to really emphasize steadiness because what looks like barely moving when you're shooting looks like an earthquake when you play it back. Rule one is to keep everything steady and smooth.

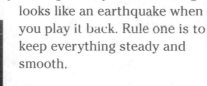

Holding the system. Steady, steady, steady. You need to really emphasize steadiness because what looks like barely moving when you're shooting looks like an earthquake when you play it back. Rule one is to keep everything steady and smooth.

To do this, try holding the housing in front, arms locked straight or with your elbows tucked against your body – whichever works best while looking through the viewfinder. Steady yourself on insensitive bottom, or if that's not possible, by controlling your buoyancy while hovering. (Pay attention to contact with the environment. Don't get so caught up in shooting that you disregard sensitive aquatic life around you.)

Angle. Underwater, your best general shooting angle is close to and slightly below your subject. This angle maximizes color and sharpness, and helps separate your subject from the background. Say it out loud: "Get close, get low, shoot up. Get close, get low, shoot up." Say it to yourself whenever you're diving with your video system.

Avoid beginner pitfalls. There are four common errors that you can avoid to greatly improve your initial efforts:

1. Failing to hold the shot. The viewer needs time to identify what's on the screen. Hold each shot at least four or five seconds, counting if necessary. It seems like a long time when you're doing it, but it's not so long when you watch it.

2. Holding the shot too long with nothing new happening. At the opposite extreme is letting the camcorder roll and roll with no new action. After 10 to 12 seconds, the viewer gets bored unless something different happens. The more new action, the longer you can hold the shot. A 20 second shot of divers swimming is boring. A shot where divers swim for 8 seconds, then a black tip reef shark swims in by the divers for 4 seconds, then vanishes and the divers turn looking for it for 4 seconds, and then it comes back in for 4 seconds, will hold attention. If you'll be using post-production editing, you can shorten the shot later, but get in the habit of holding the shot the "right" duration.

3. Rapid camera motion. Move the camera slowly, as well as steadily. It seems like a crawl when you do it, but it looks normal when you watch it.

4. Shotgun video taping. Usually, you don't want to swim around mindlessly video taping everything you see. Part of successful video includes thinking about what you've shot, what you want to show and putting together something that tells a story. Mindless video may produce some shots that interest you, but not many other people.

Videography 2

1. Water affects apparent sharpness of video by
   - ☐ a. making it appear sharper through magnification.
   - ☐ b. making it less sharp by scattering light.

2. Water _____ color.
   - ☐ a. absorbs
   - ☐ b. enhances
   - ☐ c. reverses

3. A dome port and wide angle lens benefit you by (check all that apply):
   - ☐ a. making your video system more stable.
   - ☐ b. narrowing the field of view.
   - ☐ c. allowing you to get as close as possible to your subject.

4. When using a dome port, you set the focus for infinity.
   - ☐ True   ☐ False

5. You can improve underwater video color without lights by (check all that apply):
   - ☐ a. staying shallow.
   - ☐ b. backing away from your subject.
   - ☐ c. using a color correcting filter.

6. In positioning underwater video lights, your goal is (check all that apply):
   - ☐ a. to spread the light evenly and avoid hot spots.
   - ☐ b. to light everything from the lens port to well behind the subject.
   - ☐ c. to balance the lights so you don't have to struggle to hold the system level.

7. To get maximum effectiveness from underwater video lights (check all that apply):
   - ☐ a. turn them off when you're not shooting.
   - ☐ b. set your camcorder for indoor/outdoor light as recommended by the manufacturer.
   - ☐ c. don't use a color correcting filter.

8. Hold a video camera _____.
   - ☐ a. relaxed.
   - ☐ b. steady.

9. The best all-round shooting angle is to get close, get low and shoot up.
   - ☐ True   ☐ False

10. Common errors to avoid while shooting underwater video include (check all that apply):
    - ☐ a. holding a shot too long
    - ☐ b. not holding a shot long enough
    - ☐ c. moving the camera too slow

How'd you do?

1. b.   2. a.   3. c.   4. False. You set the focus very close, typically about .3 metres/1 foot away.   5. a, c.   6. a, c.   7. a, b, c.
8. b.   9. True.   10. a, b.

UNDERWATER VIDEO SYSTEM ASSEMBLY, DISASSEMBLY AND MAINTENANCE

Okay, time to turn your attention to taking care of your video system, including putting it together, taking it apart and basic maintenance. Assembly/disassembly varies with the camcorder and housing, so consult the manufacturer's literature and your PADI Instructor for how to assemble and disassemble yours. Before you dive your system for the first time, practice setting it up and taking it apart a few times – right before you dive isn't the best time to be learning that.

While housings and video systems vary significantly, you'll find a few basic skills useful with virtually any of them: o-ring care, avoiding condensation, predive check, postdive care and recharging batteries so they last.

Basic O-ring Care

Your housing keeps your camcorder dry thanks to o-ring seals. With proper care, they're very reliable; on a typical video housing you'll have o-rings to maintain on the back cover and on the removable lens port. Check the manufacturer literature, but basically any o-ring you expose using your system, you're responsible for caring for.

First, remove the o-ring from its groove. Do *not* dig it out with a metal instrument, which can damage the o-ring and groove and cause a leak. Instead, hold it firmly in place with one finger while tracing its length with another so that it stretches slightly and forms a bulge you grasp. Gently lift it out. If this doesn't work, you can try gently lifting it out with the corner of a credit card.

Gently clean the o-ring with a clean soft cloth, avoiding excessive stretching. Inspect the o-ring for

Do not dig an o-ring out of its groove with a metal instrument. Instead, hold it firmly in place with one finger while tracing its length with another so that it forms a bulge you grasp. If this doesn't work, try gently lifting it out with the corner of a credit card.

nicks or abrasion. Replace it if it shows wear or damage.

Clean the o-ring groove with a clean cotton swab, then lightly lubricate the o-ring with silicone grease (or other lubricant if recommended by the manufacturer). The o-ring should look shiny and wet, with no silicone globs. Excess grease attracts dirt and can cause a leak.

Replace the o-ring in its groove, then check that the opposing cover is clean. There should be no sand, hair, dirt or debris, all of which can cause a leak if trapped in the seal. You're now ready to close the cover/reassemble the seal.

Ideally, repeat these steps every time you open a seal, including changing tape and batteries between dives. At the very least, closely inspect the o-ring, groove and cover for dirt or debris, recleaning everything if you have the slightest doubt.

Mechanical controls and other parts of your housing will have internal o-rings that you don't access as easily. See the manufacturer guidelines for maintenance procedures.

Condensation

There's little more annoying than getting in the water and finding your housing all fogged up. In the extreme, it can even damage your video camera. Condensation results when warm, humid air cools, allowing water vapor to accumulate as liquid water on cooler surfaces. This is exactly what happens if you open your video housing in a warm, humid climate, close it and then take it into the nice, cool water.

Since you can't avoid the temperature changes, you avoid condensation by avoiding the humidity. First, if possible assemble and seal your housing in an air-conditioned room, and don't open it before you dive. Air conditioning removes humidity, so this effectively avoids condensation. Second, if you must open your housing in warm, humid conditions, just as you reclose it, use a VERY *gentle* air stream from a scuba tank to purge the humid air. Use a slow flow for 20-30 seconds – don't blast it in there or you may damage something. Scuba tank air is very dry, so this works well.

Third, you can tape silica gel packs or other desiccant in the housing (be sure to tape it, or it will tumble right in front of the lens every time). Desiccant absorbs moisture from the air; it works, but it's a slow process requiring several hours. Your best bet is to use both desiccant and the previous steps to eliminate residual moisture.

Predive Check

Okay, you've got your system set up, sealed and ready for scuba. Are you sure? Better check. First, test all the housing/camera functions and be sure everything works. If you forgot to connect something, the time to find out is now while you can reopen the housing, not later while a humpback gives birth to quintuplets two metres away from you.

Everything go? Good. Leak check time. With the power on (to activate the leak detection system in many modern housings), immerse your video housing (ideally in to fresh water) with the lens port down. Go port down so if you have a leak, water accumulates there. (Note: Some manufacturers may recommend holding your housing a different way – do what the manufacturer says.)

Hold it there a minute and watch for bubbles. A steady stream probably means a leak – pull it up immediately. No bubbles after a couple minutes and the leak detector hasn't gone off? Pull it up, and, keeping it port down, lift the system up so you can check the port for moisture. If that's dry, then look inside the housing wherever possible. If everything's dry, put it back in the water and move all the controls to check that they don't leak when you use them.

Pull up the system as before and check again. If everything's still dry you should be good to go. Set the system aside out of the sun and power it down until you're ready to dive.

If you suspect a leak, keep the housing port down while you open it and remove the camera (turning the housing may splash the water on the camcorder). If you can't readily determine what's causing the leak, postpone shooting until you have the housing professionally serviced.

Post Dive Care
After the dive, your first priority is *immediately* rinsing your system in fresh water. Preferably, immerse it in fresh water and gently agitate it back and forth for 30 seconds to a minute. If you can't do that, use a *gentle* freshwater spray, with emphasis on nooks and crannies that trap salt and minerals.

If you can't rinse the system immediately, leave it sealed and keep it wet in sea water until you can. Allowing salt water to dry on it is far, far worse than keeping it wet in salt water until you can care for it properly.

After rinsing, dry the system off and confirm there's no water inside before opening it. Open it away from any place where moisture or spray can get water on your camcorder. If in doubt (like on a boat), leave everything sealed until you get someplace appropriate. If you plan to dive again, change the battery and tape as needed, maintain the o-ring, and do what's necessary to avoid condensation.

NiCad Batteries
By far the most common batteries for video systems and lights are rechargeable NiCads (Nickel Cadium batteries). They're very reliable, but some NiCads have a "memory," in that if you only partially discharge them and then recharge them repeatedly, after a few cycles they will only hold that partial charge.

To avoid memory, fully discharge your NiCads before recharging them. You can use your batteries to rewind tape and playback until your camcorder gives you a low battery warning. Place your sealed video lights in water and let them burn until they start to dim. Some chargers will automatically discharge your batteries before recharging them.

Fortunately, more and more "memory free" NiCads are coming on the market. Probably in the not-too-distant future – or by the time you read this – we'll have forgotten all about battery memories.

DIVING WITH YOUR VIDEO SYSTEM

Earlier you read about foundational principles that apply to shooting video while diving. Here you'll put the fin on the other foot and learn the principles that apply to diving while shooting video, which includes entry/exit considerations, your air consumption, and handling emergencies and problems.

Entries and Exits

Even in a sturdy housing, your camcorder is relatively fragile. It doesn't take getting banged around well – something to consider when planning how you start and finish your dives.

When boat diving, the simplest solution is to have someone hand you your system after you enter, and take it from you before you exit. Be sure to

When boat diving, have someone hand you your video system after you enter the water.

show that person how to hold your system, and give specific instructions about what to do with it after bringing it back aboard.

If that's not possible, lower your system on a line well below the boat. If your system floats, attach a weight so it doesn't clonk against the boat bottom. You retrieve your housing after you enter, and replace it at the end of the dive to pull up after you're back aboard. Many divers suspend their systems as 5 metres/15 feet so they can reattach them during their safety stop.

Don't suspend your system in rough conditions because the boat's rise and fall will jerk it up and down sharply, quite possibly damaging it. In very calm conditions, you may be able to put your system on a low swim step to grab after you enter.

If you're beach diving, streamline your system as much as possible, especially if you're entering through light surf. Use clips or a wrist lanyard to avoid loss, and use a port cover to protect your dome from scratches and sand. Don't set your system down in the sand at anytime; sand will cling to the o-rings, possibly damaging them and causing leaks.

If conditions look too rough to enter easily with your video system, leave it ashore. Better to miss shooting than to trash your system. Besides, if it's that rough, chances are the viz is too poor for decent video anyway.

Buoyancy, Drag and Air Consumption

Although a video system can be quite heavy out of water, in water a properly weighted system is only slightly negative or positive (if it's not, adjust it). Therefore, your video system has little effect on your buoyancy.

But your system does have mass and drag, and that means you use more energy swimming around with it. If you end up swimming a good bit on a dive, you may find you use air faster than normal. Coupled with this, videography demands concentration, so that as you shoot, it's easier to lose track of depth, direction and no stop time.

Therefore, make a habit of checking your air, computer and other instruments about twice as often as you would without a video system. This reduces the possibility of accidentally ending up in an emergency because you became so focused on shooting that you forgot basic dive safety.

Avoid the habit of holding your breath – something some videographers do unconsciously to help steady the camcorder. This, as you know, carries an unacceptable risk of lung overexpansion injury, so don't allow yourself to do this. If you find you have a headache after a video dive, pay closer attention to your breathing because this is a tip off that you might be unconsciously holding your breath.

Make a habit of checking your air, computer and other instruments about twice as often as you would without a video system. This reduces the possibility of accidentally ending up in an emergency because you became so focused on shooting that you forgot basic dive safety.

As mentioned earlier, be cautious about the environment when shooting. Don't get so distracted that you neglect buoyancy or allow yourself to hurt aquatic life. Give video third priority, after your and your buddy's safety and after protecting the underwater world.

Diving Emergencies with Your Video System

In an underwater emergency, if your video system is part of or contributes to the problem, or interferes with handling the problem then *ditch it!* It's expensive? In *that* case . . . ditch it anyway.

Video systems may be costly, but they're not worth your safety, or your buddy's, or anyone else's. They're not worth risking severe injury, nor are they worth letting get in the way of handling an emergency.

Most of the time, you'll probably be able to recover your system. Some divers prefer a slightly positive system so that if they ditch it, there's some chance of finding it floating on the surface. Others prefer slightly negative so that if they ditch it, there's some chance it won't drift away and they can find it on the bottom on a subsequent dive.

Either way, you have to consider your video system expendable when a safety question arises. If you can't, take up another hobby.

Video systems may be costly, but they're not worth your safety, or your buddy's, or anyone else's. In an emergency, ditch it if necessary.

Video Emergencies

Now let's look at what to do if your *video system* is in trouble on a dive, keeping in mind that because it's expendable, no malfunction – no matter how severe – creates grounds for compromising diver safety.

Moisture/leak warning. This almost certainly means a leak, though condensation can trigger it. Turn the housing lens port down (so any water accumulates there) or to the position the manufacturer recommends. Make a normal, safe ascent and hand the system aboard (if boat diving), instructing the person taking it to keep the housing in the same orientation.

Exit, dry yourself and the housing, again keeping it port down. Check the port for water. Open the housing and remove the camcorder. If you can't find water, it was probably condensation. If you find water, it was almost certainly a leak. If you can't find the cause, have it serviced professionally before using it again.

With the camcorder removed, reseal the housing and rinse it, then dry it thoroughly inside and out. If you suspect condensation, handle it as you already learned. If you can't determine the problem, do not dive the system until you've had it serviced. You're just asking for a ruined camcorder if you do.

Battery warning. This is an irritation, not an emergency. You may be able to finish taping the dive by turning your camcorder off between shots instead of leaving it on standby. Otherwise, you'll have to surface and change the battery. Don't let the rush to get back in the water hurry you. Do it right: Rinse the system, dry it, check the o-rings, etc. like you've already learned. Hurrying is one of the best ways of turning a low battery annoyance into a flooded housing catastrophe.

Flooded housing, minor – A "minor" flood is one in which there's definitely water coming in the housing, but it's a trickle and as far as you can tell, it has not gotten the camcorder substantially wet.

As before, turn the system off and turn the housing lens port down (or as the manufacturer recommends). Ascend immediately, but don't exceed a safe rate (18 metres/60 feet per minute, or as stipulated by your computer). Remove the housing from the water keeping it port down. Dry yourself and the housing and remove the camcorder. Don't reuse the housing until you have it serviced.

Shut off the camcorder (if it's not already), remove the battery and allow any damp air or moisture to dry out in an air-conditioned room. After several hours, if you see no moisture, you can replace the battery and see if it functions. If it does, you're probably okay, though water damage can take weeks or months to manifest itself. If it doesn't work, unfortunately it's probably beyond economical repair.

If you experience a leak, turn the system off and turn the housing lens port down (or as the manufacturer recommends). Ascend immediately, but don't exceed a safe rate (18 metres/60 feet per minute, or as stipulated by your computer). Remove the housing from the water keeping it port down.

Flooded housing, major – A "major" flood is one in which there's lots of water in the housing and your camcorder is substantially wet.

This isn't an emergency. Sorry, but your camcorder is already toast. Finí. Kicked the bucket. Play taps. Make a normal ascent and safety stop because it's beyond repair anyway, and in the very, very, very unlikely chance it is repairable, a few more minutes won't make much difference at this point. No point getting bent over it.

At the surface, open the flooded housing as soon as possible away from other people and pointed away from yourself. Wet electronics, especially batteries, put off gases that may make the housing pop or burst open. Have the housing serviced before you use it again with a brand new camcorder of the same make and model.

The worst part about flooding a housing is realizing that 99 out of a hundred times, it's your own fault. The vast majority of floods result from user error by failing to maintain o-rings, failing to assemble and test the unit or failing to maintain the system according to manufacturer guidelines. It's very rare that a housing floods due to defect.

Quick REVIEW

Videography 4

1. When entering the water with your video system (check all that apply):
   ☐ a. have someone hand it to you.
   ☐ b. don't suspend it on a line in rough conditions.
   ☐ c. avoid beach dives if conditions look too rough.

2. You can expect your video system to _____ your air consumption.
   ☐ a. decrease
   ☐ b. increase
   ☐ c. have no effect on

3. When diving with a video system, you should check your air and gauges about twice as often as you would without your video system.
   ☐ True   ☐ False

4. In the event of a diving emergency,
   ☐ a. ditch your video system if necessary.
   ☐ b. clip your video system to your weight belt.

5. In the event of a low battery warning
   ☐ a. hurry to the surface to prevent damage to your camcorder.
   ☐ b. make a safe, normal ascent, exit the water and change batteries.

6. If you have a major flood in your housing (check all that apply):
   ☐ a. it's not an emergency.
   ☐ b. you'll be buying a new camcorder.
   ☐ c. open it at the surface pointed away from yourself and other people.

How'd you do?
1. a, b, c. **2.** b. **3.** True, **4.** a. **5.** b. **6.** a, b, c.

A WORD ABOUT EDITING

In shooting a video, the idea is to tell a story. The process of taking different video segments and assembling them into a story is called *video editing*. In *post production* editing, you take your original shots and, as necessary, change their length and sequence to tell a story based on a script or outline you've planned in advance.

Editing and post production editing are beyond the scope of the Underwater Videography Adventure Dive, though you will get into it more when you take the Underwater Videographer Specialty course. But, you can apply *in-camera editing* to make your Adventure Dive tape more fun to watch.

To do this, jot down a brief story you'd like to tell – perhaps its the story of the dive itself. Make a short list, in order, of video shots that tell this story. Perhaps you begin with arriving at the dive site, then gearing up, then descending, and so on until you show everyone leaving at the end of the day. Now shoot your list, in order, so that you tell the story. Your tape will be much more watchable, and you'll be learning the basic fundamentals of editing.

Good luck.

PADI Underwater Videographer Specialty Course

Your Underwater Videography Adventure Dive may credit (at the instructor's discretion) toward the Underwater Videographer Specialty certification. In addition to what you've learned in this section and will practice on the Underwater Videography Adventure Dive, the Underwater Videographer course covers:

- video composition
- long, medium and close-up video shots
- shot sequencing
- camera moves
- editing and story lines
- producing a short video

Underwater Videography Adventure Dive Overview

- Knowledge assessment/ Knowledge Review
- Video system preparation
- Briefing
- Gearing up
- Predive safety check (BWRAF)
- Entry – retrieve video system
- Shooting with video system
- Standing
- Sitting
- Kneeling
- Lying
- Swimming
- Holding steady – at all times
- Camera motion slow and steady – all moves
- Check depth, time, air supply and location frequently throughout dive
- Maintain proper buoyancy throughout dive
- Ascent – safety stop
- Exit
- Postdive procedures
- Video system disassembly
- Debrief and review video
- Log dive – PADI Instructor signs

KNOWLEDGE REVIEW
Underwater Videography

1. Explain why the combination of a wide angle lens and dome port gives you the best sharpness, color and focus.

2. What is the best general angle for all-round underwater videography?

3. List four common errors to avoid while shooting underwater videos.

4. Describe how to prepare and check your underwater video system.

5. Describe postdive care for your underwater video system.

6. Explain how to enter/exit the water with a video system.

7. Explain how video systems may affect buoyancy, drag and air consumption.

8. How often should you check your gauges when shooting underwater videos?

9. What should you do with a video system in a diving emergency, such as having to assist a buddy's who's out of air?

10. Explain what to do if a video system has a major flood, and why.

Student Diver Statement: I've completed this Knowledge Review to the best of my ability and any questions I answered incorrectly or incompletely I've had explained to me, and I understand what I missed.

Signature _____ Date_____

WRECK DIVING

Introduction

There's nothing quite like the thrill of diving a wreck for the first time. Descending, you gaze downward, trying to catch a glimpse of it. At first, nothing. Then a hazy outline appears, and for a moment you're confused as your eyes try to sort it out. Then the wreck dissolves into clear view as you arrive upon it.

What you find next depends on the wreck and where you are. In cold, fresh water like the North American Great Lakes, you may find sunken ships nearly intact after more than 100 years underwater. In the tropical waters of Chuuk (Truk) Lagoon, Micronesia, you would find the remains of the Japanese Imperial Fleet, thickly encrusted with coral since they sank in World War II. In the Mediterranean, what might appear to be nothing more than a mound of old jars to the inexperienced eye may be a ship that sank when the Roman Empire dominated the West.

It's no wonder wreck diving is popular. While most dive sites are natural habitats, a wreck is a work of mankind. Because of this, wrecks offer diversity, attractions and opportunities not found in "natural" dive environments – but nature encroaches as the underwater world changes it into an artificial reef teeming with life. As a result, diving wrecks is an adventure in exploring humanity's loss and nature's gain.

REASONS FOR WRECK DIVING

Underline/highlight the answers to these questions as you read:

1. What are four common reasons people wreck dive?

2. What are two reasons artifact recovery is discouraged and not covered in this section or the PADI Wreck Diver course?

Why wreck dive? If you're reading this section, you probably already have an answer. With many diving opportunities on wrecks, wreck diving may interest you for any of several reasons. Four of the most common are curiosity and adventure, history, aquatic life and photography.

Curiosity and adventure. Wrecks are enigmas, especially the first time you dive them. When exploring a fairly intact wreck, you may find yourself wondering where it came from, who worked on it, what ports it called on, and why it sank. When visiting a well-known, researched wreck, it's easy to imagine the captain standing on the bridge battling the fatal storm or trying to evade a torpedo, and wonder what it was like. There's a moment of anticipation each time you look in, around or under something because, who knows what you'll find?

Wrecks quickly become artificial reefs, attracting underwater life and providing new habitats (something to grow on and hide in). In some regions, the best place to find aquatic life is on wrecks.

History. Wrecks are not just lost ships, but tangible historical resources to humanity's past. As such, many wreck divers work with or are archaeologists and historians looking for clues about our cultural past when the ship still sailed. Some wrecks contain irreplaceable historical resources, which you must respect and leave undisturbed.

Aquatic Life. As mentioned in the introduction, wrecks quickly become artificial reefs, attracting underwater life and providing new habitats (something to grow on and hide in). In some regions, the best place to find aquatic life is on wrecks. In these areas, you may engage in wreck diving not so much for the wreck, but because it is the best place to find nature.

Photography. Thanks to standing structures and the aquatic life commonly found on them, wrecks tend to be photogenic. Fairly intact wrecks present a background that nondivers recognize, making it easier

Wreck Diving
See the PADI *Wreck Diver Manual* and *Wreck Diving* video.

for them to relate to what they see. If you're fond of underwater photography, don't leave your still or video camera behind when you've diving a wreck.

About Artifact Recovery

You'll notice that neither this section nor the Wreck Diver Specialty course covers removing artifacts or other objects from shipwrecks. There are several reasons for this, but the two most compelling are: 1. Once a popular wreck has been stripped of artifacts, it's a much less interesting dive site for other divers. As you'll see for yourself, the more complete or intact the wreck, the more picturesque and compelling it is. 2. You need to leave wrecks with historical significance undisturbed for research by archaeologists. Archaeologists uncover the past by examining how objects in a wreck lie in relation to each other. You can permanently destroy some secret about our ancestors simply by moving something; therefore, only a trained archaeologist (or those working under the guidance of one) should disturb such wrecks.

Of course, not all wrecks are historical, but in any case, the actual techniques for securing and raising heavy objects require special training beyond the scope of this section. And, objects require special treatment and preservation after you get them to the surface. If these kinds of activities interest you, seek further training and diving opportunities with marine archaeological institutions and groups.

Object recovery is generally discouraged because once a popular wreck has been stripped of artifacts, it's a much less interesting dive site for other divers. If a wreck has historical significance, you need to leave artifacts undisturbed for research by archaeologists.

Quick REVIEW

Wreck 1

1. Common reasons why divers dive on shipwrecks are curiosity and adventure, history, aquatic life and photography.
   ☐ True   ☐ False

2. One reason artifact recovery is discouraged is that it makes the dive site less interesting for other divers.
   ☐ True   ☐ False

How'd you do?
1. True; 2. True.

WRECK DIVING AND THE LAW

Underline/highlight the answer to this question as you read:

1. Why must you pay close attention to local laws before planning a wreck dive?

Shipwrecks have been subject to national and international law for hundreds of years. Originally, these laws determined who owned any valuables recovered from a wreck (especially an abandoned one), but more recently laws have been passed to protect those wrecks that are submerged cultural resources.

It's important that you be aware of and heed all local laws pertaining to shipwrecks. In some areas, particularly those with many historically important wrecks, you may need a permit before you can dive on one. Other locales may allow you to dive without special permission, but it may be illegal to touch or take anything from the wreck. In yet other areas, you may dive some wrecks with virtually no restrictions, and yet others will be entirely off limits. Because in the past divers plundered and destroyed many historically important wrecks through ignorance (and sometimes greed), today governments tend to enforce antiquities laws quite vigorously.

Wreck 2

1. In some areas, _____ are required by law before you can dive on a shipwreck.
   ☐ a. special pieces of equipment
   ☐ b. permits

How'd you do?
1. b.

WRECK DIVING HAZARDS AND CONSIDERATIONS

CONCEPTS

Underline/highlight the answers
to these questions as you read:

1. What are five hazards common to wrecks, and how do you avoid them?

2. What five dive planning and equipment considerations should you make for wreck dives deeper than 18 metres/60 feet?

3. What are two reasons to obtain a local orientation to an unfamiliar wreck?

4. What are five hazards of entering a shipwreck, and why is special training mandatory to enter a shipwreck?

Old movies portray hardhat divers battling the giant octopus that inevitably hides in every sunken ship, guarding the treasure chest. If that's what you're expecting, sorry. You'll find recreational wreck diving adventurous and exciting, and like other areas of diving it has a few hazards and considerations to keep in mind. These don't generally include giant octopus, but more routine potential hazards commonly found around wrecks. You've got some considerations for diving wrecks deeper than 18 metres/60 feet, reasons why you'll want orientations to new wrecks, and you should recognize the significant hazards of entering a shipwreck.

Five Potential Wreck Hazards

There are a few hazards common to almost all wrecks that, with awareness, you can avoid pretty easily.

Sharp objects. Rusted metal, splintering wood, broken glass, coral encrustations and other objects can cut a careless diver. Although intentionally sunk wrecks tend to have fewer of these, over time a rusty edge can become knife-sharp.

Use good buoyancy control to minimize contact with the wreck, and always wear heavy-duty protective gloves when wreck diving. It's also wise to keep tetanus immunizations current in case you do accidently get a cut.

Entanglement. Entanglement is rare, but wrecks often have old ropes, monofilament and other line on them. Because wrecks attract fish, they're popular fishing grounds. Monofilament line and sometimes fishing nets end up ensnarled on the wreck. Avoid these by watching where you go. Look up as well as around to avoid swimming into or under a potential entanglement.

Use good buoyancy control to minimize contact with the wreck, and always wear heavy-duty protective gloves when wreck diving.

When wreck diving, carry a sharp knife with a smooth and a serrated edge in case you encounter entanglement too difficult to handle by hand.

Aquatic life. A wreck quickly becomes an artifical reef, so expect to find any aquatic life that can bite or sting on local natural reefs on a wreck. Avoid these the same as you would on a natural reef: watch where you put your hands, feet and knees, wear an exposure suit and gloves, and avoid contact with unfamiliar creatures.

Unstable structure. As a wreck ages and deteriorates, portions weaken, supports give way and walls shift. In some wrecks, this presents a hazard from collapsing walls and falling objects. Avoid diving around wrecks with unstable structures. If you encounter a portion of a wreck that seems unfirm and could possibly fall, get clear of the area. Don't swim under anything that could fall on you.

Surge pockets and suction. Surge and water movement through a wreck can cause periodic suction or fast currents through restricted areas and hatches. If you find surge present, be cautious for this kind of water movement and stay away from tight spaces, hatches and restricted areas. Better yet, postpone your visit to the wreck until you can do so without surge or high current conditions.

If you find surge present, be cautious and stay away from tight spaces, hatches and restricted areas. Better yet, come back when conditions are better.

Considerations for Deeper Wrecks

Many wrecks lie below 18 metres/60 feet; it's one reason many divers become interested in deep diving. Before diving on such a wreck, there are four planning and equipment considerations to take into account:

PADI Deep Diver training. Diving deeper than 18 metres/60 feet is an activity that's best learned under professional supervision. You do this first in the Deep Adventure Dive and second in the PADI Deep Diver Specialty course. These provide you practical experience in the challenges of deeper diving, while supervised by a PADI Instructor.

Extra tank at 5 metres/15 feet. As mentioned in the Deep Diving section, it's a good idea to hang a spare tank and regulator at 5 metres/15 feet in case you need to make an emergency decompression stop, or to permit a safety stop with a low air supply. Be sure you have any other equipment necessary for a deep dive in the local environment.

It's a good idea to hang a spare tank and regulator at 5 metres/15 feet in case you need to make an emergency decompression stop, or to permit a safety stop with a low air supply.

Nitrogen narcosis. Take this into account when planning your wreck dive. For example, you may be less coordinated, making it easier to bump into objects.

If you're a PADI Enriched Air Diver, wrecks in particular make good sites to take advantage of the added no stop time you get from enriched air.

Short time limits. As you go deeper, you have shorter no decompression limits and you use air faster. Keep these in mind when planning the dive.

You can gain no decompression time by following a multilevel profile with your computer or The Wheel on some wrecks, but many wrecks offer insufficient relief to allow this. If you're a PADI Enriched Air Diver, wrecks in particular make good sites to take advantage of the added no stop time you get from enriched air.

Local Orientation to a New Wreck

When diving a wreck for the first time, particularly in a new area, it's a good idea to get a local instructor, divemaster or experienced diver to orient you to the wreck. Wreck diving techniques vary from area to area and wreck to wreck, and this is a good way to find out the best techniques. Your instructor will show you the best technique for the Wreck Adventure Dive.

Another reason for a local orientation is that a wreck may have unique hazards and points of interest. A diver experienced with the wreck can help you plan your dive by letting you know what to expect in advance.

Shipwreck Penetration

One reason for an orientation to a wreck is so that you don't miss any unique points of interest.

Intact shipwrecks can have open hatchways and passages that seem to invite exploration. Going into the wreck may seem harmless, and you may see no immediate danger, **but entering a wreck without special training and equipment places you in an extremely hazardous situation.** The techniques for shipwreck penetration are beyond the scope of this section. You face five serious hazards when you enter a wreck overhead environment; it's important to understand why you should not enter a wreck without the proper equipment and training.

Loss of direction. While it may look safe from the outside, merely entering a wreck can cause confusion, made worse if the wreck is leaning on its side. Collapsed passages and obscured doorways block logical travel passages and open others. The wrong way out looks "righter" than the right way out. It's very easy to lose your sense of direction inside a wreck.

No direct access to the surface. Should you have an air supply problem or other emergency, you *must* exit the wreck before you can ascend. The emergency swimming ascent and buoyant emergency ascent are no longer options.

Restricted passages. Inside a wreck, you may find yourself in a passage so tight turning is difficult. This raises the possibility of hitting sharp or abrasive objects; it can even keep you from turning around to exit. It may be impossible for you and your buddy to go through a tight passage while sharing air in an emergency.

Falling objects. Your movement can knock loose objects that can fall on you, or behind you blocking your exit.

Silt. Most wrecks have a layer of silt (particulate matter) spread inside them that you can easily disturb with your fins, hands and even your exhaust bubbles. This can reduce visibility to almost nothing, making it nearly impossible to find your way out.

Obviously, entering wrecks is an activity reserved for those trained and equipped to handle these hazards. If you find that wreck penetration is something you have an interest in, enrolling in a PADI Wreck Diver Specialty course can teach you the techniques for limited, recreational penetration wreck dives. Ask your instructor specifically about wreck penetration and whether you make such a dive in the course (it's optional).

Entering wrecks is an activity reserved for those trained and equipped to handle these hazards.

REVIEW

Wreck 3

1. Wreck divers should wear heavy-duty gloves to
   ☐ a. protect against rusted metal and other potential injury sources.
   ☐ b. capture lobsters and other game common on wrecks.

2. When diving deeper than 18 metres/60 feet, it's a good idea to include _____ as part of your equipment.
   ☐ a. a safety tank and regulator at 5 metres/15 feet
   ☐ b. a dive computer

3. Local hazards and diving techniques vary from wreck to wreck, making an orientation to an unfamiliar wreck highly desirable.
   ☐ True   ☐ False

4. Without special training, entering a shipwreck can be very dangerous.
   ☐ True   ☐ False

How'd you do?
1. a; 2. a; 3. True; 4. True.

ASSESSING AND NAVIGATING AN UNDERWATER WRECK

When you make your Wreck Adventure Dive with your PADI Instructor, you'll practice *assessing* and *navigating* the wreck.

Assessing the Wreck

Assessing the wreck is an awareness rather than a deliberate process, though on some wrecks you may focus on it. There are three points to generally evaluate as you dive on a wreck for the first time, and which you will continuously reevaluate on subsequent visits to the wreck.

Possible hazards. Look for the hazards described earlier so you can avoid them, and be alert to any that may be unique to the wreck.

Points of interest. Look for what stands out on the wreck, and what makes it interesting. Look for key features that tell you something about the wreck. Don't forget to look closely – the most interesting parts of a wreck are not necessarily the largest and most obvious. Look for changes; what you saw last time may be gone, and something you didn't see before may be obvious now.

General condition. The wreck's condition affects the way you explore it and your safety. Pay attention to the wreck's strength – is it flimsy anywhere? Is it recognizable and intact or broken up and strewn over a wide area? This gives a feel for the wreck; after several dives, you may be able to tell a great deal even about a very broken up wreck.

Navigating the Wreck

The method you use to navigate on a wreck depends upon its condition. There are three basic ways to navigate on a wreck, and you may find it

Assessing the wreck is an awareness rather than a deliberate process; it's something you do each time you visit a wreck.

advantageous to use different techniques on different parts of the same wreck, or to combine them at times.

Following the wreck's layout. On a fairly intact wreck, the simplest navigation may be to tour the wreck much as you might if it weren't underwater. For example, you can swim along the hull, or follow the deck or a rail. This is one of the easiest ways to navigate on a wreck.

Feature reference. On a more broken up wreck, or even on an intact wreck in murky water, you may need to note unique features and their relative positions to find your way. If necessary, note these on a slate as you start the dive and use your sketch as a map for your return.

Baseline. A baseline is used on a very scattered or broken up wreck, and is a straight line through the wreckage. In clear, calm water, the baseline can be as informal as a general direction through the wreck, and in murkier water a compass heading may be used. (Note: Steel or iron objects in a wreck can affect your compass readings by attracting your compass needle. Don't expect your com

pass to be as accurate as usual when navigating in a wreck.) In poor visibility or with a strong current, your baseline might be an actual line or rope lying through the wreckage.

You use a baseline by swimming along it, leaving it for short distances to explore the wreck. The baseline forms a known heading back to the boat anchor or exit. By keeping track of the baseline, you always know where you are and the way to return at the end of the dive.

Wreck 4

1. Possible hazards, points of interest and the general condition of a wreck are always assessed the first time you dive an unfamiliar wreck.
   ☐ True   ☐ False

2. The easiest way to navigate a fairly intact wreck in clear water is to
   ☐ a. obtain a blueprint of it to use as a map.
   ☐ b. follow the natural layout of the ship.

3. A compass may not be as accurate as usual on a shipwreck because
   ☐ a. iron and steel objects may cause the magnetic needle to deviate from magnetic north.
   ☐ b. wreck environments are too restricted to take a bearing.

How'd you do?
1. True;   2. b;   3. a.

PADI Wreck Diver Specialty Course

Your Wreck Adventure Dive may be credited (at the instructor's discretion) toward the PADI Wreck Diver Specialty certification. In addition to what you've learned in this section and will practice on the Wreck Adventure Dive, the PADI Wreck Diver Specialty course includes:

- Penetration techniques
- Wreck mapping
- Origin of wreck diving laws
- Researching wrecks

Explore!

Crashed Planes.
Sunken Ships.
Lost Treasures.

*One of the most popular PADI
Specialty programs –
Check it out!*

**Take the next step in your exploration of
diving with PADI's Wreck Diver program.**

*Search out your nearest PADI Dive Center or Resort
to start your adventure today!*

PADI
padi.com

Could you say no to this face?

Support your underwater friends and our delicate aquatic environment by becoming a Project AWARE Patron. Your contributions support ongoing projects like beach and underwater cleanups, mooring buoy projects, educational programs, environmental research and more.

For a minimal, tax-deductible donation, Project AWARE Patrons are entitled to special benefits like embroidered hats or beautifully engraved recognition awards, and a quarterly newsletter detailing recent projects, activities and events sponsored by the Foundation.

For more information, or to download a Patron contribution form, visit

www.projectaware.org

You may also call the Project AWARE Foundation at

800 729 7234, ext. 2448 or **+1 949 858 7657**

The Project AWARE Foundation is the dive industry's leading nonprofit 501(c)(3) environmental organization.

© International PADI, Inc. 2002

Appendix

Recreational Dive Planner Review
IMPERIAL VERSION

To determine your current ability to solve Recreational Dive Planner calculations (with the Table or The Wheel), complete this review. Choose the best answer to each question by circling a single letter.

1. Residual nitrogen time is the total time in minutes from the beginning of descent until the beginning of final ascent to the surface or safety stop.
   ☐ True   ☐ False

2. When using the dive tables, divers must ascend no faster than a rate of _____ feet per minute.
   ☐ a. 20 ft   ☐ b. 60 ft   ☐ c. 40 ft   ☐ d. 80 ft

3. A dive to 59 feet for 30 minutes yields what pressure group?
   ☐ a. L   ☐ b. J   ☐ c. K   ☐ d. M

4. A diver in pressure group G plans a dive to 59 feet. What is the maximum allowable bottom time according to the Recreational Dive Planner?
   ☐ a. 34 minutes   ☐ c. 42 minutes
   ☐ b. 25 minutes   ☐ d. 26 minutes

5. A diver in pressure group D completes a dive to 46 feet for 29 minutes. What is his new pressure group upon surfacing?
   ☐ a. T   ☐ b. P   ☐ c. O   ☐ d. U

6. A diver makes a dive to 56 feet for 44 minutes. After a one-hour surface interval, he returns to 56 feet. Losing track of time, he notices that his bottom time is now 37 minutes. According to the Recreational Dive Planner, what action should he take?
   ☐ a. Surface immediately and contact the nearest recompression chamber.
   ☐ b. Immediately ascend to 15 feet and remain there for 3 minutes before surfacing.
   ☐ c. Immediately ascend to 15 feet and remain there for 8 minutes before surfacing.
   ☐ d. Ascend to 10 feet and remain there until air is exhausted.

7. After completing the dives indicated in question 6, what is the minimum amount of time the diver must wait prior to flying?
   ☐ a. The diver may fly immediately after the dive.
   ☐ b. 12 hours.
   ☐ c. An extended surface interval beyond 12 hours.
   ☐ d. 4 hours.

8. What is the minimum surface interval required to make a dive to 90 feet for 19 minutes, followed by a 50-foot dive for 47 minutes?
   ☐ a. 33 minutes   ☐ c. 10 minutes
   ☐ b. 20 minutes   ☐ d. 11 minutes

9. A divemaster is planning to take a group of advanced divers to two different locations. One is a reef in 54 feet of water, and he plans a bottom time of 25 minutes. The second location is on a wreck in 95 feet of water, where he plans a bottom time of 20 minutes. The surface interval between the dives will be two hours. In the interest of safety, which dive should the divemaster plan first?
   ☐ a. The order of dives is of no consequence in this example.
   ☐ b. The 54-foot dive.
   ☐ c. The 95-foot dive.
   ☐ d. Whichever the group wishes to dive!

10. A diver makes a dive to a depth of 56 feet for 24 minutes. After a one-hour surface interval, he wishes to return to a depth of 46 feet. What is the maximum allowable bottom time for the second dive?
   ☐ a. 14 minutes   ☐ c. 53 minutes
   ☐ b. 83 minutes   ☐ d. 63 minutes

How'd you do?
1. False; **2.** b; **3.** a; **4.** a; **5.** b; **6.** c; **7.** c; **8.** The Wheel: d/Table: c; **9.** c; **10.** d.

Recreational Dive Planner Review
METRIC VERSION

To determine your current ability to solve Recreational Dive Planner calculations (with the Table or The Wheel), complete this review. Choose the best answer to each question by circling a single letter.

1. Residual nitrogen time is the total time in minutes from the beginning of descent until the beginning of final ascent to the surface or safety stop.
   ☐ True   ☐ False

2. When using the dive tables, divers must ascend no faster than a rate of _____ metres per minute.
   ☐ a. 6 m   ☐ b. 18 m   ☐ c. 12 m   ☐ d. 24 m

3. A dive to 18 metres for 30 minutes yields what pressure group?
   ☐ a. L   ☐ b. J   ☐ c. K   ☐ d. M

4. A diver in pressure group K plans a dive to 17 metres. What is the maximum allowable bottom time according to the Recreational Dive Planner?
   ☐ a. 26 minutes   ☐ c. 29 minutes
   ☐ b. 44 minutes   ☐ d. 27 minutes

5. A diver in pressure group D completes a dive to 14 metres for 29 minutes. What is his new pressure group upon surfacing?
   ☐ a. T   ☐ b. P   ☐ c. O   ☐ d. U

6. A diver makes a dive to 17 metres for 44 minutes. After a one-hour surface interval, he returns to 17 metres. Losing track of time, he notices that his bottom time is now 37 minutes. According to the Recreational Dive Planner, what action should he take?
   ☐ a. Surface immediately and contact the nearest recompression chamber.
   ☐ b. Immediately ascend to 5 metres and remain there for 3 minutes before surfacing.
   ☐ c. Immediately ascend to 5 metres and remain there for 8 minutes before surfacing.
   ☐ d. Ascend to 3 metres and remain there until air is exhausted.

7. After completing the dives indicated in question 6, what is the minimum amount of time the diver must wait prior to flying?
   ☐ a. The diver may fly immediately after the dive.
   ☐ b. 12 hours.
   ☐ c. An extended surface interval beyond 12 hours.
   ☐ d. 4 hours.

8. What is the minimum surface interval required to make a dive to 24 metres for 23 minutes, followed by a 15-metre dive for 47 minutes?
   ☐ a. 33 minutes   ☐ c. 8 minutes
   ☐ b. 20 minutes   ☐ d. 15 minutes

9. A divemaster is planning to take a group of advanced divers to two different locations. One is a reef in 16 metres of water, and he plans a bottom time of 25 minutes. The second location is on a wreck in 29 metres of water, where he plans a bottom time of 20 minutes. The surface interval between the dives will be two hours. In the interest of safety, which dive should the divemaster plan first?
   ☐ a. The order of dives is of no consequence in this example.
   ☐ b. The 16-metre dive.
   ☐ c. The 29-metre dive.
   ☐ d. Whichever the group wishes to dive!

10. A diver makes a dive to a depth of 17 metres for 24 minutes. After a one-hour surface interval, he wishes to return to a depth of 14 metres. What is the maximum allowable bottom time for the second dive?
   ☐ a. 14 minutes   ☐ c. 41 minutes
   ☐ b. 83 minutes   ☐ d. 80 minutes

How'd you do?
1. False; **2.** b; **3.** The Wheel:a/Table: c; **4.** The Wheel: d/Table: a; **5.** c; **6.** c; **7.** c; **8.** a; **9.** c; **10.** The Wheel: d/Table: b.

⊕PADI Equipment Checklist

Basic Equipment

- [ ] Gear Bag
- [ ] Fins, Mask, Snorkel
- [ ] Wet Suit
  - [ ] Jacket
  - [ ] Pants
  - [ ] Vest
  - [ ] Hood
  - [ ] Boots
  - [ ] Gloves
- [ ] Dry Suit
  - [ ] Undergarments
  - [ ] Inflation Hose
  - [ ] Repair and Care Items
  - [ ] Hood
  - [ ] Boots
  - [ ] Gloves
- [ ] Weight Belt
- [ ] BCD *(Buoyancy Control Device)* With Whistle
- [ ] Tank *(filled)*
- [ ] Regulator *(with SPG and alternate air source)*
- [ ] Compass
- [ ] Depth Gauge *(altitude adjustable)*
- [ ] Knife
- [ ] Watch
- [ ] Dive Computer *(altitude adjustable)*

Accessory Equipment

- [ ] Float and Flag
- [ ] Thermometer
- [ ] Slate and Pencil
- [ ] Marker Buoy
- [ ] Buddy Line
- [ ] First Aid Kit
- [ ] Emergency Oxygen
- [ ] Inflatable Signal Tube
- [ ] Flashing Signal Light
- [ ] Goodie Bag

Specialty Equipment

- [ ] Recreational Dive Planner (Wheel or Table)
- [ ] Theoretical Depth at Altitude Charts *(from Adventures in Diving manual)*

- [ ] Deep Diving Surface Support Station
  - [ ] Reference Line
  - [ ] Spare Tank
  - [ ] Regulator(s)
  - [ ] Spare Weights
- [ ] Diver Propulsion Vehicle and Accessories
- [ ] Drift Diving Surface Float with Line
- [ ] Fish Identification Slates
  - [ ] Marine Life ID Books
- [ ] Underwater Camera, Film and Accessories
- [ ] Underwater Video Camera, Tape and Accessories
- [ ] Dive Lights
  - [ ] Primary, Backup
  - [ ] Shore Lights for Navigation
- [ ] Search and Recovery Equipment
  - [ ] Lift Bag and Rigging
  - [ ] Search Line with Reel

Spare Equipment

- [ ] Tanks (filled)
- [ ] Weights
- [ ] Straps
- [ ] O-ring
- [ ] Tools
- [ ] Regulator HP Plug
- [ ] Bulbs and Batteries
- [ ] Nylon Line

Personal Items

- [ ] Swimsuit, Towel
- [ ] Jacket
- [ ] Extra Clothes
- [ ] Money
- [ ] Tickets
- [ ] Certification Card
- [ ] Log Book
- [ ] Sunglasses
- [ ] Suntan Lotion
- [ ] Medications
- [ ] Personal Articles
- [ ] Lunch, Thermos
- [ ] Eating Utensils
- [ ] Ice Chest
- [ ] Sleeping Bag

⊕PADI Boat Diving Information Sheet

Date of trip _____ Name of vessel _____

Landing _____ City _____

Directions _____

Destination _____ Cost _____

Departure time _____ Estimated return time _____

Items Needed

- ☐ Diving equipment
- ☐ Gear bag
- ☐ Extra tank
- ☐ Warm clothes

- ☐ Jacket
- ☐ Towel
- ☐ Suntan lotion
- ☐ Medication

- ☐ Ticket
- ☐ Money
- ☐ Lunch, snacks
- ☐ Drinks

Terminology

Bow	Front end of the boat	Leeward	The downwind side, sheltered side
Stern	Rear end of the boat	Windward	Side facing into the wind; windy side
Port	Left side of the boat when facing the bow	Galley	Kitchen
Starboard	Right side of the boat when facing bow	Head	Restroom
Bridge	Wheelhouse, vessel control area		

General Instructions

- Double-check to be sure you have all required equipment and needed items.
- Board vessel at least one half hour prior to departure time.
- Ask crew where and how to stow your gear.
- Place clothes, cameras, lunch, and all items to be kept dry, inside.
- Place all diving equipment outside on the deck.
- Wait in the stern area for pre-departure briefing (if applicable).
- Keep dockside rail clear during docking operations.
- If susceptible to seasickness, take madication prior to departure.
- If seasick, use the leeward rail, not the head.
- Learn toilet operation and rules before using head.
- Stay off the bow during anchoring operations.
- Work out of your gear bag. No loose gear on deck.
- Check out and check in with the divemaster for all dives.
- Pack and stow all gear before return trip.
- Be available for visual roll call before boat is moved.
- Check to be sure nothing is left behind when disembarking.

General Rules

- No trash or litter overboard. Use trash cans.
- Bridge and engine room are off-limits.
- Do not sit on the rails when underway.
- Follow the instructions of the crew.

PADI Dive Planning Checklist

Advance Planning

- ☐ Dive buddy(s) _____
- ☐ Date and time (check tide tables) _____
- ☐ Dive objective _____
- ☐ Location _____
- ☐ Alternate location(s) _____
- ☐ Directions _____
  _____
- ☐ Meeting place and time _____
- ☐ Any special or extra gear needed _____
- ☐ Precheck of weather and water conditions _____

Preparation

- ☐ Tank(s) filled
- ☐ Equipment inspected
- ☐ Equipment marked (ID)
- ☐ Spare parts inventoried
- ☐ Weights adjusted
- ☐ Equipment packed
- ☐ Transportation arranged
- ☐ Obtain information on new location
- ☐ Get local emergency contact information

Last Minute

- ☐ Make sure you are healthy, rested and nourished.
- ☐ Have a good, confident feeling about the dive.
- ☐ Check weather and water conditions.
- ☐ Pack food, snacks, drinks.
- ☐ Leave dive plan information with someone not going.
  (dive site, expected return time, what to do if you do not report back by agreed time, etc.)
- ☐ Be sure you have
  - ☐ Tickets
  - ☐ Money
  - ☐ Medications
  - ☐ Directions
  - ☐ Swimsuit
  - ☐ Towel
  - ☐ Jacket
  - ☐ Sunglasses
  - ☐ Other _____

Pre-Dive Planning

- ☐ Evaluate conditions decide whether or not to dive.
- ☐ Locate and check nearest communications (telephone, radio).
- ☐ Select entry/exit points, alternates, methods.
- ☐ Discuss buddy system techniques.
- ☐ Agree on
  - ☐ Pattern or course for the dive
  - ☐ Limits for the dive (depth, time, minimum air)
  - ☐ Emergency procedures

Problems? Call _____ or _____

English-Metric Conversions

Length

1 inch	=	2.54 centimetres	1 centimetre	=	0.39 inches
1 foot	=	0.30 metres	1 metre	=	3.28 feet
1 yard	=	0.91 metres	1 metre	=	1.09 yards
1 fathom	=	1.83 metres/6 feet	1 metre	=	0.55 fathoms
1 statute mile	=	1.61 kilometres/5280 feet	1 kilometre	=	0.62 statute mile
1 nautical mile	=	1.85 kilometres/6080 feet	1 kilometre	=	0.54 nautical mile

Capacity

1 cubic inch	=	16.38 cubic centimetres	1 cubic centimetre	=	.06 cubic feet
1 cubic foot	=	.03 cubic metres	1 cubic metre	=	35.31 cubic feet
1 cubic foot	=	28.32 litres	1 cubic metre	=	1.31 cubic yards
1 cubic yard	=	0.76 cubic metres	1 litre (1000cc)	=	.04 cubic yards
1 pint	=	.57 litres	1 litre	=	.22 gallons
1 gallon	=	4.55 litres	1 litre	=	1.76 pints

Weight

1 ounce	=	28.35 grams	1 cubic ft. fresh	=	62.4 pounds
1 pound	=	.45 kilogram	1 cubic ft. salt	=	64 pounds
1 kilogram	=	2.21 pounds	1 litre fresh	=	1 kilogram
			1 litre salt	=	1.03 kilograms

Pressure

1 pound per square inch	=	0.07 kilograms per square centimetre
1 kilogram per square centimetre	=	14.22 pounds per square inch
1 atmosphere	=	14.7 pounds per square inch
1 atmosphere	=	1.03 kilograms per square centimetre

Temperature

To convert degrees Fahrenheit to Centigrade, deduct 32 and multiply by 5/9.
To convert degrees Centigrade to Fahrenheit, multiply by 9/5 and add 32.

Conversions *(approximate)*

Miles to kilometres	multiply by 8/5
Kilometres to miles	multiply by 5/8
Statute miles to nautical miles	deduct 1/8
Nautical miles to statute miles	add 1/7
Pounds per square inch (psi) to atmospheres	divide by 14.7
Water depth (feet) to bars absolute	divide by 33, add 1 bar
Water depth (metres) to bars absolute	divide by 10, add 1 bar
Bars absolute to feet of water depth	subtract 1 bar, multiply by 33
Bars absolute to metres of water depth	subtract 1 bar, multiply by 10

Wind Direction, Speed and Measurement

Direction is specified always as the direction from which the wind blows.
(For example, a westerly wind blows west to east.)
Speed is in knots by mariners/airmen, in mph by landsmen/coastal navigators.
Measurement: 1 knot = 1.7 feet/.51 metres per second   1 mph = 1.61 kph
1 foot per second = .3 metres per second   1 kph = 5/8 mph

Student Transcript Request

Mail To: Office of Academic Transcripts • International PADI, Inc.
30151 Tomas Street   •   Rancho Santa Margarita, CA 92688-2125

Personal Information – (please type or print clearly)

Student Name _____

Student Mailing Address _____

City _____ State/Province _____

Country _____ Zip/Postal Code _____

Phone (_____)_____ Fax (_____)_____

email_____ Birth Date _____

Sex ☐ M ☐ F Social Security No. _____

Transcript Mailing Information

☐ Self: Mail _____ transcript(s) to address indicated in Personal Informaiton section.

☐ College or University: one transcript will be sent to the institution listed below.

Name of Institution _____

Address _____

City _____ State/Province _____

Country _____ Zip/Postal Code _____

Note: if you need more than two transcripts sent, please include the adresses on an additional sheet of paper. All transcripts sent to a college or university are addressed to the Registrar's Office.

Transcript Fee – $15 for the first transcript and $5 for each additional transcript ordered.

Payment Method

☐ I am requesting _____ transcript(s) at $15 for the first one and $5 for each additional
   TOTAL Enclosed $ _____

☐ Check – make payable to PADI in US dollars and drawn on a US bank

☐ MasterCard   ☐ VISA   Expiration Date _____

   Card No. _____ _____ _____ _____

   Cardholder's Name (please print) _____

   Authorized Signature _____

Verification of Certification – Please Read Carefully
For ***each*** recognized PADI course you want to have listed on your transcript, you must submit proof of course completion by one of the two following methods:
1) Include this form with either a PIC envelope or Divemaster Application **OR**
2) Attach a clear photocopy of the **front and back** of your certification card(s) or validation card(s) to this form.

Receive College Credit for PADI Diver-Training Courses

The American Council on Education (ACE) recommends college credit for certain PADI scuba diver courses. ACE represents all colleges and universities before the U.S. federal government and as such is the unified voice of higher education. ACE evaluates educational courses according to established college-level criteria and recommends college credit for those that measure up to these standards.

The ACE credit recommendations for PADI courses may help you in receiving college credit at an American university or college – *even if the courses aren't conducted on a university or college campus*. Courses offered through PADI Dive Centers, Resorts and other locations qualify.

Take a Course – Use the Credit

A university or college may use the ACE credit recommendations in a variety of ways. The institution may apply the credit to your major replacing a required course. They may also use the credit as a general elective to possibly waive a prerequisite course.

College Credit at No Extra Charge

Universities and colleges that accept ACE credit recommendations for PADI courses typically handle them like transfer credit. Transfer credit is often awarded without an additional fee. This may save you tuition fees while at the same time allowing you to possibly meet graduation requirements.

How Much College Credit Can I Earn?

ACE has set forth the following college credit recommendations for PADI courses:

Course	Semester Credit Hours	Division*	Instructional Area	Course	Semester Credit Hours	Division*	Instructional Area
Open Water Diver	1	Lower	Recreation/PhysicalEducation	Wreck Diver	1	Lower	Recreation/PhysicalEducation
Advanced Open Water Diver	1	Lower	Recreation/PhysicalEducation	Enriched Air Diver	1	Lower	Recreation/PhysicalEducation
				Apprentice Tec Diver	1	Lower	Recreation/PhysicalEducation
Night Diver	1	Lower	Recreation/PhysicalEducation	Tec Deep Diver	1	Upper	Recreation/PhysicalEducation
Deep Diver	1	Lower	Recreation/PhysicalEducation	Divemaster	2	Lower	Recreation/PhysicalEducation
Dry Suit Diver	1	Lower	Recreation/PhysicalEducation	Assistant Instructor	1	Lower	Recreation/PhysicalEducation
Search and Recovery Diver	1	Lower	Recreation/PhysicalEducation	Instructor Development Course	3	Upper	Recreation/PhysicalEducation or Education
Underwater Navigator	1	Lower	Recreation/PhysicalEducation	Course Director Training Course	3	Upper	Recreation/PhysicalEducation or Education
Underwater Photographer	1	Lower	Recreation/PhysicalEducation				
Rescue Diver	1	Lower	Recreation/PhysicalEducation				

Lower – typically freshman/sophomore level; Upper – typically junior/senior level

In addition to ACE credit recommendations, various international organizations, such as the Canadian Learning Bank, recommend PADI courses for college credit.

Ordering an Official PADI Transcript

To secure credit for a PADI course at a college or university you need an official transcript as proof of course completion. *Colleges and universities will not accept certification cards or wall certificates as proof of course completion*. PADI will send your transcript directly to you or the college or university you are currently attending or planning to attend. It is recommended that you also order a transcript for your own records. To order an official transcript, complete the application on the previous page and enclose the indicated processing fee.

Index

focus, 292-293
food chain, 249
forward, 43
framing, 310
free descent, 60

G

galley, 43, 55
gear line, 59
grease, silicone, 290

H

half hitch, 239
hard-hull day boat, 46
hazards, 55
hazards, multilevel diving, 175-177
hazards, search and recovery, 229-231
hazards, wreck diving, 349-350
head, 43, 55
hot spot, 328
housing, video, 323-324
how to use this manual, xi
hypothermia, 5-6, 146, 175
hypoxia, 4-5

I

inflatable, 45, 53, 57
interaction, with aquatic life, 255-258
ISO, 304-305

J

jackstay pattern, 237

K

kick cycles, 265-266

L

law, wreck diving, 348
leak, video housing, 334, 338
leeward, 43
lift bag, 238-239
light failure, 199

light loss, 297-298
light meter, 304
light, and photography, 297-299
light, and videography, 326-327
light, video, 324-325, 328
lights, 190-194
live-aboard, 41, 45-46, 57
local orientation, wreck, 351-352
local regulations, 55
lung overexpansion injury, 169

M

maintenance, dive lights, 193
maintenance, DPV, 102
malfunction, DPV, 109-111
Master Scuba Diver, x
measured line, 268
mooring line, 58
multilevel and computer diving, 165-181
Multilevel Diver Specialty course, 77, 181
mystery fish, 37

N

natural light, 297-298
navigation, natural, 269-273
navigation, night, 206-207
navigation, wreck, 354-356
Night Diver Specialty course, 198, 208
night diving, 185-208
nitrogen narcosis, 67, 70, 88-90, 351
no decompression limit, 67, 166, 167, 351
no-stop times, 70
noise, 273

O

o-ring, 191, 290-291, 315, 332-333
Open Water Diver course, 48, 146
oxygen, 48-49
oxygen toxicity, 78